The Cambridge Technical Series

EXPERIMENTAL
BUILDING SCIENCE

VOLUME ONE

EXPERIMENTAL BUILDING SCIENCE

BY

J. LEASK MANSON

B.Sc., Eng. (Lond.); M.I.Struct.E.; M.R.San.I.

VOLUME ONE

INTRODUCTION TO SCIENCE AS APPLIED
IN BUILDING

*This volume will be found sufficient for the first
two years' work in Building Science in National
Certificate Courses*

Cambridge

at the University Press

1940

CAMBRIDGE
UNIVERSITY PRESS

University Printing House, Cambridge CB2 8BS, United Kingdom

Published in the United States of America by Cambridge University Press, New York

Cambridge University Press is part of the University of Cambridge.

It furthers the University's mission by disseminating knowledge in the pursuit of education, learning and research at the highest international levels of excellence.

www.cambridge.org
Information on this title: www.cambridge.org/9781107666214

© Cambridge University Press 1940

First edition 1917
Reprinted 1922, 1929
Second edition 1940
First published 1940
First paperback edition 2014

A catalogue record for this publication is available from the British Library

ISBN 978-1-107-66621-4 Paperback

PREFACE

BUILDING SCIENCE is a term which may be conveniently used to cover the selection, arrangement and development of scientific knowledge and experience which has, or which may have, a bearing upon the practical problems of architecture and building.

For the present, however, it is with the more limited definition of the term as applied to a subject for class instruction that we are concerned, although the purpose and necessity for such instruction is only clearly realised in the light of the full possibilities of the scientific treatment of building problems.

In the past the lack of some such instruction has not only greatly restricted the field of work possible in the Building Departments of the technical schools of this country, but has also rendered ineffectual much of the knowledge gained by building students in other and more technical subjects.

In preparing this volume the author has assumed that students will possess some knowledge of elementary science and simple calculations; but even where such is not the case no insuperable difficulties need arise for the careful and thoughtful student, particularly if he is fortunate in working under the guidance and inspiration of a skilful and enthusiastic teacher.

In approaching the subject for the first time the chief object to be aimed at is to obtain a grounding in all essential elementary science and to become familiar with the practical, experimental and mathematical methods of investigation adopted. Next the student should endeavour to obtain, by experiment and by actual handling, an intimate and reliable acquaintance with the nature and properties of the chief building materials. Finally it ought to be possible, by means of the knowledge and experience gained in working through this and the succeeding volumes, to understand, discuss and possibly investigate some of the larger problems which arise in connection with the production and use of building materials and the design and occupation of buildings.

To gain the maximum benefit it is necessary that many, if not all, of the experiments described should be carried out, particularly in the early stages of the instruction, and the student should supplement this with close and persistent observation of building operations and the behaviour of building materials in actual use. He should be instructed at an early stage in the fact that different degrees of accuracy are possible or necessary under different circumstances, and the experimental results obtained should always be the best possible under the particular conditions of each experiment. The numerous numerical results set out in full should serve to show on what lines a laboratory notebook should be kept. Such notes should always be made up and completed at the time of the experiment. From time to time also the teacher should explain the main principles which a series of minor facts and experiments is intended to support, and he should at the same time emphasise all interesting and useful links between the work in the laboratory, in the mathematics and construction classes and in the actual processes of building.

While much of the work dealt with in this volume is necessarily common to most books on elementary science, the elimination of all work not absolutely essential to the building student, the close association from the first with building interests and the experimental treatment of many simple building problems should go far to economise time, improve the instruction and retain the student's interest throughout. The association with building terms, problems and materials must of course be obvious and truthful and in such a form as to appeal to the young student, whose acquaintance with actual building practice may be slight.

The details of construction have not been touched upon in this volume, although the importance of many of the experimental illustrations and investigations given is only fully realised when the practical aspects of the problem to be faced are fully understood. Hence it is essential that the study of construction should run concurrently with the study of building science, and a companion volume in this series, *Architectural Building Construction*, will be found to provide an excellent book for this purpose, since it has been written with the production of such a book as this volume in view and should hence form a link between the science and the art of building of a most interesting and satisfactory nature.

In closing this preface the author would like to express his thanks to Mr F. E. Drury, F.I.S.E., M.C.I., Mr W. R. Jaggard, F.R.I.B.A., Mr J. B. Johnston, B.Sc. (Lond.), and Mr L. Rowland, B.Sc. (Lond.), A.M.I.C.E. During the strange times of the past two years, when it has been exceedingly difficult to concentrate on a task of this character and when more immediate tasks have greatly restricted the time available for its completion, the generous and informed assistance rendered by each of these gentlemen has gone far to make it possible to produce the book now with, the author hopes, a minimum of error or mis-statement. For whatever that is faulty the author must alone be held responsible, but he hopes that such blemishes will not be sufficient to defeat his endeavour to render, in as simple, interesting and instructive a form as possible, a statement of those items of elementary science which go far to make even the simplest operations of building work more interesting and more attractive. It is not unreasonable to hope that if instruction in this subject be developed systematically and intelligently it will help to improve both the standing and the powers of accomplishment of the building industry in the future.

J. LEASK MANSON.

January, 1917

PREFACE TO SECOND EDITION

THE years which have elapsed since the issue of the first volume of this book have seen a great expansion of the subject of Building Science, as a subject of technical instruction, as a matter for scientific research and in its practical applications in architecture and building. Some of the items introduced in an elementary form in the first edition have been developed almost beyond recognition, and there is now a wealth of advanced technical knowledge and experimental material not previously available. The problem of selection therefore becomes increasingly difficult. In this connection attention is drawn to the "List of Experiments" given at the end of this volume. This will serve as an example of the way in which this important but difficult problem of selection can be tackled. Where the field is so wide it is inevitable that others will draw up lists which will differ from this to a considerable extent. Some methodical basis of selection should be adopted.

Experience has shown that a sound knowledge of elementary chemistry is of great value in the early stages of the subject. The opportunity has been taken therefore to add a further chapter so as to complete the treatment of elementary chemistry. A chapter has also been added giving a simple introduction to the important subject of loaded beams. This should bring the student to the interesting stage where he is able to calculate the sizes of timber and steel beams for simple cases. With these additions the volume should cover the work generally asked for in the first two years of study in National Certificate Courses in Building, and in a similar period in courses for architectural and other professional students. It should in fact provide a suitable general basis for more specialised studies in the later years of these courses.

A number of problems have been added to those given at the ends of the chapters. An up-to-date set of examination papers has also been added, including some devised for students of the separate building trades. While these latter students are not normally expected to cover the whole field of Building Science, they should find various sections of it to be of great value in relation to the work of their particular trades.

J. L. M.

November, 1939

CONTENTS

CHAPTER I

THE WEIGHTS AND DENSITIES OF BUILDING MATERIALS

The Properties of Matter. Before proceeding to discuss the weights and densities of building materials, it will be convenient for us to make here a very brief reference to the more important properties of matter, leaving to the later stages the discussion, in such detail as may be necessary, of the general and particular properties peculiar to building materials.

All substances around us—air, water, brick, stone, wood, etc. —are forms of matter and may be distinguished from such things as heat, light and electricity by certain properties.

The fact that **all matter occupies space** (the property of Extension) is a statement of a property which needs little elaboration; similarly with the accompanying property of Impenetrability, the statement of which is that **no two (or more) portions of matter can occupy the same space at the same time.**

A further property of matter is apparent when we note that, if any body be in a state of rest it will remain so unless some *force* acts upon it so as to cause it to move, or, if the body be in a state of uniform motion, e.g. a ball rolling along a smooth horizontal table, it will continue to move until some force or forces—the friction of the table top and the resistance of the air—bring it to rest. This property, in virtue of which a body is unable of itself to change its state of rest or state of motion, is known as the inertness or **Inertia** of matter; it enables us to define **Force** as *that which changes or tends to change a body's state of rest or of uniform motion in a straight line.* Particularly in considering building problems concerning force is it important to realise that forces may be acting without motion taking place; a load suspended in the air from a crane hook or a man supporting a weight are both cases where forces are producing a *tendency* to move but not actual motion. (See Chap. VI.)

All particles of matter are known to attract other particles of matter, the attractive force varying according to the *quantity of matter* contained in the particles and the *distance* separating them.

The Earth is a body so immeasurably greater than any other with which we are acquainted, that the force of attraction it exerts upon all bodies on or near its surface is the only force of this kind which we need consider. This force is known as *the attraction of gravity* and tends to cause all bodies to "fall" towards the centre of the earth. In everyday language we speak of this force as "the weight of a body" and since all forms of matter are affected in this way we may say that **all matter has weight**.

Weight and Mass. From time to time it will be necessary for us to ascertain *the quantity of matter* contained in a body. This quantity is usually referred to as **the mass of a body**. We may distinguish mass from other quantities by noting, (1) that the masses of different portions of the same substance are proportional to the spaces they occupy, and (2) that the mass of any particular body is always the same and is not affected by altering the size of the body (by compressing or otherwise). For example there is just twice as much matter in one pound of iron as there is in a half-pound of the same iron. Again if it were possible, by the exercise of great force, to compress either or both of these amounts of matter until they occupied only half the original spaces the quantities of matter would still remain unaltered. Thus it would appear that while volume is not necessarily a measure of mass it is possible to measure it by weighing, and it might be shown, more fully than space allows us to do here, that **the weight of a body gives us a measure of its mass**. The operation of weighing a body is usually carried out by means of a "pair of scales" or by a "physical balance," the body to be weighed being placed on one pan and balanced by placing on the other pan pieces of metal containing a standard quantity of matter and known as "weights." With the systems in common use the *unit of mass* is either the *pound* or the *gram*.

Practical Hints on Weighing. It will be convenient for us to refer briefly to the means at our disposal for obtaining the weights of various bodies.

The Heavy Scales. These should be used for all approximate weighing and for heavy bodies; they should for our purpose be capable of weighing anything up to 20 lbs. and sensitive enough to show a change of weight of about $\frac{1}{4}$ oz. A suitable pair of scales is shown in fig. 1.

In using such scales the points to note are:

(*a*) See that the pans are kept clean and free from dust or grease (use a soft duster).

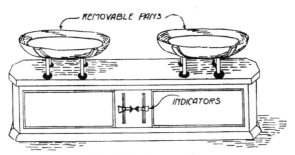

Fig. 1. The heavy scales.

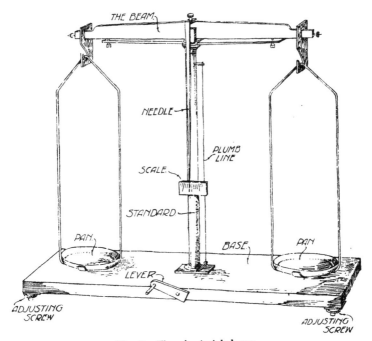

Fig. 2. The physical balance.

(*b*) Before commencing to weigh see that the empty pans balance. If there is a slight discrepancy adjust by the addition of some lead foil. If the error is considerable the scales should be corrected.

(*c*) Start your weighing with a weight that appears likely to exceed the weight of the body, then try the other weights in descending order *without omitting any.*

The Physical Balance. This is an instrument capable of a much higher degree of accuracy than the scales and it should only be used where accuracy in weighing is really essential. A suitable balance for elementary work should be capable of weighing up to 250 grams and sensitive to 5 milligrams when fully loaded. In these balances the beam and pans are suspended from delicate knife-edges. When the balance is not in use these knife-edges are freed from strain by lowering the beam on to rigid supports projecting out from the standard, see fig. 2. A small lever is provided to raise and lower the beam.

The following additional points should be noted:

(*d*) Do not place any wet or loose substance directly on the pan but always into a weighed receptacle. The weight of the substance may then be obtained by subtracting the weight of the receptacle from the total weight of substance and receptacle. This is known as the method of "difference."

(*e*) The body to be weighed is placed on the left-hand pan and the weights on the other.

(*f*) The weights must only be placed on the pan when the beam is down on the supports. To test whether the weights are correct raise the beam, keep the lever in the hand and, as soon as it is apparent that the weights are incorrect, lower the beam again. Only when it appears that a correct balance has been obtained should the lever be turned right over and the pointer be allowed to swing for some little time. If its movements on each side of the centre mark are equal then the correct weight has been found. Lower the beam again before removing the weights.

(*g*) The total of the weights should be obtained by counting them up while still on the pan and also checked by counting them again whilst they are being replaced in the box.

The Unit Weights of Building Materials. In considering the question of the weights of the various materials used in building, it will be as well to point out at once that with most of these materials, whether manufactured or natural (e.g. bricks or stones), considerable variation in weight exists; among the same batch of bricks will be found some which weigh above and others below what we may call the *average weight* of this particular kind of brick. Similarly for stones, timber, slates, etc. Hence for these materials very careful weighing is not essential. For such materials as iron, lead, zinc, cement and lime, however, much more careful weighing is necessary since their composition, and therefore their weight, is much more uniform.

Such materials as bricks, slates and tiles are used in small *units* and it is useful to know approximately the weight of each variety of these materials in the form used in building.

Similarly lead and zinc—materials largely used for covering roof surfaces—are usually described by their *weight per square foot*. If small pieces be cut off, measured and weighed, the weight per square foot may be readily calculated. For calculating roof loads or floor loads the weight *per square foot* for flooring, rough boarding, felt, slates and tiles may be similarly found.

Finally for such articles as lead piping, iron piping, rolled steel sections and timber joists the weight "*per foot run*" or per foot of length may be found experimentally by finding the weights of short lengths of each material.

It has not been thought necessary to introduce any experimental details here, as the methods to be adopted in finding the above weights are direct and simple, but a number of suggestions for adding variety to the experimental work and calculation will be found in the problems given at the end of this chapter.

Some Useful Unit Weights.

Note. Most of the following weights are only approximate. For local and special materials the reader should prepare his own list, obtaining the values experimentally as already suggested.

Material	Dimensions (inches)	Weight (lbs.)
Common Stock Brick ...	$8\frac{3}{4} \times 4\frac{1}{4} \times 2\frac{7}{8}$ (average)	$7\frac{1}{4}$
London ,, ,, ...	$8\frac{3}{4} \times 4\frac{1}{4} \times 2\frac{1}{4}$,,	$6\frac{3}{4}$
Pressed Facing ,, ...	$\begin{cases} 8\frac{3}{4} \times 4\frac{1}{4} \times 2\frac{7}{8} \text{ ,,} \\ \text{to } 9 \times 4\frac{1}{2} \times 3 \text{ ,,} \end{cases}$	8 9
Common Blue ,, ...	$9 \times 4\frac{1}{2} \times 3$,,	$9\frac{1}{2}$
Pressed ,, ,, ...	,, ,, ,, ,,	10 to 11
Glazed Brick	,, ,, ,, ,,	$7\frac{1}{2}$ to 9
Welsh Slates	20×10	$3\frac{1}{2}$
Lake District Slates ...	,, ,,	$5\frac{1}{4}$
Common Tiles	$10\frac{1}{2} \times 6\frac{1}{2} \times \frac{1}{2}$	$2\frac{1}{4}$
Pantiles	$13\frac{1}{2} \times 9\frac{1}{2} \times \frac{1}{2}$	$5\frac{1}{4}$
1 Gallon of Water ...	277 cu. ins. (approx.)	10 lbs. (at 17° C.)
Deal Boarding	1 sq. foot, 1″ thick	3
Lead	,, ,,	59
Zinc	,, ,,	37
Copper	,, ,,	46
Cast Iron	,, ,,	$37\frac{1}{2}$
Wrought Iron	,, ,,	40
Steel	,, ,,	41
Slab Slate	,, ,,	15
Glass	,, $\frac{1}{16}$″ thick	14 ozs.

The Densities of Building Materials. We have just found the weights of several materials taken in various units; now these weights are obviously not in such a convenient form for the comparison of various materials as they would be if we weighed an equal volume of each material every time. The quantity of matter in a unit of volume of any substance is known as the "density" of that substance; in other words, **density is the weight per unit volume.**

In expressing density we may use any units we like, but it is usual to give the weight of a cubic foot of a substance in pounds and the weight of a cubic centimetre in grams, according to the system of weights and volumes used.

Since it is not easy to obtain an exact cubic foot or an exact cubic centimetre of any substance, we must usually calculate the density from the known weight and volume of a given piece of the substance. To find the weight of a unit volume we divide the known weight by the known volume, thus:

$$\text{Density} = \frac{\text{Weight}}{\text{Volume}}.$$

Proceeding thus find first the density of substances, such as brick, stone, wood and lead. These substances may be easily obtained in pieces of regular shape.

When the materials, of which we require the density, can only be obtained in irregularly shaped pieces then we must proceed along somewhat different lines.

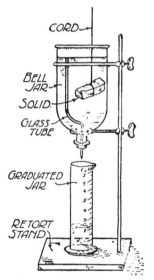

Fig. 3.   Volume of a solid by displacement.

Experiment 1. To find the volume of an irregular solid by displacement. We have seen that matter occupies space and that no two substances can occupy the same space at the same time; hence if a solid body be lowered into water it will *displace an amount of water equal in volume to the solid*. This is the principle of the apparatus described below and shown in fig. 3. This form of apparatus is very suitable for the fairly large specimens of materials likely to be used in a building laboratory. A smaller form of the same type of apparatus is shown in fig. 6.

In both pieces of apparatus the vessel is filled with water until the water begins to overflow down the glass tube. When this has ceased the solid is lowered gently into the vessel and the displaced water—which evidently equals the volume of the solid—overflows, passes down the tube and is collected in a graduated measuring jar below. For good results the experiment should be repeated two or three times, the overflow being caught each time in the same jar. By finding the average of these results we obtain a fairly accurate estimate of the volume of the solid.

The method may be utilised to find the densities of irregular pieces of lead, zinc, iron, copper, brass, wood, stone and brick.

Porous substances like brick or stone should first be weighed then soaked for about an hour before being immersed in the bell-jar. This procedure is necessary to prevent the solid absorbing water when placed in the bell-jar. Substances, such as wood, which float in water should have a sinker of lead

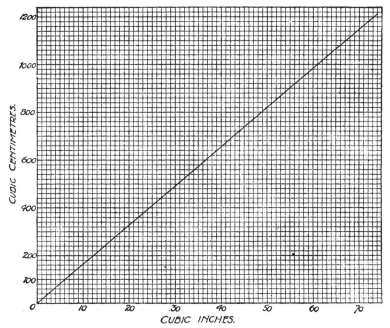

Fig. 4. Relation between cubic centimetres and cubic inches.

attached to them by a piece of string, the string being of such a length that when the sinker rests on the bottom of the jar the wood specimen is fully immersed. The solid is first suspended over the jar with the sinker *in* the water and the solid clear of the water. The level is then adjusted as already described, after which the solid is lowered and the displacement noted.

The method of recording the results of such an experiment is given below.

To find the density of Portland stone.

Weight of stone (dry) = 0·75 lb.

Stone was then immersed in water for an hour, taken out and wiped with a dry cloth.

The displaced water was collected three times and gave:

Total volume displaced = 28·35 cubic inches.

$$\text{Volume of solid} = \text{average volume displaced}$$
$$= \frac{28·35}{3}$$
$$= 9·45 \text{ cubic inches}$$
$$= \frac{9·45}{1728} \text{ cubic feet.}$$

∴ Density of sample of Portland Stone $= \dfrac{\text{Weight}}{\text{Volume}} = \dfrac{0·75}{9·45 \div 1728}$

$$= 136 \text{ lbs. (approx.) per cubic foot.}$$

Note. If jars graduated in cubic inches are not available then a jar graduated in cubic centimetres will probably be used. In this case it will be found convenient to construct a graph similar to that given in fig. 4, by the aid of which cubic centimetres may be readily converted to cubic inches. A similar graph showing the relation between grams and pounds should also be prepared.

$$1 \text{ centimetre} = ·3937 \text{ inch (approx.)},$$
$$∴ \text{ 1 cubic cm.} = (·3937)^3$$
$$= ·0610 \text{ cubic inch (approx.)}$$
$$1 \text{ kilogram} = 2·2 \text{ lbs. (approx.)}$$
$$\text{or} \quad 1 \text{ gram} = ·0022 \text{ lb.}$$

The Density of Liquids. To obtain the density of a liquid it is only necessary to obtain *the weight of a known volume of the liquid.* A simple form of apparatus is shown in fig. 5 and consists of a flask which if filled up to a certain mark on the neck is known to contain a certain volume, say 100 cubic cms.

Experiment 2. To find the density of water. Find the weight of the flask when empty. Then fill it with water nearly up to the mark on the flask. Take a small quantity of water into a pipette and by allowing only a drop to fall into the flask

Fig. 5. Measuring flask.

at a time, adjust the level of the water until it just reaches the mark (see p. 20). Weigh flask and water and obtain the weight of the water by subtraction. Divide the weight of the water in gms. by its known volume in cubic cms. and we have the approximate weight of water under the conditions of the experiment. This you ought to find as very nearly 1 gm. per cubic cm.

If this experiment were conducted at a temperature of 4° C. (39·1° F.) and all experimental errors were eliminated then the **weight of 1 cu. cm. would be exactly one gram.** This value is commonly used in experimental work although it is not absolutely correct at other temperatures.

By calculation it is possible to obtain the **density in lbs. per cubic ft.** (see Prob. I, 6), which at 4° C. is **62·43 lbs.** (approx.). This value will be used throughout this book so as to be consistent with the "gram per cubic centimetre" of the metric system.

For rough calculations the density is frequently taken as 62½ lbs. per cubic foot.

Relative Density and its use in Building. In comparing the densities of various materials it would obviously be an advantage if we could take one substance as a *standard*, calling its density "1." The comparative or *relative* value of the density of any other substance would then also be expressed by a number, e.g. if it had twice the density of the standard substance its "relative density" as compared with the standard substance would be "2" and so on. We take water (strictly at a temperature of 4° C.) as our standard substance and the number which gives the ratio between the density of the substance and the density of water we call the **Relative Density** or **Specific Gravity** of the substance, so that:

$$\text{Relative Density} = \frac{\text{Density of Substance}}{\text{Density of Water}}.$$

But, since it is immaterial whether we take a cubic foot or any other volume of the substance and of water so long as we take *equal volumes,* our expression may be put in a more useful form as follows:

$$\text{Relative Density} = \frac{\text{Weight of substance}}{\text{Weight of equal volume of water}}.$$

Note. (1) We shall shortly proceed to obtain the relative density of materials in various ways, but it is most important to realise that the above expression for relative density holds good in every case no matter how the numerator and denominator of the expression are obtained.

(2) Since, as we have seen (Experiment 2), the density of water is 1 gram per cubic centimetre in the metric system and by definition its relative density is also 1, therefore the relative density of any substance in this system is given by the number expressing its weight in grams per cubic centimetre.

(3) In addition to the results obtained when ascertaining the density of a solid we require to know in this case the weight of an equal volume of water. If the volume of the solid be known in cubic cms. we have at once (from the last paragraph) the number of grams in an equal volume of water.

(4) The method usually adopted to find the volume of the solid is that of displacement, in which case "the weight of an equal volume of water" may be found directly by weighing the water displaced using the apparatus shown in fig. 3.

A very satisfactory and interesting method of dealing with this problem is based upon what is known as the **Principle of Archimedes.** This law states that when a body is immersed in water (or any fluid) it apparently loses weight, the reduction being equal to the weight of the water (or fluid) displaced by the body. That this is so may readily be shown as follows.

Experiment 3. Attach a large body, such as a brick, to a spring balance. Note its weight. Now lower the brick into a pail of water. Note the sensible reduction in weight and ascertain its approximate amount by means of the balance. Calculate the weight of a volume of water equal in volume to the brick. This calculated weight and the *reduction in weight* as given by the balance should be approximately equal.

Experiment 4. To obtain a more exact verification of the law we may use the displacement apparatus already described. Fig. 6 shows it in a form suitable for finding the volume of small specimens.

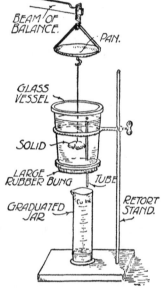

The body is suspended from a special balance pan so as to hang in the displacement vessel. This is at first empty and the weight of the body is obtained when hanging thus *in air*. The body is now taken out of the vessel and the vessel filled up with water. When all the overflow has passed down the tube, a small (weighed) measuring glass is placed beneath and the body carefully lowered into the water in the larger vessel. It will now be found that the balance needs readjusting, some of the weights having to be taken off. When equilibrium has been restored note *the apparent reduction in weight*. Obtain also the weight of the water displaced and *note the approximate equality of the two weights.* Hence we have: weight of water

Fig. 6. Loss in weight equals weight of water displaced.

displaced = apparent reduction in weight. It ought not to be difficult for the reader to see that this change in weight is evidently due to upward acting forces, which originally supported the water now displaced by the solid body, and these upward acting forces must be equal to the weight of the water displaced since they originally supported it.

Floating Bodies. Before proceeding to utilise the above law experimentally it will be as well for us to try to realise more fully the significance of this apparent loss in weight. As we have seen, an immersed body experiences an upward force which is just equal in magnitude to the weight of the water displaced by the body. Thus we may think of two forces acting on the immersed body, the upward thrust, of which we have just spoken, and the weight of the body itself, acting vertically downwards. When the weight of the body exceeds the upward thrust the body sinks; when the weight just equals the upward thrust the body is in a state of equilibrium and will float in any position in the water; lastly when the up-thrust exceeds the weight of the body, the body rises in the liquid and *floats*. When the floating body comes to rest on the surface of the water, the upward and downward forces must be equal and the body in equilibrium; but since the up-thrust equals in magnitude the weight of the water displaced, we deduce that, **a floating body displaces an amount of water equal in weight to its own weight.** A barge weighing 100 tons will sink in the water until it just displaces 100 tons of water. If an upward force of 1 lb. is required at the end of the lever of a ball-cock in a water cistern, then the copper ball will sink until this amount of water is displaced (see Problems I, 11).

Experiment 5. To find the relative density of cast iron, using the principle of Archimedes. The following setting out of the data obtained in an experiment will make the method of procedure sufficiently clear. Any suitable vessel may be used to contain the water since there is now no need to measure or weigh the amount of water displaced.

$$\begin{array}{ll} \text{Weight of piece of iron in air} & = 296\cdot6 \text{ gms.} \\ \text{,,} \qquad \text{,,} \qquad \text{,,} \quad \text{water} & = 255\cdot4 \quad \text{,,} \\ \therefore \text{ Reduction in weight} & = \overline{\;41\cdot2\;} \quad \text{,,} \end{array}$$

and this gives the weight of an "equal volume of water."

$$\therefore \text{ Relative density of cast iron} = \frac{\text{Weight of specimen}}{\text{Weight of equal volume of water}}$$

$$= \frac{296\cdot6}{41\cdot2} = 7\cdot2 \text{ (approx.).}$$

Experiment 6. To find the relative density of red deal, using the law of flotation. Prepare from the wood to be tested a piece about 6 inches long and of uniform section, say $\frac{5}{8}$ inch by $\frac{5}{8}$ inch or thereabouts. (To prevent absorption the specimen should be thinly varnished or gone over lightly with some vaseline.) Measure the length of the piece accurately. Fit into a glass jar some simple wire supports as shown in fig. 7 so that when the rod is floating it will be upright and clear of the sides of the jar. Mark the point to which the rod sinks in the water and measure the length immersed. Now, remembering that the weight of the water displaced equals the weight of the rod, we proceed as follows:

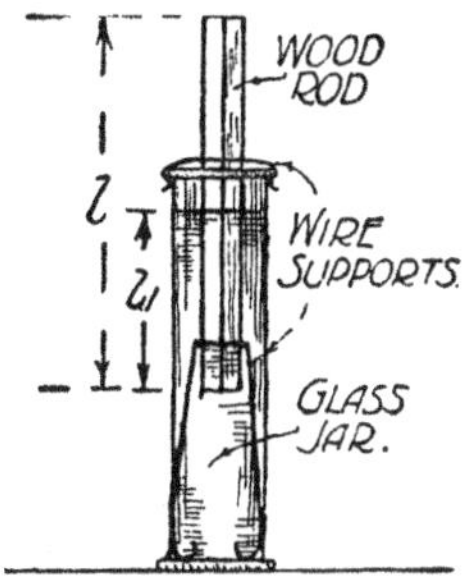

Fig. 7. Relative density of wood by flotation.

Let A be the area of the cross section of the rod,

l ,,   length of the rod,

l_1 ,,   ,,   ,, immersed,

d ,,   density of the wood and

w ,,   ,,   water in the same units

(inches, feet or centimetres and pounds or grams as the case may be).

Then   Weight of rod $= l \times A \times d,$

              Volume of water displaced $= l_1 \times A,$

and   Weight of water displaced $= l_1 \times A \times w;$

but　　　　　Weight of water displaced = weight of rod,

$$\therefore\ l_1 \times A \times w = l \times A \times d,$$

i.e.　　　　　　　　　$l_1 \times w = l \times d,$

or　　　$\dfrac{l_1}{l} = \dfrac{d}{w} = \dfrac{\text{density of the wood}}{\text{density of water}}$ = relative density of wood.

Hence　　Relative density of wood = $\dfrac{\text{length immersed}}{\text{total length of rod}}$.

In conducting this experiment some slight difficulty will be experienced in eliminating the friction between the wood and the wire supports, hence the average result of several trials should be used in the calculation (see Problems I, 7).

The Relative Densities of Liquids. Various methods are available for ascertaining the relative densities of liquids. The method just adopted for ascertaining the relative density of a floating body furnishes us with a rough but handy method of obtaining an approximate value.

Experiment 7. To find the relative density of turpentine by the law of flotation. Take the rod prepared in the last experiment (or a similar one), float it as before in water and note the length immersed. Take it out, dry it, float it next in a jar of turpentine and note the length immersed. Let l_1 and l_2 be the lengths immersed in water and turpentine respectively, and let w_1 and w_2 be the densities of water and turpentine respectively.

Then since weight of water displaced = weight of rod,

and　　　,,　　　turpentine　,,　　=　　　,,　　,,

$\therefore$　weight of water displaced = weight of turpentine displaced,

or　　　　　　　$l_1 \times A \times w_1 = l_2 \times A \times w_2,$

i.e.　　　　　　　$l_1 \times w_1 = l_2 \times w_2,$

i.e.　　　$\dfrac{l_1}{l_2} = \dfrac{w_2}{w_1} = \dfrac{\text{density of turpentine}}{\text{density of water}}$ = relative density of turpentine,

or　Relative density of turpentine = $\dfrac{\text{length immersed in water}}{\text{length immersed in turpentine}}$.

For a sample of turpentine the values were:

$$l_1 = 3.87 \text{ ins.,}\qquad l_2 = 4.45 \text{ ins.}$$

$\therefore$ Relative density of the turpentine = $\dfrac{l_1}{l_2} = \dfrac{3.87}{4.45} = 0.87.$

(See Problems I, 8.)

As already stated this method is not capable of giving a high degree of accuracy but is easy of application. For very accurate results the **hydrometer,** the principle of action of which is exactly the same as for the wood rod, may be substituted. A hydrometer is shown in fig. 8; the stem is graduated and the mark to which it sinks gives the relative density of the liquid.

When testing the purity of such liquids as turpentine or linseed oil the hydrometer may be used; another method available is to fill a vessel of known volume first with water and then (after careful drying) with the given liquid. By weighing we may thus obtain the weight of equal volumes of water and of the given liquid. A measuring flask such as was described on p. 8 may be used but a relative density bottle is preferable. These bottles differ in capacity: this, however, is usually marked on the bottle as "grams of water at a certain temperature," see fig. 9. Thus it is usually unnecessary to obtain the weight of the water, the weight of an equal volume of the liquid being all that is required. The stopper is carefully "ground in" to give a good fit, a small

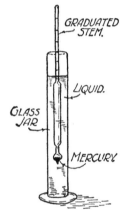

Fig. 8. The relative density of a   Fig. 9. The relative
liquid using a hydrometer.   density bottle.

hole passes through it and allows the surplus liquid to escape. The bottle is carefully dried on the outside before weighing. After filling the bottle should not be handled with the hot hand or placed near a hot body.

The Relative Densities of Limes and Cements. In building, one of the most important uses of the relative density number occurs in testing the quality of Portland Cement and in distinguishing it from cheaper substitutes or from other finely ground materials such as ground lime. While it is not our purpose at this stage to go into the question of the real significance of this test it will be convenient for us to deal here with the simpler methods available for carrying out this test.

The liquid used. Since water has a chemical action upon the substances now being discussed some other liquid has to be used—usually either turpentine or paraffin-oil.

Types of apparatus used. Quite a number of forms of apparatus for carrying out this test may be obtained, they are all based, however, upon the principle of the displacement of an amount of liquid equal in volume to the powder used. Two types will be dealt with here.

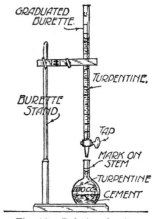

Fig. 10.   Relative density of cement.

Experiment 8. To find the relative density of cement or ground lime.

(a) The apparatus shown in fig. 10 is of quite a simple form and may be fitted up in any building laboratory. A graduated flask (100 cu. cms. is convenient) is taken and into this is introduced about 50 gms. of the cement (or 25 gms. of lime) to be tested, (the weight is obtained by "difference" after the cement is in the flask). The burette is now filled up with turpentine and a reading taken. Some turpentine is then run into the flask and shaken up with the cement, to get rid of all air-bubbles. Finally sufficient turpentine is run in to bring the level up to the mark (see p. 20) and the reading of the burette noted again. The results may be set out as follows:

To find the relative density of a sample of ground hydraulic lime.

Weight of flask and lime	= 58·73 gms.
Weight of flask	= 31·52 gms.
∴ Weight of lime	= 27·21 gms.
Capacity of flask	= 100 cubic cms.
First reading of burette	= 0·5 cubic cms.
Second „ „	= 91·28 cubic cms.
∴ Amount of turpentine used	= 90·78 cubic cms.

Then volume occupied by the lime = 100 − 90·78 = 9·22 cu. cms.

∴ Weight of equal volume of water = 9·22 gms.

∴ Relative density of sample of lime = $\dfrac{27\cdot21}{9\cdot22}$

= 2·95 (approx.).

(*b*) Fig. 11 shows a flask specially designed for this test. The stem is of uniform bore and the flask when filled up to the mark "14" holds exactly 64 cubic cms.

50 cubic cms. of turpentine are run carefully into the flask (without wetting the sides of the stem). About 50 gms. of cement are then introduced into the flask and the air-bubbles got rid of by stirring or shaking. The liquid will now have risen to some mark between "14" and "17" and *the reading will give the volume displaced by the cement.*

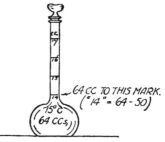

Fig. 11. Blount's volumeter.

The Densities of Building Materials (approx.).

Material	Density (lbs. per cu. ft.)	Relative density (water 1)
Water	62·43 (at 4° C.)	1
Sea Water	64 ,,	1·025
Limestone (average)	140	2·2
Sandstone ,,	145	2·3
Granite ,,	170	2·7
Sand (dry and in bulk)	95	—
,, (wet ,, ,,)	110	—
Gravel	116	—
Clay	120	—
Cast Iron	450	7·2
Wrought Iron	480	7·7
Steel	490	7·9
Lead	707	11·3
Zinc	450	7·2
Copper	550	8·9
Fir (average)	36	·56
Pitch Pine (average)	46	·74
Mahogany ,,	43	·69
Oak (average)	54	·83
Teak ,,	48	·77
Lignum Vitae (average)	80	1·3
Portland Cement	90 (in bulk)	3·1 (R.D. of grains)
Fat Lime (lump)	55 ,, ,,	3·0 (R.D. of lumps)
Hydraulic Lime (ground)	54 ,, ,,	2·9 (R.D. of grains)
Lime Mortar (2 to 1)	125 (average)	—
Cement Mortar (2 to 1)	130 ,,	—
Stock Brickwork (lime mortar)	112 ,,	—
Blue ,, (cement ,,)	135 ,,	—
Concrete	140 ,,	—
Turpentine	—	·862 to ·873
Linseed oil (raw)	—	·930 to ·937
,, ,, (boiled)	—	·937 to ·952
Mercury	—	13·6

PROBLEMS

Note. (i) Under the above heading will be given, at the end of each chapter, a series of problems intended (a) to revise the work of the chapter, (b) to correlate with the work of previous chapters and (c) to suggest problems, experiments and practical applications *additional* to those already given in the text.

(ii) The information dealt with in Chapter I gives rise to a large number of useful practical applications. These include the calculation of weight per 1000 bricks, per square of flooring, tiling or slating, the number of cubic feet of stone per ton, the weight of given lengths of piping or joisting, the weight of given masses of brickwork and concrete, etc. As these problems are, however, more suitable for treatment under the head of Building Mathematics they will not be detailed here.

(iii) The numerical answers are given as they would be obtained by means of logarithms or by a slide rule, i.e. correct to 3 or 4 significant figures.

PROBLEMS I

1. A rectangular piece of sheet lead 5″ × 7″ weighs 1·7 lbs. Calculate (a) its weight per foot super and (b) its thickness. Density of the lead is 707 lbs. per cubic ft.

2. A roll of wire containing 100 ft. is lowered into water and displaces 3·684 cubic ins. of water. Calculate the diameter of the wire.

3. A piece of glass tubing is filled with mercury over a length of 100 cms. The increase in weight due to the mercury is 171·1 gms. Calculate the internal diameter of the tubing, given that the relative density of mercury is 13·6.

4. A relative density bottle weighs 18·5 gms. when empty and 62·0 gms. when filled with turpentine. If the capacity of the bottle is 50 cubic cms. what is the relative density of the turpentine?

5. A piece of glass is suspended from the pan of a balance as in fig. 6. "In air" it weighs 18·9 gms., "in water" 11·9 gms. and in some raw linseed oil 12·38 gms. Calculate the relative density of the oil.

6. Given that 1 cubic cm. of water weighs 1 gram at 4° C., calculate the density of water in lbs. per cubic foot at this temperature.

7. A rod of red deal of uniform section was floated in water as described in Exp. 6, and on three trials sank to a depth of 3·87 ins., 3·9 ins., and 3·84 ins. Given that the total length of the rod was 5·9 ins. calculate the density of the red deal.

8. The rod used in question 7 was afterwards floated in some boiled linseed oil and three trials gave depths of 4·15 ins., 4·09 ins. and 4·12 ins. Calculate the relative density of the oil.

9. A piece of rough concrete weighed 4·7 lbs. when dry and 5·2 lbs. after soaking for a day in water. It was then suspended from a scale pan and lowered into some water, when it weighed 3·06 lbs. Calculate the density of the concrete.

10. Given a measuring flask of 50 c.c. capacity, a 50 c.c. burette, some turpentine and a physical balance, describe how you would proceed to find the relative density of a sample of Portland cement. What value would you expect to get with a good cement?

11. The copper ball to a ball-cock (see fig. 38, p. 43) has a diameter of 3½ ins. Neglecting the weight of the ball itself, find what upward force will be exerted when the ball is fully immersed in water. (Volume of a sphere = $\frac{4}{3}\pi r^3$.)

CHAPTER II

FLUID PRESSURE. HEAD OF WATER AND WATER PRESSURE

Solids and Fluids. Matter may exist in three different states—as a solid, a liquid or a gas—and we are all more or less familiar with the general properties associated with these states. It is necessary, however, to make our notions of these properties more precise.

Briefly, a solid may be defined as a body which tends to keep a definite shape which may not be changed without the application of considerable force. Iron, stone, brick and timber are examples of solids. This property of *rigidity* is characteristic of solids and is not possessed by either liquids or gases.

Both *liquids* and *gases* are classed as fluids and of these water and air are familiar examples. **Fluids** are substances which will flow from one vessel to another, and which change their shape to that of the containing vessel.

In order to be able to resist pressure a fluid must be entirely enclosed in some vessel, so that it cannot escape from the effects of the pressure. When so enclosed it may be shown that the pressure exerted on a fluid is *transmitted equally in all directions*. Thus if water be taken up into a syringe and the nozzle closed, the water will tend to escape equally at all points when pressure is brought to bear upon the piston. Similarly with air enclosed in a bicycle pump. Further it will be observed that while it is possible to compress the air in the bicycle pump until it occupies a much smaller space than it did originally, the volume of the water is not so affected even though great pressure be brought to bear upon the piston. This fact is contained in the statement that liquids *are practically incompressible*, (for all ordinary purposes they may be considered to be actually incompressible).

Gases, unlike liquids, are not constant in volume but always *tend to occupy as large a space as possible*. Thus if a certain volume of gas be introduced into a closed vessel it will expand and fill the vessel no matter how large it may be.

The free surface of a liquid at rest is horizontal. This is an important property of all liquids and may be simply explained as follows. From the fact that a liquid is easily stirred and readily changes its shape we may conclude that the particles of the liquid are free to move in any and every direction unless constrained by other forces. But each particle of the liquid has weight—in other words each particle is drawn towards the earth by the force of gravity—thus every particle of the liquid will tend to seek the lowest possible level. Hence it is not possible for a liquid at rest to have a surface of the form suggested in fig. 12, for so long as there are portions of the surface, as at *A*, at a higher level than other portions of the surface, movement will take place and continue until all the particles of water at the surface have reached the same level, as suggested by the dotted line. As we shall see later if the same body of liquid has several surfaces, all will rise or fall to the same level in accordance with this property.

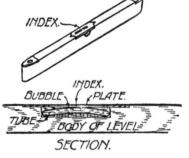

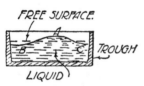

Fig. 12. Horizontal surface of a liquid at rest.

Fig. 13. The spirit-level.

The Spirit-Level, as used in building and surveying operations, is an example of the practical application of the property of liquids which we have just discussed. A builder's level is shown in fig. 13, an enlarged section showing the essential parts of the instrument. These consist of a glass tube, closed at both ends and filled almost completely with spirit (alcohol or ether), the tube is suitably bedded in a wooden body and secured above with a brass plate; over the tube is a slot continuous except for a small bridge (the index) at the centre. The bubble of air left in the tube constitutes a small free surface to the liquid and, since the liquid will always occupy the lower parts of the tube if free to do so, the bubble tends to set itself at the highest part of the tube. The tube is slightly bent in its length (exaggerated in fig. 13) and is so set in the base that the highest part comes immediately beneath the index. If the tube be correctly set the length of the bubble will be bisected by the index when the lower surface of the instrument is horizontal. To allow for any errors due to wear or bad setting the level is usually reversed in position over the same portion of the surface being tested. If this surface is truly horizontal the bubble will extend an equal distance on the same side of the index in each position.

The level used by the surveyor consists of a telescope with a large and sensitive level attached which is set parallel to the axis of the telescope.

Fluid Pressure. It will be convenient for us in dealing with fluid pressure to deal particularly with "water pressure" and "air pressure." The properties and laws ascertained in this way may, however, be taken as applying generally to other liquids and gases. It is necessary to point out, however, that our investigation deals only with *fluids at rest*, on no account must it be assumed that the same laws apply to fluids in motion.

Liquid Pressure due to Weight. If we consider a heavy liquid, such as water, at rest, since each layer of liquid has to support the weight of the layers of liquid above—unless it be at the surface —the pressure in the lower layers must be greater than in those above. For example, if a long vertical tube be filled with water the pressure near the bottom will be greater than it is near the top and may be sufficient to thrust a cork out of a hole at the bottom of the tube while not able to do so higher up. The insides of cisterns, tanks, reservoirs and water-pipes are subjected to this type of pressure and it is with such pressures that we are now about to deal.

The other type of fluid pressure, such as occurs in closed vessels like pumps and other hydraulic machinery, though important need not be dealt with in detail at this stage.

How to compare fluid pressures experimentally. Any form of apparatus which can be used to measure or compare pressures in liquids or gases is known as a **manometer**. These manometers vary in design, the simple type which we describe here is known as a *mercury manometer* since the pressures are measured by the relative movements of two surfaces of mercury in a bent tube. Fig. 14 shows a type of manometer suitable for our present purpose, it consists of a tube suitably bent and containing mercury at the bend of the tube. When this manometer is lowered into

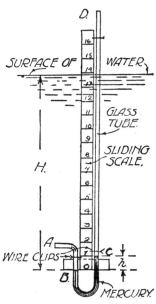

Fig. 14. Mercury manometer in water.

2—2

water—or any other liquid—water enters at the open end A and
the pressure acting on the surface of the mercury at this side of the
bend depresses it to B (say) with a consequent elevation of the
surface in the other tube to C (say). The greater the pressure
the greater the *difference in levels* (h), hence the pressures at various
depths in the liquid may be compared by noting the values of h
and the corresponding values of H, the total depth from the surface of the water to the surface of the mercury at B. The sliding
scale attached to the tube as shown will be found convenient in
practice since as soon as the cross-bar is adjusted to the surface B
in one tube both the heights h and H may be read off together.
The scale may be graduated in inches or centimetres.

Experiment 9. **To show that the pressure in a liquid increases
directly with the depth.** Take a tall jar of sufficient diameter to admit
the manometer and fill it with water. Lower the manometer into the water
and note the values of H and h in various positions. Tabulate the values thus
obtained and note the direct increase of pressure with depth, e.g. at twice the
depth the pressure will be twice as great, etc. This relation between pressure
and depth will be more strikingly shown if the various values be plotted on
squared paper when—allowing for experimental errors—a *straight-line graph*
will be found to pass through all the points thus obtained (see fig. 21).

Meniscus. Probably before reaching this stage the student will have
experienced difficulty when trying to read the level of the surface of a liquid

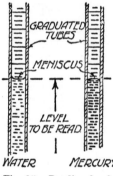

Fig. 15.   Reading levels
in tubes.

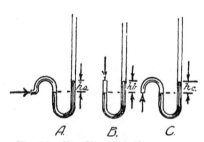

Fig. 16.   Equality of fluid pressure
in all directions.

in a small tube, since that surface does not appear flat but curved. This
formation is known as the *meniscus* and is due to surface tension (see p. 71).
It occurs at all free surfaces with all liquids but is more noticeable on small
surfaces. Fig. 15 shows the appearance of surfaces of water and of mercury
in the tube of a burette. In both cases the curved surface near the side is
disregarded and the level read to the central portion of the surface.

Experiment 10. **To show that at any given depth the pressure in a
liquid acts equally in all directions and is not affected by the shape of
the vessel.** Lower the manometer to any convenient depth and whilst there

turn it round so that the opening points in *all directions*—the pressure is not changed. Now substitute successively manometers with the lower tube arranged as shown in *A*, *B* and *C* of fig. 16. These respectively test the pressure acting horizontally, downwards and upwards; note that at the *same depths* no difference in pressure is noted in these directions. If now the manometer

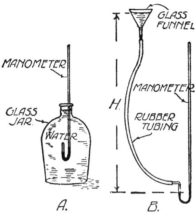

Fig. 17. Liquid pressure independent of shape of vessel.

be lowered into any large vessel of *irregular outline*, fig. 17 *A*, the pressures at stated depths will be found to be as before. Instead of the irregular vessel a piece of rubber tubing and a glass funnel may be fitted up as shown in fig. 17 *B*, when it will be found that the pressure is only affected by the depth *H* from the free surface, and that the shape that the tube may take up between the funnel and the manometer does not affect the pressure.

Effect of Density. If sea water, turpentine or any other liquid be substituted for water in Experiments 9 and 10 it may be shown that the same laws apply and, in addition, that at the same depths in the different liquids the pressures vary directly with the densities of the liquids.

We may now summarise these facts concerning liquid pressure as follows:

(1)   The pressure in a liquid varies directly with the depth;
(2)   it is independent of the shape of the vessel;
(3)   it is the same in all directions at the same depth, and
(4)   it varies directly with the density of the liquid.

Pressure on a Surface. When two bodies in contact press against each other the two forces exerted by the bodies are said to form a **thrust**; thus on p. 19 we spoke of a cork being forced out of the pipe by a thrust exerted by the water in the pipe. Now that thrust would be exerted over the whole area of the end of the cork equally and when the effect of a given thrust is distributed over a surface in this way we generally refer to it as a **pressure**, thus we have steam pressure in a boiler, air pressure in a bicycle tyre and water pressure in a water supply system.

If we wish to compare the intensities of various pressures we do so by ascertaining the pressures exerted on unit areas (the square foot, square inch or square centimetre); this we call the "intensity of pressure" or merely the "pressure."

If then the pressed surface have A units of area and the total thrust be P whilst the intensity of pressure is p, then evidently:

$$P = pA$$

or   total thrust = (pressure per unit area) × (area),

and it follows from this that

$$p = \frac{P}{A},$$

or   intensity of pressure $= \dfrac{\text{total pressure}}{\text{area of surface}}.$

Example. *If the total pressure on the flat bottom of a cistern is 2000 lbs. and the bottom is 3 ft. long by 2 ft. wide, find the pressure on a square inch.*

Total pressure = 2000 lbs.

„   area   = 3 × 2

= 6 sq. ft.

= 864 sq. ins.

∴ Pressure $= \dfrac{\text{total pressure}}{\text{area}} = \dfrac{2000}{864}$

= 2·31 lbs. per sq. inch.

Uniform Pressure. In all calculations in this volume involving pressure on a surface it will be assumed that the pressures are uniformly distributed in each case, i.e. no matter where a unit area of the surface be taken the intensity of pressure is the same.

The Intensity of Water Pressure due to **Weight.** It will now be possible for us to obtain an expression which will enable us to calculate the pressures at various depths in water. Consider a column reaching down from the surface of a body of water for a depth H, the end of the column having unit area, see fig. 18. Then it may be shown that the pressure on the area a of the bottom of the column at the depth H is equal to the weight of the column of water enclosed in this

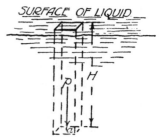

Fig. 18.   Intensity of fluid pressure.

way. If the units be feet and lbs. and w be the density of the water (62·43 lbs. per cubic ft.) then the total weight of the column would be wH lbs. Hence:

Pressure at depth H ft. $= wH$ lbs. per sq. ft.

$= 62\text{·}43\,H$ lbs. per sq. ft.

$= \text{·}434\,H$ lbs. per sq. inch.

Over any other area, say A sq. ft., the

total pressure $= wAH$ **lbs.**

Head of Water. These pressures as we have seen are independent of the shape of the vessel, hence our imaginary column need not actually exist so long as the water exerting the pressure is at a depth H below the free surface of *the same body of water*, see fig. 17 *B*. This is generally the condition which exists in a water supply system, in which, when the water is at rest, the pressure at any point depends upon the vertical distance which that point is below the free surface of the reservoir supplying the system. This vertical distance is usually referred to as the "head of water at that point" or briefly the **head**.

If "H" in the preceding expressions be taken to stand for "head" they may be applied to all such cases of water pressure. As an easily remembered (but very approximate) statement, plumbers frequently speak of pressure in water pipes as "increasing $\frac{1}{2}$ lb. per sq. in. for every foot of head."

For liquids other than water the density (say d) should be substituted for w. Then:

total pressure = dAH lbs.

The U-tube method of finding the relative densities of liquids. If two liquids, which do not mix and are of differing densities, are poured carefully into a U-tube as shown in fig. 19 they will come to rest with a definite dividing surface as shown at *A*. Imagine a horizontal line drawn through *A* and cutting the other tube in *B* and let the heights of the liquids above this line be H_1 and H_2 at *A* and *B* respectively.

Now it is possible to show, that in the same body of any liquid at rest *the pressures are the same at all points on the same horizontal plane* passing through the liquid. Let *AB* represent such a horizontal plane, since the liquid beneath it is continuous and all of the same kind, the *pressure at A equals the pressure at B.* Further let the

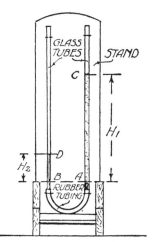

Fig. 19. Relative densities of liquids by the U-tube method.

column AC consist of water of density w and the column BD of some other liquid of density d (at present unknown), then:

$$\text{intensity of pressure at } A = wH_1,$$

and   ,,   ,,   ,, $B = dH_2;$

but these pressures have been shown to be equal,

$$\therefore\ wH_1 = dH_2,$$

i.e. $$\frac{H_1}{H_2} = \frac{d}{w} = \frac{\text{density of liquid}}{\text{density of water}} = \text{Relative density of liquid,}$$

or $$\text{Relative density of liquid} = \frac{\text{Height of column of water}}{\text{Height of column of liquid}}.$$

If two liquids are to be used which mix, mercury may be placed in the bend of the tube to separate them. In this case the amounts of the liquids are adjusted until the two surfaces of the mercury are on the same level. The heights of the columns are then measured from these surfaces.

Experiment 11. To find the relative density of mercury (water and mercury do not readily mix).

Height of column of water $= H_1 = 73 \cdot 5$ cms.

,,   ,,   ,, mercury $= H_2 = 5 \cdot 4$ cms.

$$\therefore\ \textbf{Relative density of mercury} = \frac{H_1}{H_2} = \frac{73 \cdot 5}{5 \cdot 4} = 13 \cdot 6.$$

Experiment 12. To find the relative density of sea water. (The two liquids would mix and are therefore separated by mercury as described above.)

Height of water above mercury $= H_1 = 68 \cdot 5$ cms.

,,   sea water ,,   ,, $= H_2 = 66 \cdot 75$ cms.

$$\therefore\ \textbf{Relative density of sea water} = \frac{H_1}{H_2} = \frac{68 \cdot 5}{66 \cdot 75} = 1 \cdot 025.$$

How to graduate and test a Mercury Manometer. After reading the preceding paragraphs on the U-tube method of finding the relative densities of liquids, the similarity in principle between that apparatus and the mercury manometer should be apparent. In both pieces of apparatus we may balance a column of water or other liquid against a column of mercury.

So far we have used the mercury manometer only for the *comparison* of pressures, but it will be possible for us now to graduate or mark off a scale which, on being suitably attached to the manometer, will give us not merely the difference in levels of the surfaces but also the corresponding *heads of water* and the *pressures*.

To set out the scale. This may be done directly by calculation alone but the following method will be found both interesting and economical of time and effort.

We have seen that mercury is 13·6 times as heavy as water, hence a column of water 13·6 ft. high would balance a column of mercury 1 ft. high when placed in a U-tube as already described. Use this ratio to con-

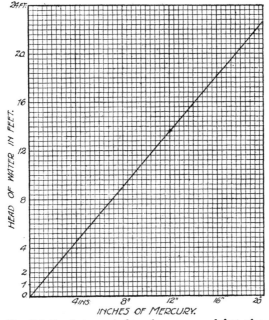

Fig. 20. Relation between inches of mercury and feet of water.

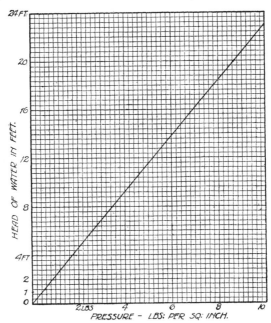

Fig. 21. Relation between head and pressure.

struct a graph to show the relation between inches in the mercury column
and feet in the column of water, see fig. 20. (*Note.* No other values need be
calculated since we know that the heights of the columns vary directly, hence
the graph is a straight line passing through zero.)

Utilising the expression given on p. 23, note next that with a head of say
10 ft.

$$\text{the pressure per sq. inch} = wH$$
$$= \cdot 434 \times 10$$
$$= 4 \cdot 34 \text{ lbs.}$$

Use this ratio to construct a graph to show the relation between head of
water and pressure, see fig. 21.

Finally take a piece of $\frac{1}{10}''$ squared paper wide enough to go between the
tubes of the manometer, paste a strip of plain paper down the centre and,
utilising the two graphs just drawn, mark off the "heads" and "pressures"
corresponding to "inches of mercury," as shown in fig. 22.

The construction of the Manometer. While the principle of the
manometer shown in fig. 23 is exactly the same as in those already used,
the form has been considerably altered for reasons which will be apparent as
we proceed. The scale just set out is attached to a board which is capable
of sliding up and down between the two tubes of the manometer, the zero of
the scale may thus be adjusted to the lower surface at A and the height
h to the surface B read off on the opposite side with its equivalent head and
pressure.

Above A the tube of the manometer is continued to the top of the stand
where it turns over and continues down to the bottom. At this point it is
connected to the tubes or vessel, the pressure in which is being measured.
On being connected to the pressure system the water will rise in this outer
tube compressing the air between the surfaces C and A; unless, however, the
pressure is considerable the water will not reach to the top of the bend and
the mercury will be kept free of water; this is a great advantage and explains
the design of the manometer. Between C and A the pressure will be *transmitted* through the compressed air in the tube, see p. 17. Within the
limits of the apparatus it may be used for measuring air pressure as well as
water pressure.

To test the scale, connect the manometer to a long vertical tube and by
means of a branch connection as shown fill the tube with water (this branch
may be used for emptying the tube at the close of the experiment). At intervals
measure the difference in levels of the surfaces of the water at C and D and
note whether this corresponds to the "head" as given by the scale.

Water Pressure Tests on Drains. One of the tests utilised
in the examinations of drains is to submit them to water pressure.
The lower end of the portion of the drain to be tested is closed
with a special form of rubber plug or drain stopper. The drain
is then filled with water to a level previously settled and the free
surface carefully watched. A continuous fall is then taken to
indicate a leak, which must be located and remedied before the
drain can be considered satisfactory. If the school laboratory
contains a short length of drain set up for the purpose of tests
such as these it will be interesting to ascertain experimentally
the magnitude of the pressures usually obtained in these tests.

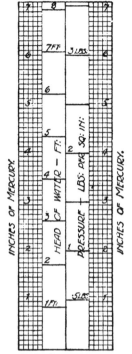

Fig. 22. Scale for mercury manometer.

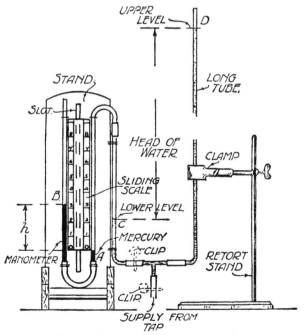

Fig. 23. Testing a mercury manometer.

Failing such a drain the following or similar connections may be
made at each end of a short length of drain pipe and the experiment carried out in that way (see also p. 36).

Experiment 13. **To ascertain the pressures in a drain under test.**
Close the lower end of the drain, fig. 24 A, by means of a rubber stopper
provided with a nozzle.   Connect the nozzle to the manometer with as long
a piece of tube as space allows; add a branch connection to the tap as before.
The drain may be filled in this way from the bottom.   The upper end of the
drain, fig. 24 B, may be left open unless the "fall" be not great, in which

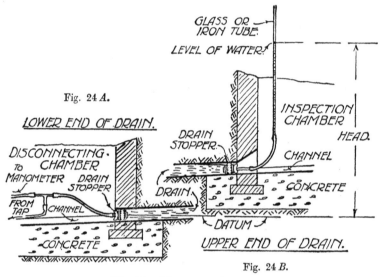

Fig. 24.   Water test of a drain.

case another stopper should be used to the nozzle of which is attached a long
vertical tube. Fairly considerable heads may thus be obtained, the procedure
being exactly the same as in testing the manometer. The "heads" should
be measured from a *datum line,* which may conveniently pass through the
centre of the lower stopper as shown, and the corresponding pressures
obtained by the manometer.

**The surface or surfaces of a liquid at rest rises every-
where to the same level.** If a number of branches ran into
the drain just tested and were all equally open to the atmosphere,
then we should find that when the water had come to rest the
level of the free surface in each pipe would be exactly the same.
This is a fact of great importance in designing water supplies. As
already stated it is the cause of pressure in the system and it also
explains why it is that water will not rise to any level in the system
higher than the free surface of the reservoir supplying the system.

Experiment 14. To ascertain the fall in a length of drain. Fit a stopper and tube, similar to that shown in fig. 24 B, to the *lower* end of the portion of the drain selected. Fill the drain with water until it reaches the upper end and note the height of the surface of the water in the tube above the centre of the stopper. This evidently gives the "fall."

Pressure in Water-logged Soils. Ground which is beneath the level of a river or pond situated close by is often water-logged. If a building with a basement is erected on such a site special precautions have to be taken not only to keep the basement dry (see Chap. v) but also to meet the pressure which exists owing to the presence of the water. We have seen that in a liquid, at any level, pressure is exerted equally in all directions, in the case we are now considering the additional thrusts on the side walls and the floors which arise in this way may be very considerable. Similar pressures are exerted on concrete centering when the concrete is laid in a wet condition, particularly in tall column boxes. In both cases special precautions must be taken to meet these thrusts.

Example. *The underside of a basement floor, 15′ × 12′, is 5 ft. below the "saturation line" (water level), calculate the upward pressure exerted on the floor.*

With a head of 5 ft. the upward pressure $= 62\cdot43 \times 5 = 312$ lbs. per sq. ft.

$$\therefore \quad \text{Total pressure on floor} = 312 \times 15 \times 12$$
$$= 56,300 \text{ lbs.}$$
$$= 25 \text{ tons (nearly).}$$

Experiment 15. To illustrate the presence of upward pressure in water-logged soils. Partly fill a strong glass jar with coarse sand and on it place an empty beaker or any suitable metal vessel with a smooth exterior surface. Now fill the jar right up with sand so as to enclose the beaker, see fig. 25, and push down into the sand a tube provided with a funnel as shown.

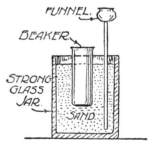

Fig. 25. Upward pressures in water-logged soils.

Pour water down the tube as rapidly as it passes into the air spaces in the sand and note the rise of the level on the outside of the jar. As soon as this level passes the bottom of the beaker it will commence to rise steadily out of the sand, being pushed up by the thrust exerted from beneath. A rough estimate of the magnitude of this thrust may be obtained by loading the beaker in any convenient way and removing the weights until it just commences to rise. The weight of the beaker and the remaining weights will be a measure of the upward thrust less the friction on the sides of the vessel.

PROBLEMS II

1.   If the bottom of the jar shown in fig. 17 A is circular and 5″ diameter, calculate the total pressure upon it if the depth of the water is 21″.

2.   What is the total pressure (in grams) on a horizontal surface 8 cms. × 6 cms. at a depth of 38 cms. below the free surface of the water?

3.   If the jar in question 1 were filled with turpentine (R.D. 0·87), calculate the pressure per sq. inch on the bottom, depth 21 ins.

4.   What is the depth of the water in the tank mentioned in the example on p. 22?

• 5.   Calculate the pressure per sq. inch in the boiler of a hot water system given that the free surface of the water in the supply cistern is 40 ft. above the boiler.

6.   Calculate (a) the head of water necessary to give a pressure in a drain of 3·5 lbs. per sq. inch and (b) the corresponding difference in levels in a mercury manometer.

7.   By suitable drainage the saturation line in water-logged soils may be lowered.   Calculate the *reduction in total pressure* on the floor mentioned on p. 29 if the water level is lowered by 2 ft.

8.   (See also Problems I, 11.)   In a ball-cock the upward force of the floating ball is transmitted and multiplied by a lever and presses a flat valve against the end of the water supply pipe (see fig. 38, p. 43).   If the internal diameter of the pipe at the valve is ⅜″ and the water pressure 35 lbs. per sq. inch, calculate the minimum force necessary to keep the valve against the end of the pipe.

9.   In some tests of very coarse drain pipes it was found, (a) that a considerable amount of water came through the body of the pipes when the pressure was 12 lbs. per sq. inch and (b) that the pipes were fractured at a pressure of 160 lbs. per sq. inch.   Calculate the equivalent head in feet of water at these two pressures.

10.   In testing a length of drain the lower end is closed with a drain stopper and the drain filled with water until the level rises 6 ft. above the stopper. What would be the pressure per sq. inch, and also the total pressure on the stopper, given that the drain was 4 ins. internal diameter?

11.   What is meant by the term "head of water"?   Describe some practical problems in which a knowledge of this term is of value.   By how much does the pressure per sq. foot increase for each foot increase in depth of water?

12.   The safety valve to a hot-water boiler is designed to "blow off" at a pressure of 30 lbs. per sq. in.   What is the head of water equivalent to such a pressure?   If the area of the valve subjected to this pressure has a diameter of 0·5 inch, what must be the total weight of the valve to allow it to "blow off" at this pressure?

CHAPTER III

AIR PRESSURE. SIMPLE PUMPING APPLIANCES AND SIPHONS USED IN BUILDING

The Density of Air. So far as the scope of this volume is concerned the question of gaseous pressure need only be considered in relation to air. This gas—or mixture of gases (see Chap. x)—is familiar to us all as forming the atmosphere which we breathe. Considered as a whole the atmosphere completely surrounds the earth and is held to it by the force of gravitation, in other words **air has weight** and the following simple laboratory experiment may be carried out to verify this fact.

Experiment 16. To show that air has weight. Take a strong round-bottomed flask of about 750 cu. cms. capacity and fit it with a rubber stopper, glass tube and tap as shown in fig. 26. By means of a short rubber tube connect the flask to an air-pump (see p. 39) and pump the air from the flask. Turn the tap, disconnect from the pump and weigh the flask. By turning the tap again admit air to the flask and note that the pan of the balance is depressed and more weights are necessary to restore equilibrium. The weights added will be a rough indication of the weight of air contained in the flask.

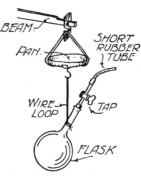

Fig. 26. · The weight of air.

The density of air is 1·29 grams per litre or 1·29 ozs. per cubic foot, *at 0° C. and a pressure of 760 mms. of mercury, see p. 33.* (Note the coincidence in the values given.)

Gaseous Pressure. In the preceding chapter it was stated that all gases tend to occupy as large a space as possible, this statement leads directly to another of equal importance, viz. that all gases when contained in closed vessels exert *pressure* on the sides of the vessels.

If, as suggested on p. 17, the nozzle of a bicycle pump be closed and force be applied to the piston, the air in the barrel of the pump will be compressed and occupy less space. On the removal of the force the pressure in the barrel will be sufficient to move the piston back to its original position. Hence we may conclude that *the reduction in volume* of a given mass of gas is accompanied by an *increase in pressure*. Conversely it may be shown that an increase in volume is accompanied by a reduction in pressure, assuming throughout that the temperature remains constant.

We have already mentioned the air-pump and we shall presently explain its action; let us for the present, however, consider its effect upon the pressure within the flask in the experiment described on p. 31. As each portion of air is withdrawn from the flask the air still remaining expands and fills the flask. As this effect corresponds to the increase in volume mentioned above it is accompanied by a decrease in pressure within the flask. When all the air has been removed from the flask we have a **vacuum**, i.e. a space empty of all matter and *the pressure would be zero*. (In practice it is not possible to obtain a perfect vacuum, there is always a small residue of air, or other gases, and therefore a slight pressure.)

Atmospheric Pressure. We have already shown that air has weight and, since we may consider the atmosphere as an immensely thick layer of air resting on the surface of the earth, it must evidently exert pressure upon the earth in virtue of its weight (compare with water pressure). This pressure is known as **atmospheric pressure** and the following simple experiments should serve to verify its presence and show something of its intensity.

Experiment 17. To show that pressure is exerted by the atmosphere
(a) Over the large end of a bell-jar pass a piece of thin flexible rubber sheeting, binding it securely below the rim with several layers of soft cord. Fit the jar with a rubber stopper and glass tube and connect to an air-pump. As the air is withdrawn from the jar the pressure inside the jar is reduced. Outside

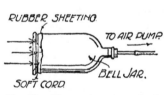 

Fig. 27. Illustrating atmospheric   Fig. 28. Illustrating atmospheric
pressure.   pressure.

the jar the atmospheric pressure remains constant and being now the greater of the two pressures (equal at the commencement of the experiment) it is able to force the sheeting into the jar as shown in fig. 27. (Refer to the "siphonage" of the contents of a trap, p. 45, in which a similar effect is produced.)

(b) Obtain a cubical box, of about 3" or 4" sides, of thin sheet tin and solder a short piece of brass tubing to a hole in the lid, see fig. 28 (test the box under water to see that it is air-tight). Fill the box about one-quarter full with water and heat the whole over a bunsen burner. When steam has been issuing from the tube for a few minutes, and the box may be assumed to be full of steam, cork the tube and quickly drop the box into cold water. The box will at once crumple up and be completely destroyed.

When the box is dropped into cold water the steam, which fills the box, is quickly converted into water owing to the large fall in temperature. Since the water thus formed occupies only about $\frac{1}{1720}$th of the volume occupied by the steam a partial vacuum is produced, accompanied by a considerable reduction in the pressure within the box. Outside the box the atmospheric pressure remains constant and is sufficiently in excess of the internal pressure to cause the collapse of the box.

The Intensity of Atmospheric Pressure. Having noted the presence of atmospheric pressure we may now proceed to discuss the means at our disposal for *measuring its intensity.*

Experiment 18. To balance the pressure of the atmosphere against a column of mercury in a U-tube. Take a U-tube, of which the longer arm is about 44 inches and the shorter one about 36 inches. Put in sufficient mercury to reach at least 18 ins. above the bend in each tube and connect the shorter arm to an air-pump, see fig. 29. As the air is exhausted the pressure over the mercury in the short arm is reduced below that of the atmosphere and the atmospheric pressure, acting on the surface at B, is able to depress the mercury at that side forcing it higher and higher in the other arm. If it were possible to produce a perfect vacuum over A, then the difference in levels would be about 30 inches and it ought not to be difficult for the student to see that, when such is the case, the atmospheric pressure acting on B is supporting a column of mercury of this height.

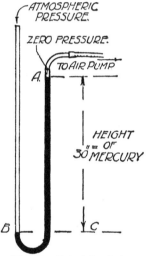

Fig. 29. Principle of the barometer.

Further, knowing the density of mercury, we may calculate the intensity of pressure at the base of the column $A\hat{C}$ and on a level with the surface at B, this will evidently equal *the intensity of the atmospheric pressure* acting on B.

Taking the height of the column of mercury as 30″ (or 760 mm.), the density of mercury as 13·6 and of water 62·43 we have:

Standard **Atmospheric Pressure** = height × density × area

$$= \tfrac{30}{12} \times 13\cdot 6 \times 62\cdot 43 \text{ per sq. ft.}$$

$$= \frac{30 \times 13\cdot 6 \times 62\cdot 43}{12 \times 144} \text{ per sq. inch}$$

$$= 14\cdot 7 \text{ lbs. per sq. inch}$$

$$= 1033 \text{ gms. per sq. cm.}$$

This is known as *a pressure of one atmosphere* and is sometimes used as a unit of pressure.

The Barometer. Owing to the mechanical difficulties involved in producing and maintaining a vacuum the U-tube described in Experiment 18 is not convenient for practical use. Instead we use the familiar **barometer** (weight measurer), either in the form of a *mercury barometer* or an *aneroid barometer*.

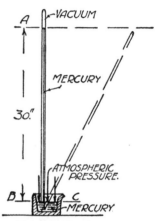

Fig. 30. The barometer.

If a glass tube, closed at one end and about 33 inches long, is filled with mercury and inverted over a bowl of mercury, with its open end beneath the surface, the mercury will fall away from the upper end of the tube as the tube approaches the vertical position, see fig. 30. When it has come to rest the height of the surface of the mercury in the tube, above the surface of the mercury in the bowl, will be found to be about 30 inches. Since no air has been introduced into the tube, the space at the top of the tube must evidently be a vacuum and the conditions of equilibrium of the mercury in the tube are evidently the same as those shown in fig. 29.

This explains the construction of the ordinary **mercury barometer.** There are several types of these in use, the chief difference being in the mode of measuring the difference in levels between the two surfaces of mercury.

The **aneroid barometer** depends for its action upon the movements of the sides of a hermetically sealed metal box, from which the air has been partially removed. The variations in atmospheric pressure cause slight movements in the sides of the box and these are communicated to the pointer of the instrument through multiplying levers. The graduations on an aneroid barometer are made to correspond to those of the mercury barometer, that is they are equivalent to inches or millimetres of mercury.

Uses of the barometer. (1) Anyone who has watched a barometer from day to day will have noticed the variations in pressure that are continually taking place; these variations are directly connected with the state of the atmosphere and explain the use of the barometer for registering and forecasting the weather.

(2) As we have already seen the volume of a gas is considerably affected by pressure, and what is probably the most important scientific use to which the barometer is put is to ascertain the pressure at the time of any particular experiment in which it is an important factor.

(3) Just as the pressure in a column of water varies with the depth so the atmospheric pressure decreases as we rise from the surface of the earth. Unlike water, however, gases are very compressible hence variation in pressure results in a variation in density, since if a given mass of gas be compelled to occupy less space it will obviously be more dense. Conversely reduction in pressure results in reduction in density. Thus it arises that the reductions in pressure which are experienced as we rise from the surface of the earth are not capable of such simple calculation as are pressures in water, since they are affected by the reduction in density as well as by the reduction in pressure due to weight alone.

These variations, however, are all registered by the barometer and this explains the use of this instrument to measure the heights of mountains. The calculations necessary, if really satisfactory values are to be obtained, are not simple. For very approximate results it is useful to note that at sea-level and with a temperature of 20° C. a change in level of about 95 ft. corresponds to a difference in reading of the barometer of $\frac{1}{10}''$.

A manometer to measure pressures less than one atmosphere. The principle underlying the construction of the U-tube shown in fig. 29 furnishes us with a method of constructing a manometer capable of measuring pressures less than atmospheric

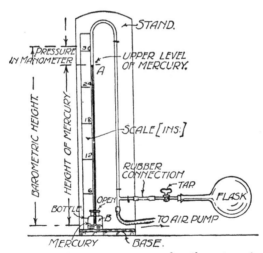

Fig. 31. A manometer to measure pressures less than atmospheric pressure.

pressure. This will be found convenient when dealing with the exhaustion of air from a vessel since it will enable us to ascertain the state of exhaustion reached at any instant.

The instrument is shown in fig. 31. It consists of an inverted U-tube, the longer arm of which is 36 ins. long and dips into a glass bottle containing mercury. The shorter arm is connected to the air-pump with a T-piece interposed so as to afford a connection to the vessel to be exhausted.

As the air is pumped out of the tube and vessel the pressure is reduced above the surface A of the mercury in the longer arm. The atmospheric pressure acting on the surface of the mercury in the bottle then forces the mercury up the tube until equilibrium is restored, when the pressure on the mercury in bottle (atmospheric pressure) is balanced by the column of mercury *plus* the pressure of the partially exhausted air in the tube of the manometer acting on the surface of the mercury at A. Suppose, for example, that the mercury column is 24 ins. high and that the barometer at the time of the experiment registers 30 ins. Then if p be the pressure in the manometer and flask we have:

$$24 + p = 30,$$
or
$$p = 30 - 24,$$
$$= 6 \text{ ins. of mercury.}$$

Hence the pressure above A at any moment in inches of mercury is given by the difference between the height of the mercury column and the barometric height at the time of the experiment. *The height to the surface A must be measured from the surface of the mercury in the bottle.*

The measurement of air pressures above that of the atmosphere may be carried out by means of the manometer shown in fig. 23 provided that they are not very great. For high pressures a suitable form of manometer is described at the end of this chapter, see fig. 45.

Air-pressure Tests on a Drain. If the drain mentioned in Chap. II is available such a test may be carried out. Both ends of the drain are stopped and an inlet for the air-pipe provided at one end. The pressures are obtained by means of a suitable compression air-pump (a motor-pump is convenient) and the values may be read off on the manometer shown in fig. 23, any continuous fall in pressure may be taken to indicate a leak. If the manometer has been marked so as to show "feet of water" as well as "lbs. per sq. inch," then the *equivalent head of water* may be noted.

With air-pressure tests on drains the pressures do not usually exceed $2\frac{1}{2}$ lbs. per sq. inch above atmospheric pressure. For water tests the maximum head is usually stated as 10 ft., equivalent to 4·34 lbs. per sq. inch. With an air test the leaks are difficult to locate, hence smoke is usually driven in with the air. This test differs from the water test in that *all parts of the drain are subjected to the same pressure.* With the water test the pressures vary, being greater at the lowest levels. As, however, the latter test approximates more closely to the actual conditions which would exist if the drains were blocked it may be considered more satisfactory; it is undoubtedly the most severe. It is not, however, suitable for testing soil pipes or other long vertical lengths of pipes owing to the high pressures produced at the bottom.

Simple Pumping Appliances in Building. Since the action of pumps may be largely explained in terms of air and water pressure it will be convenient for us to deal at this stage with some simple forms of pumps.

The Common Lift Pump. This type is used for raising water from shallow wells, cisterns or trenches, where the quantities to be dealt with are not great. Fig. 32 gives a diagrammatic section of the pump showing the various parts. The piston, which has a valve opening upwards, is made to move vertically in the barrel of the pump by means of a connecting rod and cranked handle. The bottom of the barrel is connected directly to the suction pipe into which the water enters through a strainer at the bottom. An upward opening valve covers the top end of the suction pipe. For lifts above 5 ft. another valve, known as the foot valve, should be placed at the bottom of the suction pipe to prevent the return of the water in this pipe.

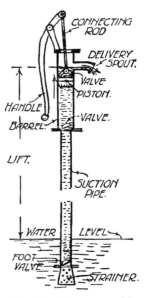

Fig. 32. The common lift pump.

The action of the pump is as follows. As the piston is raised from its lowest position a partial vacuum is formed beneath it, reducing the pressure in the suction pipe and causing the water to flow into it. On the return stroke the valves at the bottom of the barrel and at the foot of the suction pipe close, the air is compressed in the barrel and some of it passes out through the valve in the piston. This cycle of operations is repeated until the barrel is full of water when, on the next downward stroke of the piston, water passes through to the upper side of the piston and the next upward stroke raises this water which then flows from the spout.

Contractor's Pumps for Excavations. For raising the water which accumulates in trenches and excavations a simple form of lift pump may be used, but as considerable quantities of water may have to be dealt with, containing sand and gritty matter, a diaphragm pump is usually preferred. This type of pump is shown in fig. 33. The moving piston is replaced by a leather or rubber diaphragm having an upward opening valve at its centre. Another valve is placed at the bottom of the barrel.

The action of the valves is similar to that of the lift pump.   The small movement of the diaphragm is compensated for by its large diameter; 12″ is a common size.   The diaphragm may be replaced by a piston when the pump becomes a lift pump of large diameter and short stroke.

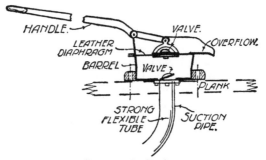

Fig. 33.   Contractor's diaphragm pump.

The Lift and Force Pump.   The power of the pumps already treated to "lift" water through a certain head is limited by their power to reduce the air pressure over the water in the suction pipe. But, even if it were possible to create a perfect vacuum in the suction pipe, the water could not rise higher than 34 ft., for, as we have seen, atmospheric pressure is capable of supporting a column of mercury 2·5 ft. high, but mercury is 13·6 times heavier than water, hence the equivalent water column is 2·5 × 13·6 or 34 ft. high.   In practice, owing to the fact that it is impossible to make pistons absolutely air-tight and also because water gives off a vapour at low pressures destroying the vacuum, the maximum "lift" is reached at about 25 ft.

When water has to be raised to greater heights than this a **lift and force pump** is used.   A simple form, suitable for raising water from deep wells or up to high cisterns, is shown in fig. 34. This type is similar to the lift pump shown in fig. 32, except that the top of the barrel is closed and the delivery pipe provided with a non-return valve, which prevents the return of the water into the barrel on the down-stroke of the piston.   Such a pump would be placed near the water at the bottom of the well and the piston worked through a long connecting rod reaching from the top of the well.

In order to give a steady delivery an air chamber is usually attached to this type of pump.   The air in the chamber is compressed by the rising water and during the down-stroke of the piston this pressure is sufficient to keep the water moving steadily up the delivery pipe, see fig. 34.

If the delivery pipe is led from the bottom of the pump, as at *A* in fig. 34, the valve in the piston may be omitted and a heavy

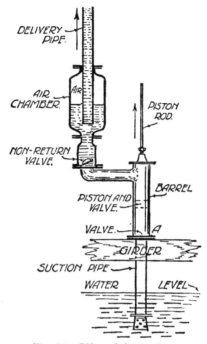

Fig. 34.   Lift and force pump.

solid ram substituted for the piston. In this form the pump is known as a **force pump** and is used for creating hydraulic pressure for power and other purposes.

Air-pumps for Laboratory Use. We have already mentioned the use of air-pumps in experimental work. There are several types of these available, two of which are described below; these have been selected because they are simple in action and give results sufficiently satisfactory for our purpose.

Tate's Double-acting Air-pump. A sectional elevation of this type of pump is given in fig. 35, which shows the air being exhausted from a glass receiver. Two solid pistons are connected to the piston rod, at a distance apart a little less than half the length of the barrel of the pump. They are capable of moving close up to the end plates of the barrel. Each end of the barrel is provided with an outward opening valve of oiled silk.

In the drawing the pistons are shown moving towards the right. The air enclosed at the right-hand end is being compressed and forced through the valve *A* against atmospheric pressure. At the other end the small amount of air left in the pump when the piston started to move away from that end is being gradually expanded and its pressure reduced. When this latter piston

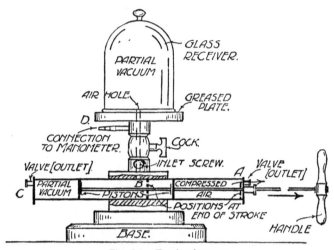

Fig. 35.   Tate's air-pump.

passes the opening *B*, leading from the receiver, air rushes in from the receiver to equalise the pressure; this, in its turn, is compressed and forced through the valve *C* into the air. This action is repeated until the exhaustion is complete. A connection is provided at *D* for a manometer and also an inlet screw to let the air in at the close of the experiment.

The "Filter" Pump. This is a handy little pump for laboratory use, being both cheap and efficient, see fig. 36. It is worked by water-pressure and with pressures of not less than 25 lbs. per sq. in. will give a good degree of exhaustion. This type of pump may be obtained in glass or metal and may if preferred be connected permanently to the water supply system. (For pressures exceeding 30 to 35 lbs. per sq. inch this should always be done since in these cases rubber pressure tubing is not strong enough.) There are no moving parts to the pump.

The water under pressure passes down the tube *AB* inside the bulb *C*. At *A* this tube narrows down and expands again at *B* where it finishes just in the neck of the bulb. The water passing through the tube is thus "broken up" and on continuing down the discharge pipe at D it carries bubbles of air forward with it. Air is thus drawn from the bulb and also from any vessel connected to it at E. The tap at E should always be turned before stopping the water, otherwise water will be drawn back and over into the vessel.

The efficiency of the above and any other form of air-pump may be readily compared by connecting them in turn to the mercury manometer described on p. 35.

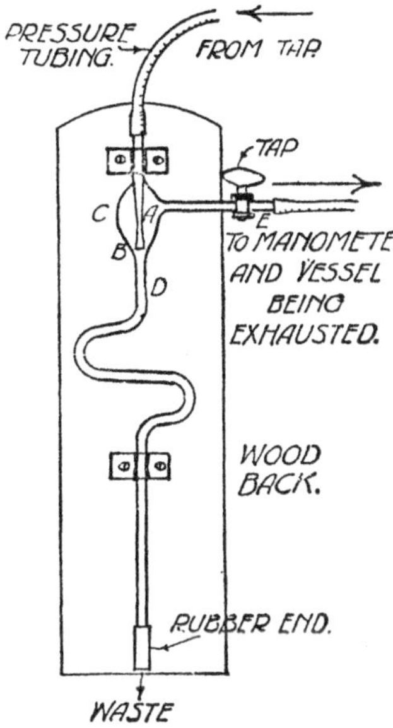

The Siphon. This piece of apparatus is met with in a variety of forms in building. It consists essentially of a tube for discharging a liquid from a tank or vessel of any kind to some point at a lower level, the tube having to pass over some obstacle between the two points. In fig. 37 a siphon is shown in use for drawing oil or

Fig. 36. The "filter" pump.

other liquid from a heavy drum not provided with a tap. Using the same figure the action may be simply explained as follows. Assume the two arms of the siphon full of liquid with both ends of the tube closed. Then the pressure at F would be that due to the column of liquid BF while at C it would be that due to the column BC, which is the greater of the two. When the ends of the siphons are opened the liquid would be subjected in each case to atmospheric pressure but owing to the greater weight of the column of liquid in BC the net pressure at C would be *less* than at F and water would flow from F to C. This action would continue so long as C was below the surface of the liquid in the drum and the tube remained full.

When used as suggested in fig. 37 the two arms of the siphon may be conveniently filled, preparatory to starting the siphon, by means of the suction tube DE. C is closed and on drawing air from E atmospheric pressure forces the liquid up the arm AB and over the bend filling the siphon.

The filling of a siphon by a suction tube ought to suggest to the reader that while in action the pressure at the bend B in a siphon is less than atmospheric pressure. If a leak occurs at B

air is drawn in and both arms of the tube empty. Leaks at the highest point in a siphon are a frequent cause of trouble in large siphons. In this connection it should be noted that the height over which a siphon will carry water is only limited by the amount

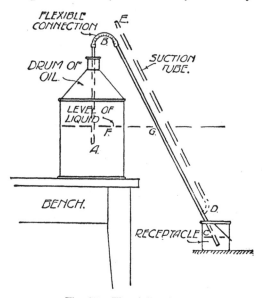

Fig. 37. The siphon in use.

of atmospheric pressure, 34 ft. being the theoretical maximum Siphons are not so effective at high altitudes owing to the reduction in atmospheric pressure.

SIPHONS IN BUILDING

Water-waste Preventers. These are used for flushing purposes; for obvious reasons they must be so constructed as to be capable of emptying their contents quickly without the adoption of large valves likely to get out of order. Some form of the siphon is usually adopted for this purpose, the variations in design being chiefly limited to the means selected for starting the siphon.

Fig. 38 shows a reliable type of action not likely to go wrong. The top of the flush pipe *A* is carried above the highest level of the water in the cistern and is completely covered with a heavy metal dome *C*. This hood is enlarged at the bottom and fits loosely into a cylindrical depression *D* in the bottom of the cistern. The figure shows the cistern full and ready for use. To start the siphonic action the dome is raised by pulling on the chain and then allowed to fall. Its weight causes it to fall with sufficient speed to force the water up from D into the top of the dome and over

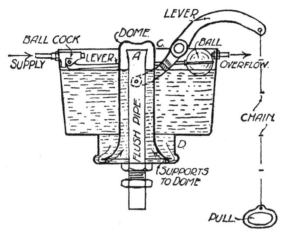

Fig. 38. Action of a water-waste preventer.

into the flush pipe, this starts the action which goes on until the cistern is emptied. The space between the dome and the flush pipe and the flush pipe itself form the two "arms" of the siphon.

Automatic Flush Tanks. These tanks are so constructed that they give a flush at definite intervals, the interval being regulated by the rate at which the tank is filled. A well-known

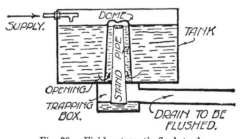

Fig. 39. Field automatic flush tank.

type is the Field flush tank which is illustrated in fig. 39. The stand pipe A is covered over with a metal dome provided with openings at the bottom to allow the water to enter and rise inside. The lower end of the stand pipe dips slightly into a small

secondary tank connected directly with the drain to be flushed.
As the water rises in the hood the air in the stand pipe is compressed
and forced out at the lower end, the water there forming a trap
and preventing its return.   Finally water begins to overflow at
the top of the stand pipe, the top of which is so formed that the
overflowing water is broken up and carries air-bubbles with it,
some of these escape through the trap at the bottom and the
pressure inside of A is reduced, water comes over more quickly,
finally the siphon is started and the cistern emptied rapidly.   This
form of tank is very valuable where small driblets of water are to
be collected and utilised for flushing purposes.

Experimental illustrations.   The actions of both of the cisterns
mentioned above may be readily illustrated experimentally.   Fig. 40 shows
a simple piece of apparatus designed to illustrate the Field tank.   The water
flows into a bell-jar, through the cork of which passes a straight tube.   The
top end of the tube is covered by an inverted test tube, weighted to keep it
in position.   The lower end of the tube dips into a small vessel full of water.
The action is as already described.   If the vessel be removed at the bottom
of the tube the siphon will only act with a quick supply.   The action of the
water-waste preventer may be illustrated by choosing a test tube which fits
loosely into the neck of the bell-jar (which should be fairly long).

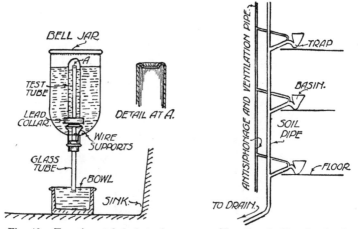

Fig. 40. Experimental flush tank.   Fig. 41. Outline sketch of
                                                  arrangement of closets.

The "Siphonage" of Traps in Water-closets.   In buildings
of several storeys it is usual to arrange the water-closets on each
floor so that they are vertically over each other and discharge
into one soil pipe, see fig. 41.   Fig. 42 shows one of the closets to
a larger scale with the usual connections; let this represent the
closet on the ground floor and let us suppose that the contents

of one of the closets above has been discharged into the soil pipe and that no opening is provided in the branch, as at *F*. In passing the end *A* of the branch pipe *AB*, this *broken body* of water will cause the same action as was set up in the filter pump described on p. **41**, that is *air will be drawn from the branch pipe*. This withdrawal of air will cause a reduction of pressure in the branch *AB*, that is over the water surface *B* in the trap. If the reduction of pressure be sufficiently great the atmospheric pressure acting on the water surface *C* will force the whole body of water into the branch and no *water seal* will be left in the trap. In practice the action is not usually so complete as this, but sufficient of the water may be

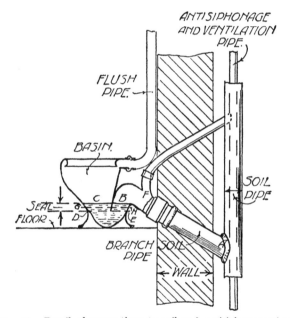

Fig. 42.   Detail of connections to soil and antisiphonage pipe.

carried over to reduce the water level from *BC* to say *GH*, thus reducing the "seal." Again if the lower end of the soil pipe be trapped or in some way obstructed the falling body of water will compress the air in the soil pipe and branches, the variation in pressure causing the water in the trap to oscillate with a consequent reduction of the seal. Finally if a pail of water be thrown suddenly into the closet it may be sufficient to fill the branch pipe and start a true siphonic action which would empty the trap and destroy the seal.

All these effects are due to variation in pressure taking place over B and they may to a large extent be prevented by forming an opening into the branch at F and connecting it to an anti-siphonage pipe, which communicates with the open air, keeping the pressure on each side of the trap equal and in addition serving to ventilate the branch pipe.

Experiment 19. **To illustrate the action of an antisiphonage pipe.** The effects described above may be readily illustrated by the apparatus shown in fig. 43. The soil, branch and antisiphonage pipes are represented by short lengths of glass tubing. The antisiphonage pipe may be closed by means of a clip. The contents of the vessel at C may be discharged suddenly

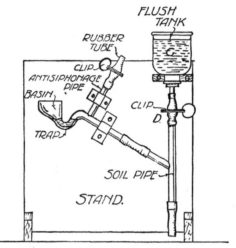

Fig. 43. Apparatus to illustrate the "siphonage" of a trap.

down the soil pipe by releasing the clip at D. (To ensure that this body of water is sufficiently broken up the cistern should empty through a tube of smaller bore than the soil pipe.)

Fill the trap with coloured water and note the effect upon it of a sudden discharge down the soil pipe both when the antisiphonage pipe is open and when it is closed.

Boyle's Law. We have already seen how air, or any other gas, is affected by the increase or decrease of pressure, we shall now proceed to investigate this more thoroughly. The most important law for us to deal with at this stage is known as **Boyle's Law**; this states that **the volume of a given mass of gas varies inversely as the pressure, the temperature being kept constant.** In other words if we have gas occupying a given *volume v* at a known pressure *p*, then if the pressure be *doubled* the volume will be *halved*, if the pressure be *quadrupled* the volume will only be *one-quarter* of the original volume, etc.   Thus

if   at pressure p volume of gas is v,

then   „   „ $2p$ „   „   will be $\frac{1}{2}v$,

            „   „ $3p$ „   „   „ $\frac{1}{3}v$,

            „   „ $4p$ „   „   „ $\frac{1}{4}v$.

If the *pressure* in each case is multiplied by the *corresponding volume* it will be found to give the same result every time, thus: $p \times v = pv$, $3p \times \frac{1}{3}v = pv$, $4p \times \frac{1}{4}v = pv$, etc.   This leads to the important statement of the law that *for a given mass of gas at a constant temperature the product of the pressure into the volume is constant.*

Experiment 20.   To verify Boyle's Law. For our purpose the simple form of apparatus shown in fig. 44 will suffice.   Mercury is poured into the bend and adjusted until it reaches the same level in each tube, say AA, the gas enclosed in the short arm being then at atmospheric pressure.   (This adjustment may be omitted.)   The length l_1 is then measured. Since the bore of the tube is uniform the length occupied by the air may be taken to be proportional to its volume.   Mercury is now poured into the longer arm and the height h_2 and the length l_2 measured.   Evidently the pressure on the enclosed air is equal to the atmospheric pressure plus the pressure due to the column of mercury of height h_2; this total pressure is found for each case and tabulated along with l as shown below.   The products in the last column should be fairly constant. The readings given were obtained as described.

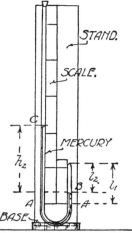

Fig. 44.   Apparatus to illustrate Boyle's law.

Height of Barometer, (1).	Values of h, (2).	Total pressure $=(1)+(2)=P$.	Values of $l=V$.	$P \times V$.
75·4 cms.	0 cms.	75·4 cms.	17·0 cms.	1280
75·4 „	4·7 „	80·1 „	16·05 „	1286
75·4 „	12·7 „	88·1 „	14·6 „	1287
75·4 „	23·7 „	99·1 „	12·9 „	1279
75·4 „	47·8 „	123·2 „	10·4 „	1282
75·4 „	60·4 „	135·8 „	9·47 „	1284

Experiment 21.   To construct a manometer to measure high pressures and to measure pressure at a water tap.   The following experiment describes a useful and interesting application of Boyle's Law.   The manometer

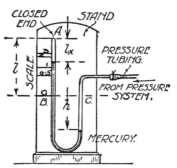

Fig. 45. A manometer for pressures above atmospheric pressure.

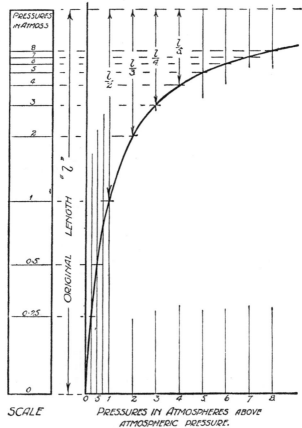

Fig. 46. Marking out a scale for the manometer.

consists of a U-tube having the end A closed. Mercury is introduced into the bend of the tube as before. Let the original levels of the mercury be B, C and let the length of air enclosed between B and A be l. If this air be subjected to pressure, l will be reduced in accordance with Boyle's Law and *from its length we may calculate the intensity of the pressure.*

Remembering that the original pressure of the air in the tube, with both levels of mercury the same, would be 1 atmosphere, if the pressure be increased to 2 atmospheres l will be halved; 3 atmospheres and l will be one-third of its original length. Thus for pressures measured *above that of the atmosphere* we have: an *increase* of 1 atmosphere reduces l to $l/2$, an increase of 2 atmospheres reduces l to $l/3$, etc. A graph may then be constructed, as shown in fig. 46, from which it is not difficult to mark out a suitable scale and attach it to the manometer. If l alters in length after the manometer has been in use for some time, it is a simple geometrical problem to increase or decrease the total length of the scale whilst keeping the ratios of the divisions the same (use radiating lines).

So long as the pressures are not too great this manometer may be used to measure pressures in water supply systems. An interesting experiment consists of testing the pressures on several floors of a high building to show the effect of height on the pressures. The equivalent pressures in lbs. per sq. inch may be readily marked on the scale. (See Problems III, 5.)

PROBLEMS III

1. Calculate the total resultant pressure acting on each face of the box, shown in fig. 28, given that a perfect vacuum is obtained inside the box, a $3\frac{1}{2}''$ cube, and that the barometer registers $28\cdot5''$ at the time of the experiment.

2. Calculate the pressure in lbs. per sq. inch in a gas main if, when tested with the manometer shown in fig. 23, and using water instead of mercury, the difference in levels of the surfaces is $2\frac{1}{2}''$.

3. Calculate the difference in pressure on the two surfaces of a water seal, see fig. 42, when it is sufficient to cause a difference in levels of $4''$.

4. If the barometer register $29\cdot8''$ what is the pressure in the manometer shown in fig. 31 when the mercury stands $23''$ above that in the bottle, (a) in inches of mercury, and (b) in lbs. per sq. inch?

5. In measuring the pressure at a tap with the manometer shown in fig. 45, the length l (originally $5''$) was reduced to $1\frac{1}{2}''$. Calculate (a) the pressure in the system in atmospheres above atmospheric pressure and (b) the pressure in lbs. per sq. inch.

6. Calculate the pressure in the barrel of a lift pump when the excess of the atmospheric pressure is able to support a column of water in the suction pipe of a height of 10 ft. Atmospheric pressure equal to $30''$ of mercury.

7. Given that the density of the air in a room at a given pressure and temperature was $1\cdot2$ oz. per cubic ft., calculate the weight of air passing into a room, 16 ft. by 14 ft. by 11 ft., in an hour if the air is changed completely five times during that period.

8. If the air chamber of the pump shown in fig. 34 contained $\frac{1}{2}$ cubic ft. of air at atmospheric pressure, what space would this air occupy when the water in the delivery pipe stood 30 ft. above the air chamber?

9. If the pressure in the room in question 7 rose from say 29″ to 30″ of mercury (a) what space would each cubic foot of the air originally in the room occupy and (b) what would then be the density of the air in the room?

10. In sinking deep foundations in water-logged soils caissons are used. These consist of an inverted cylindrical box, the bottom being open and the edges formed into cutting-edges. Through suitable doors men pass into the caisson from the top and excavate the earth at the bottom. The water is kept out by compressing the air within the caisson until it slightly exceeds the pressure due to the water in the soil.

If a caisson 6 ft. in diameter and weighing $2\frac{1}{4}$ tons has been sunk until its lowest edge is 12 ft. below the saturation line, calculate (a) the minimum weight necessary to keep the caisson from rising when full of air (neglecting friction on the sides), (b) the minimum pressure of the air within the caisson at this depth.

11. Describe, with sketches, the action of a flushing cistern (a) of the water waste preventer type and (b) of the automatic flushing type.

12. Explain why, in the gas supply services to buildings, the pressure of a gas increases with the height of the building.

If gas is delivered at the ground level of a building at 1 inch water gauge pressure, and the building is 80 ft. high, calculate the water gauge pressure and the pressure in lbs. per sq. in. of the gas at the top of the building, given that the gas pressure increases by $\frac{1}{100}$ inch water gauge pressure for every additional foot in height.

13. Explain what is meant by the term "atmospheric pressure." What is the intensity of pressure equal to "one atmosphere"? If the volume of a gas at atmospheric pressure is 100 cu. ft., what will be its volume at pressures of 20 and 50 atmospheres respectively if the temperature remains constant? Give the law upon which your calculation is based.

14. The compressed gas cylinders used in lead burning, welding, etc., have pressure gauges marked in atmospheres, since this affords a ready means of calculating the amount of gas in the cylinder.

(a) If when the cylinders are full the pressure is 120 atmospheres calculate the size of cylinders required to hold (i) 80 cu. ft., (ii) 100 cu. ft., (iii) 150 cu. ft.

(b) In an "80 cu. ft. cylinder" calculate the gas used when the pressure falls from 100 atmospheres to 40 atmospheres, given that the volume of the cylinder is $\frac{2}{3}$ cu. ft.

15. In the case of dissolved acetylene the method described in (14) does not give very accurate results. The amount of gas used is therefore calculated from the loss of weight of the cylinder. If a cylinder loses 20 oz. in weight calculate the volume of acetylene used, given that the density of air is 1·29 oz. per cubic foot (see p. 31) and acetylene has a density of 0·92 if the density of air is 1.

CHAPTER IV

THE STRUCTURE OF MATTER; ITS BEARING ON THE PREPARATION OF MORTAR AND CONCRETE

The Structure of Matter. All kinds of matter possess the property of **divisibility**, that is they are capable of division into very small portions; for example if a piece of chalk be ground up, exceedingly small particles will result and may be observed by means of a magnifying glass. It is known, however, that even such small particles as these may, by suitable means, be still further divided into what are known as molecules, but for our present purpose it will be sufficient to consider the much larger particles of which many building materials consist. In this chapter is given a series of experiments intended to explain the part which the *size* and the *arrangement* of these particles play in the production of substances such as mortar and concrete.

Cohesion and Adhesion. The powder obtained as described above is in one respect at least different from the original chalk; while there may be still the same quantity of matter it exists now as separate particles, and it must be evident that we have robbed the chalk of some property by virtue of which these small particles clung together to form the solid substance—chalk. This force is known as **cohesion.**

Any material like sand or gravel, which is composed of a large number of separate particles, may be described as a *discrete material,* and one of the important problems to be dealt with in building is the combining of these particles into a united or *concrete material* forming eventually a solid body. When by natural or artificial means *separate particles* of the same or different materials are made to hold together, then the force holding them together is known as **adhesion.** Any substance which possesses the power of uniting particles of other substances in this way is known as an "adhesive"; glue and cement are familiar examples. Separate particles of the same or different substances can only be united together by the force of *adhesion.* It should be noted that *cohesion* can only act between particles of the same substance when forming a solid piece of that substance.

Mortar and Concrete. Such materials as mortar and plaster, which consist of the separate materials lime (or cement) and sand, and concrete (which requires in addition broken brick or stone), are well-known examples of solids built up from discrete materials and which may, in their plastic condition, be moulded to any desired form.

With these materials the adhesion is provided by the lime or cement, the sand and coarse material serving chiefly to increase the bulk and lessen the cost of the resulting materials. With some limes the addition of sand up to a certain limit increases the strength of the mortar, but with cement mortars and concretes the addition of sand and other inert materials decreases the strength. In the present volume, however, we will limit ourselves to the consideration of some facts which will assist us in deciding what are the correct proportions in which the separate materials should be used.

Voids and Air-spaces in Discrete Materials. If a test tube be filled with sand and the sand examined through the sides of the tube it will be seen that there exists much space not filled by sand grains. These air-spaces are known as the **voids** of the sand and it is possible to obtain a measure of their volume by pouring in water to displace the air. The voids are usually calculated as a percentage of the whole volume occupied by the material.

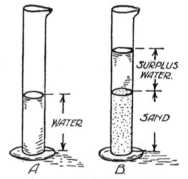

Fig. 47. Voids in sand.

Experiment 22. To ascertain the voids in loose materials. (*a*) For coarse sands and small aggregates the following method is simple and sufficiently exact for our present purpose. Place about 500 cu. cms. of the sand into a 1000 cu. cms. graduated jar, see fig. 47. Pour over this a measured quantity of water, *A*, sufficient to more than cover the sand; agitate the whole by stirring or shaking—so as to displace all air bubbles—tamp the sand down gently and after all fine dust has settled read off the volume of the sand and the volume of water *standing above* the sand, see fig. 47 *B*. Some of the water poured in will have filled the voids and its volume may be ascertained by subtracting the "surplus" water from the total amount used. Set out the working as follows:

Volume of sand (after wetting and tamping) = 500 c.c.s.
Total volume of water used ... ... = 350 ,,
Surplus water above sand ... ... = 160 ,,
∴ Water filling voids ... ... = 190 ,,

$$\therefore \quad \text{Voids} = \frac{190 \times 100}{500} = 38 \text{ per cent.}$$

(b) For dealing with large aggregates the use of narrow fragile measuring jars is unsatisfactory. Several types of apparatus have been devised to give more or less accurate values in this case, but since, for our present purpose, we do not require a high degree of accuracy, a simple form of apparatus will do and will be more suitable for the rough practical tests which it may be desired to carry out away from any laboratory.

Any strong metal vessel capable of standing rough usage will do and the aggregate should be filled into this and consolidated by tamping or by knocking the vessel on the bench. After the top has been levelled off, water should be poured in *slowly* until it rises level with the rim of the vessel. The vessel should stand on a horizontal bench top and the amount of water poured in may be measured by using a large measuring jar. The volume of the vessel should be ascertained from time to time (to allow for possible alterations in shape due to knocking) by weighing the vessel when empty and again when full of water; the volume may then be calculated from the weight of water contained. The calculations for the voids are as already described.

With porous materials a difficulty arises since they absorb water readily. In this case the aggregate should be soaked in water for about an hour and then spread out on a sieve to drain for about 15 minutes. The voids may then be found as already explained. (See Problems IV, 3.)

On p. 56 are given some values of the voids for several materials, but the reader is warned against using these in preference to values experimentally obtained from samples of the actual materials being considered.

The Grading of Discrete Materials. With all discrete materials like sand, broken brick or stone, considerable variation in the sizes of the particles exists (unless special means are adopted to prevent it). The presence or absence of this variation may be detected by a superficial examination of the material, but for purposes of comparison and classification a more exact method is essential.

The usual means adopted for sorting out the grains of sand, or of any similar material, is to use sieves, which consist of wire meshes through which all the particles pass save those which are larger than the mesh. The larger sieves are classified according to the size of the mesh as 2″, 1″, ½″, etc., whilst the smaller sieves are classified according to the number of openings to a *linear inch* as a "20" sieve, a "30" sieve, etc. A "30" sieve will have 30 × 30 or "900 holes to the square inch" and may be so described. Fig. 48 shows a good form of sieve. This type of sieve is provided with a lid and a series may be arranged as shown. A cheaper form consists of an open box with the sieve beneath.

The term "grading" is used to refer to the arrangement, as regards size, of the particles in a discrete material. When the particles have been sorted out according to size a sand is said to have been "ungraded," or the same term may be used to refer to a sand in which all the particles are practically of the same size. Sand may be any natural or artificially prepared rocky substance, the particles of which are small enough to pass a $\frac{1}{4}''$ mesh. Generally it is taken to refer to the small particles of quartz found so abundantly in nature and commonly spoken of as sand. A "coarse" sand is one the bulk of which would be retained on a "20" sieve, whilst a "fine" sand would entirely pass through this sieve.

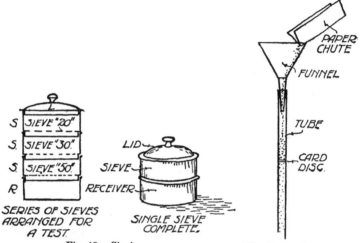

Fig. 48.   Sieving.   Fig. 49.   Filling the tubes.

The result of sieving any material may be gauged "*by weight*" (see Problems IV, 4) or "*by volume after separation.*" Except in the case of cement there is no standard method. In our case it will be convenient to use the latter method as it shows the results more graphically.

Experiment 23.   To test a sand for the grading of its particles. Take a number of glass tubes about 18″ or 20″ long and not less than $\frac{1}{2}$″ in diameter.   Cork one end of these tubes and nearly fill each of them with some of the sand to be tested, see fig. 49.   Next arrange a series of sieves according to the kind of sand being tested—coarse or fine—and place the contents of the tube on the top sieve.   Shake the sieves for about 10 minutes, then separate them; the approximate grading of the sand will now be apparent.   Next empty the contents of each sieve—starting with the finest grade—into the tube, separating each grade by a small disc.   When all the sievings have been emptied in, cork the tube and calculate the percentage amounts of each grade, taking the length of each portion compared with the total length occupied as giving the ratio of the volumes *after separation.*   Fig. 50 shows three different sands after treatment in this way.   "Standard sand" is an ungraded sand specially prepared for testing purposes.

The Effect of Grading upon Voids.   If we assume that the four largest spheres A, A in fig. 51 represent the largest grade of particle in such materials as we are now considering (the particles

of which, however, are usually irregular in shape), the voids would
evidently be made up of the spaces existing between these spheres.
If then other and smaller spheres B were introduced into these

A. An ungraded sand. Standard sand (Leighton Buzzard).

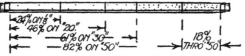

B. A naturally graded sand (Bournemouth).

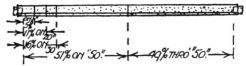

C. A naturally graded sand (red pit sand, Leicestershire).

Fig. 50. The grading of sands.

spaces, of such a size that though they touched the larger spheres
they did not push them apart, the voids would evidently be
reduced. A still further reduction could be obtained by intro-

Fig. 51. The effect of grading on voids.

ducing other spheres of yet smaller size as is suggested at C. Thus
we could go on with smaller and smaller particles until theoretically
the mass would become practically solid. Hence we may conclude

that (a) proper grading of the particles reduces the voids and (b) a "well graded" sand or aggregate is one with a low percentage of voids. As we shall see presently, it is an advantage to have a sand or a large aggregate with as few voids as possible.

It should be carefully noted that "sieving" of itself does not tell us whether a sand is well graded or not; *the percentage of voids present must always be the test of good grading.*

Generally speaking, however, a good sand should have a fair proportion of each size of grain from the largest to the smallest—most sands are deficient in the larger grains—and not too large a proportion of fine grains—passing "50." Further we may take it that, though large particles give higher voids than small particles, grading has much more effect upon the voids than the size of particles. Also rounded aggregates like gravels usually have less voids than angular aggregates like crushed brick or stone (this apart from the "sand" accompanying them).

A series of interesting experiments on grading and voids may be arranged by ascertaining the voids for a variety of sands and then making trial mixtures to find with which *mixture* the voids are least. Finally, the original sands and the mixtures may be sieved, when the results should give a rough indication of the proportions in which the various grades should be present.

After reading the above paragraphs the following list and the tubes shown in fig. 50 should be carefully studied.

Voids for various Materials (average values).

Material	Size	Voids %
Broken Brick	2″ and under	47
Broken Stone	1″ ,, ,,	46
,, ,, ...	2″ ,, ,,	45
Sand with many fine grains (see fig. 50 C)	Below ¼″	38
Standard sand (ungraded, see fig. 50 A)	Through "20," on "30"	36
Coarse sand	Through ¼″, on "20"	35
Ballast and sand	¾″ and under	34
Sand naturally graded (see fig. 50 B)...	Below ¼″	33
Sand artificially graded, by trial mixings.	Below ¼″	25

The Reduction in Volume on mixing Mortars and Concretes. It would be noted in Experiment 23 that, after sieving out the various grades in a sand, the total volume occupied by the ungraded particles was greater than the volume they occupied when mixed together in the original sand. This variation in volume may be simply explained by the fact that in the mixture the smaller particles will tend to occupy the spaces between the larger particles without greatly increasing the total volume. When ungraded these spaces are unoccupied by the smaller grains, and the total space occupied is increased. Hence, as we might expect, when sand and lime (or cement) are mixed to make mortar there is an apparent shrinkage of the materials used, similarly with concrete, the particles in each case being roughly graded and therefore packing well when mixed.

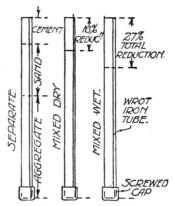

Fig. 52.   Reduction on mixing a concrete.

As it is very necessary that the amount of this shrinkage should be known when calculating the amounts of the separate materials required we will explain how this may be ascertained experimentally for any given mix.

Experiment 24. To show the reduction on mixing concrete. Let the sample to be tested be a concrete suitable for reinforced concrete in which the coarse material will all pass a $\frac{3}{4}''$ sieve. Prepare a wrought iron tube, not less than 1″ internal diameter and about 2 ft. long and closed at one end with a screwed cap, see fig. 52. Measure the internal length of the pipe and, assuming that the proportions for the concrete are 4 parts of coarse material, 2 parts of sand and 1 part of Portland cement, divide this length into 7 parts $(1 + 2 + 4 = 7)$ and fill 4 with aggregate, 2 with sand and 1 with cement, separating each with a card disc and gently knocking the bottom of the tube as the materials are filled in, so as to make them take up a minimum volume. Note the length occupied.

Now empty the contents of the tube on to a smooth board or slate mixing-slab, carefully turn them over at least four times with a trowel and finally return the mixture to the tube. Note the reduction (see fig. 52).

Once more empty out the contents of the tube and mix the whole up with water until it is of such a consistency as to be just unable to keep its shape on a flat board. Using a large-mouthed funnel and a little extra water to wash it down, return this wet mixture to the tube, tamp it thoroughly into position and note the final volume occupied, see fig. 52. Any surplus water should be disregarded. (The tube should be emptied and cleaned before the mixture has had time to set.)

For the mixture mentioned the final reduction will be between $\frac{1}{4}$ and $\frac{1}{3}$ of the total volume before mixing and most concretes will be found to lie within these limits. A great deal, however, depends upon the materials used and tabulated values should not be accepted in preference to those obtained in an actual test of the materials to be used.

With lime or cement mortars the reduction is less and for ordinary materials it may be taken that *approximately* a 1 to 1 mortar will show about $\frac{1}{6}$ reduction, 2 to 1 a reduction of $\frac{1}{5}$ and 3 to 1 a reduction of $\frac{1}{4}$.

The reduction which takes place on wetting is probably due to the lubrication of the particles allowing them to pack more closely. Portland cement shrinks about 15 per cent. on wetting and lime a little less. Sands and aggregates vary considerably in this respect.

The Calculation of Materials to be used in the Preparation of Mortars and Concretes.

(*a*) When the proportions in which the various materials are to be used in mixing a concrete are settled by specification, the amount of materials required *per cubic yard of concrete* may be readily calculated. Let the concrete be a $1 : 2 : 4$ concrete. If on experiment the actual reduction accompanying mixing is 28 per cent., then every cubic yard of mixed concrete will correspond to $\dfrac{(100-28)}{100}$ or $\dfrac{72}{100}$ of the volume of dry materials required.

$$\therefore \text{ Total volume of dry materials} = 27 \times \tfrac{100}{72}$$
$$= 37\cdot5 \text{ cu. ft.}$$

Dividing this into three parts in the ratio of $1 : 2 : 4$ we have:

$$\text{Volume of coarse material required} = 37\cdot5 \times \tfrac{4}{7}$$
$$= 21\cdot4 \text{ cubic ft.}$$
$$\therefore \text{ Volume of sand required} = 10\cdot7 \quad ,,$$

and $\quad\quad\quad$,, $\quad$ cement ,, $\quad = 5\cdot35 \quad ,,$

$\therefore$ Weight of cement at 90 lbs. per cubic ft. (see p. 15) = 480 lbs.

From these values the amount of materials for any given number of cubic yards of concrete may be found. Mortars may be dealt with similarly.

(*b*) In mixing such a concrete by hand it is convenient to use a gauge-box, (a bottomless box in which the coarse aggregate and sand are measured before mixing), of such a size that a "cental" of 100 lbs. or a "bag" of 200 lbs. of cement is required to complete the mixture.

To find the required volume of the gauge-box to use with a bag of cement for the above concrete proceed as follows:

$$\text{Volume of 200 lbs. of cement} = \tfrac{200}{90} \quad = 2\cdot22 \text{ cubic ft.}$$
$$\therefore \text{ Volume of sand} = 2\cdot22 \times 2 = 4\cdot44 \quad ,, \quad ,,$$

and $\quad\quad\quad$,, ,, aggregate $= 2\cdot22 \times 4 = 8\cdot88 \quad ,, \quad ,,$

$$\therefore \textbf{ Volume of gauge-box} = \textbf{13·32} \quad ,, \quad ,,$$

Since the total volume of separate materials is 15·54 cubic ft. evidently *for every bag of cement we have* 15·54 × $\frac{72}{100}$ or 11·2 *cubic ft. of concrete.* From this value may be calculated the number of bags of cement required for a given quantity of concrete.

The Proportioning of Concrete. As with other building materials, concrete will be dealt with more fully in the succeeding volume but, even without detailed knowledge, most readers of this book will realise that the two most necessary properties are *strength* and *waterproofness.* It is not always that both these qualities are required together, but it should be fairly obvious that, apart from the actual strength of the separate materials, both the strength and the waterproofness of the concrete will be increased if we reduce the air-spaces and voids to a minimum. In other words it is important that a concrete should be as dense as possible. The investigation we have already made into the question of voids and grading furnishes us with a powerful method of ensuring this and of understanding what the problem requires.

There are two types of solution to this problem of producing a dense concrete; the one is to ascertain the voids of the materials used and calculate the proportions of the materials so that theoretically these voids should be filled; the other is to proceed by the method of trial mixtures until the densest concrete is obtained. In practice the latter method usually gives the best results.

(*a*) **Proportioning by Voids.** The simplest method is to fix the proportions of the "mortar" (cement and sand) and provide sufficient of it—allowing for shrinkage—to fill the voids of the coarse material with a margin of 10 per cent. (reckoned on the total volume of coarse material). For example let the mortar consist of 1 part of cement to 2 of sand and shrink $\frac{1}{8}$ on mixing wet, and let the aggregate have 42 per cent. of voids; to find the ratio in which the coarse aggregate should be used.

Let the volume of aggregate per unit volume of concrete be x units. Then each unit volume of concrete will be made up of x units of aggregate plus the 10 per cent. margin of mortar, that is

$$x + \tfrac{10}{100}x = 1 \text{ unit volume of concrete,}$$
$$\therefore \tfrac{11}{10}x = 1,$$
and $$x = \tfrac{10}{11} = ·91 \text{ of unit volume.}$$

Volume of voids = ·91 × $\tfrac{42}{100}$ = ·38 of unit volume.

∴ *Volume of mortar* = volume of voids + 10 per cent. of ·91
$$= ·38 + ·091$$
$$= ·471 \text{ of unit volume.}$$

Hence total volume of sand and cement before mixing

$$= \cdot471 \times \tfrac{5}{4}$$
$$= \cdot59 \text{ of unit volume.}$$

That is, volume of sand $= \tfrac{2}{3} \times \cdot59 = \cdot4$ of unit volume (approx.),

and ,, ,, cement $= \tfrac{1}{3} \times \cdot59 = \cdot2$,, ,,

Therefore suitable proportions for the given materials are $20 : 40 : 91$ or $1 : 2 : 4\tfrac{1}{2}$ nearly.

If preferred, the cement—allowing for shrinkage—may in the same way be proportioned to give a 10 per cent. margin over the voids in the sand.

Proceeding on somewhat similar lines it is possible to ascertain whether a given mix will give a dense mortar or concrete, the necessary margin of cement or mortar having been previously fixed. Take the case of a 3 to 1 cement mortar, the sand for which has 34 per cent. of voids. For, say, 3 cubic ft. of sand, 1 cubic ft. of cement would be taken which after wetting would shrink to ·85 cubic ft. The total volume of voids in 3 cubic ft. of the sand would be $3 \times \tfrac{34}{100}$ or 1·02 cubic ft. But the cement would only fill ·85 cubic ft. of voids and hence the resulting mortar would be porous. This is actually the case with all 3 to 1 mortars and while with some limes this is an advantage (see Chap. XIV), such mortars should not be expected to be waterproof. (See Experiment 31.)

(b) Proportioning by Trial Mixtures.

(i) One method is to prepare a mixture in proportions which are likely to be suitable, mix it with water and put it into the tube mentioned in Experiment 24. After tamping it down in the tube the height to which the concrete rises should be noted, after which the sample is thrown away. Another mixture is then prepared using the same weight of cement and the same *total weight* of sand and coarse material but varying the ratio in which they are present. This is also placed in the tube and the height again noted. This second trial should prove a guide in preparing further mixtures. For the same materials and total weights *the mixture which occupies the least volume will give the densest concrete.*

(ii) Another and less troublesome method is to mix in succession 1 part of sand with varying quantities of coarse aggregate and note which mixture gives *the least voids.* These proportions are then taken and sufficient cement used to give—after shrinkage—a 10 per cent. margin over the voids.

Where concrete is needed for filling in spaces, over arches, or under hearths a light porous concrete will do, so long as it has sufficient strength, and the above methods for obtaining dense concretes do not apply.

Clean and Dirty Sands. As we have seen some sands contain a large proportion of very fine grains which, if they pass a "50" sieve, are usually considered objectionable. In addition, however, finely divided clay, dust or organic matter may be present and, as these may have a deleterious effect upon mortars or concretes in which these sands are used, it is an advantage to be able to apply a simple test to show the presence of such substances and roughly measure the amount.

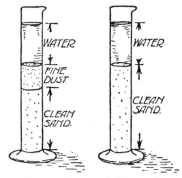

Fig. 53. Clean and dirty sands.

Experiment 25. If a sample of the sand to be tested be shaken up in a tall jar, or the sand be poured into water contained in the jar and stirred, it will be found, after settlement, that nearly all the impurities mentioned above, being lighter than the sand grains, will settle last and form a distinct layer above the comparatively clean sand. We may consider that the depth of the dust settling in this way should not exceed about 5 per cent. of the total depth. No standard as yet exists and it must not be assumed that a sand need be perfectly clean before it is fit for use. It is known from experience that washing may not improve a sand and that a small percentage of finely divided clayey matter may increase the waterproofness of the concrete without reducing its strength. Coarse aggregates may also be tested for fine dust as explained above.

PROBLEMS IV

1. In a test carried out as explained on p. 52, 160 c.c.s of water were poured over 220 c.c.s of sand. After settling, 82 c.c.s of water stood above the sand. Calculate the percentage voids in the sand.

2. The voids in sands or aggregates may be calculated if the densities of the solid and of the discrete materials be known. (a) Calculate the voids in a quartz sand weighing 98 lbs. per cubic ft., assuming solid quartz to weigh 164 lbs. per cubic ft. (b) If a broken brick aggregate weighs 64 lbs. per cubic ft., what are the percentage voids, given that the bricks before breaking $(9'' \times 4\frac{1}{2}'' \times 3'')$ averaged 8 lbs. each?

3. A metal vessel weighs 1·5 lbs. when empty and 5·18 lbs. when full of water. (a) Calculate its volume. When this vessel is filled with soaked coarse material it weighs 5·25 lbs. Water is then poured in until it rises level with the rim when the total weight is 6·91 lbs. (b) Calculate the voids in the aggregate. (It should be clear to the reader, after working the second part of this question, that the only values required are, the weight of the water to fill the vessel and the weight to fill the voids when the coarse material is in the vessel.)

4.   2 lbs. of a sand are taken and sieved in a series of sieves.   Calculate the *total percentage amounts* which would be retained on each sieve if 7·36 ozs. were retained on the "20" sieve, 7·68 ozs. passed the "20" and were retained on the "30" sieve, 13·43 ozs. passed the "20" and "30" and were retained on the "50."   What percentage passed all the sieves?

5.   If a sand with 35 per cent. of voids were used to fill the interstices of a stone aggregate with 45 per cent. of voids, what would be the theoretical percentage of voids in the mixture?   Assume that the sand can fill the voids of the aggregate without increasing the latter's volume, i.e. without pushing the stones apart.

6.   Assuming a shrinkage of $\frac{1}{3}$ on mixing, calculate the quantity of cement (in lbs., at 90 lbs. per cubic ft.), sand and coarse material for a cubic yard of a 1 : 3 : 6 concrete.

7.   Assuming a shrinkage of $\frac{1}{8}$ calculate the amount of sand necessary and the amount of 2 to 1 cement mortar produced with 5 bags of cement.

8.   A concrete is made with cement (shrinking 12 per cent. on wetting), sand with 33 per cent. of voids and an aggregate of crushed stone with 45 per cent. of voids.   Calculate suitable proportions for the materials so as to produce a dense concrete.
Assume that the wetted cement must exceed the voids in the sand by 10 per cent., that the mortar produced shrinks $\frac{1}{8}$ on mixing and wetting and that it must be present in sufficient quantity to exceed the voids in the stone by 10 per cent.

9.   For the approximate proportions obtained in the last question calculate the sizes of gauge-box to be used in measuring the sand and stone necessary to mix with one bag of cement.

10.   If the materials mentioned in question 8 were used in the proportions 1 : 3 : 6, calculate the theoretical margin of mortar over the voids in the coarse material.   Assume that the mortar shrinks $\frac{1}{4}$ on mixing.

11.   Describe a series of simple tests which may be carried out on sands and aggregates to be used in concrete.

12.   How is it that a dense concrete can often be obtained more economically by mixing cement, sand and gravel than by mixing cement and gravel alone?

13.   How would you proceed to determine the most suitable proportions in which to combine a given sand and a given aggregate in order to obtain a dense concrete on mixing with cement?

General note on the mixing of concrete. Considerable work has been done in recent years on the problems associated with concrete mixing. In particular it has been shown that the most important qualities of concrete—density, impermeability, strength—may be markedly improved by (a) using only sufficient water to ensure reasonable workability and (b) ramming or vibrating the concrete while it is being placed in position. Simple laboratory tests may be devised to illustrate these effects. (See Lists of Experiments in Building Science (S 2).)

CHAPTER V

THE POROSITY OF BUILDING MATERIALS AND THE PREVENTION OF DAMPNESS

Porosity. In the preceding chapter we discussed in an elementary way the effect of structure upon the density and the amount of air-spaces in any substance built up from separate particles; but, even where the structure cannot be so simply conceived, it is generally held that the packing of the molecules (see p. 51) is never so perfect as to exclude all air-spaces. It is not possible to illustrate this statement simply, but the fact that all substances may be reduced in volume if sufficient force is exerted is usually explained by saying that the molecules have been compelled to pack more closely with a consequent reduction of the air-spaces. Thus we may say that *porosity is a general property of matter*.

The Porosity of Building Materials. Since one of the first essentials of a good building is the ability to resist the penetration of wet and damp, the need for the careful examination of building materials for the presence or absence of porosity should be obvious. Unfortunately there does not appear to exist any very clear notion as to the exact relation between the porosity or non-porosity of building materials and their suitability for use under various circumstances; however, while it is not possible in a volume of this character to treat the matter with the fullness it deserves, sufficient may be said to suggest possible lines along which this investigation may proceed and also to prepare the reader for a fuller discussion in the succeeding volume. Even with but a superficial knowledge of such materials as wood, brick and stone, the reader will be quite prepared for the statement that most building materials are very porous and one of the points which this chapter should serve to emphasise is, that even with such materials a satisfactory building may be erected if suitable methods of construction are adopted. Since, however, materials of the same type—e.g. bricks—may be put to a variety of uses, it is an advantage to be able to classify them in respect to this property in order to settle their suitability for various kinds of work. For example, bricks may be used in interior walls where, so long as their strength is sufficient, porosity will be a positive advantage since it will reduce their weight; again bricks may be used as facings to exterior walls, in which case they will have to resist the penetration of rain and probably of rain driven against them by strong winds, but even here a much more porous brick might be used than would be possible say in the sides of a brick-built reservoir.

In this connection it should not be overlooked that *porous materials will allow the passage of air* or other gases equally with water. Thus while a more or less porous wall may be considered an advantage, as affording an indirect means of ventilation, to lay a *porous concrete* over the site of a house would be to defeat the very object which this site concrete is intended to fulfil, viz. to exclude "ground air" from the house.

Lastly, it should not be forgotten that the *appearance* of a material is to some extent associated with porosity. Hence, to obtain desired effects in colour or texture, materials may be used which are admittedly not the most efficient from the weather-resisting point of view, when it may be necessary to take special precautions to overcome their weaknesses in this respect.

The Examination of Materials for Porosity

Surface examination affords us a simple and oftentimes sufficient test of the presence or absence of porosity. Samples of stone, brick, slate, tile, mortar and concrete may be prepared by grinding one face flat and finishing it on one or two grades of emery cloth. These surfaces may then be examined by means of a magnifier, see fig. 54, and the samples classified in a simple way according to their apparent porosity.

A useful classification may be made of the porous substances by arranging them according to whether the pores are uniformly distributed through the material or occur in a haphazard way.

Facing materials such as facing bricks, tiles and glazed bricks may have their special faces compared with rough fractures of these materials.

Wood may be placed in a class by itself, since its structure is entirely different from that of any of the materials we have so far considered. Both the longitudinal and the cross section should be examined. A knowledge of the relative amounts of porosity of woods is useful, for this property is closely related to strength and density and affects such questions as the suitability to receive paint, polish or treatment with liquid for preserving and fire-resisting purposes.

Absorption as a Measure of Porosity. Various methods, more or less elaborate, have been devised for ascertaining the exact amount of air-space present in any given material. These depend almost entirely upon the power of a porous material to absorb water. If we could ensure that all the air-spaces might be filled with water in this way, the *increase in weight* of the body after

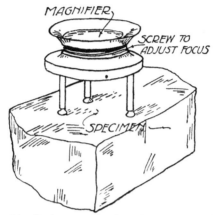

Fig. 54. Surface examination of porous materials.

immersion would give us the weight of water absorbed, from which we could readily obtain the volume of the air-spaces. Unfortunately, however, we cannot always be sure that all the air-spaces would be filled in this way, since some of the air-spaces may be more or less detached from the rest and the air in them not easily displaced. To get over this difficulty the substance may be crushed to a powder and the volume of "solid" matter obtained, from which the air-spaces in the original substance may be calculated (see Problems IV, 2). Another method is to immerse the substance in water, which is subjected first to a reduction in pressure and afterwards to an increase in pressure; this results in a more perfect filling of the air-spaces (compare impregnation of timber with creosote and see Problems V, 5). These are elaborations, however, which are unnecessary at this stage since the simpler methods will suffice to give us results which may be compared amongst themselves.

Experiment 26. To compare the porosity of various bricks (or stones). To carry out this experiment the brick to be tested is first weighed and then wholly immersed in a trough as shown in fig. 55. It should then be taken out at stated intervals, dried with a piece of cloth and weighed; this should be repeated until *no further increase in weight is apparent,* when it may be assumed that the brick has absorbed all the water possible under the circumstances of the experiment. The *amount absorbed* is then calculated *as a percentage on the weight of the brick when dry.*

It is generally stated that a good brick should not absorb more than ⅛th of its dry weight in 24 hours but, since there is such a great variation in the amounts absorbed by the different classes of bricks—a blue brick may not absorb more than $\frac{1}{20}$th of its weight—there is distinct need for a more detailed standard.

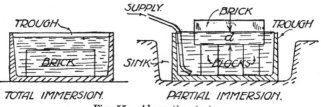

TOTAL IMMERSION.   PARTIAL IMMERSION.
Fig. 55.   Absorption tests.

If preferred the specimens may be only *partially immersed* to any suitable depth (*d*) and a convenient arrangement for maintaining this depth is shown in fig. 55.   It will be found that, whichever method is adopted, practically *the same comparative results* will be obtained.   (Total immersion gives quicker results.)

In order to be able to compare the results obtained in this way it is important that, so far as possible, the *conditions of the experiment* should be the same in each case, so that whether bricks, stones, tiles or slates are being tested, the specimens in the case of each material should be of approximately the same size and shape.

In addition to the maximum absorption it is interesting to ascertain the *rate* at which the water is absorbed, and as this may be done without much extra trouble the method is described below.

Experiment 27. To obtain a curve showing the rate at which water is absorbed by a brick.   Proceed exactly as in the last experiment but let the intervals between the weighings be very short at first—say 10 mins.— gradually increasing them until the point is reached when no further increase in weight is apparent.   Tabulate the amounts absorbed and by plotting these values on squared paper set out a curve as shown in fig. 56.

Curves are given for five varieties of bricks showing the rate of absorption during the first 10 hours and also during a period of days up to 20, the latter curves showing when the "point of saturation" was reached for each brick.   The figures in brackets give the weights of the bricks used.   The curves given are from values obtained by the author; they may be considered typical for each type of brick treated, but the actual values obtained would of course vary for examples of these types of brick obtained from different parts of the country.   Curves for individual bricks will usually show slight irregularities at various points; these have

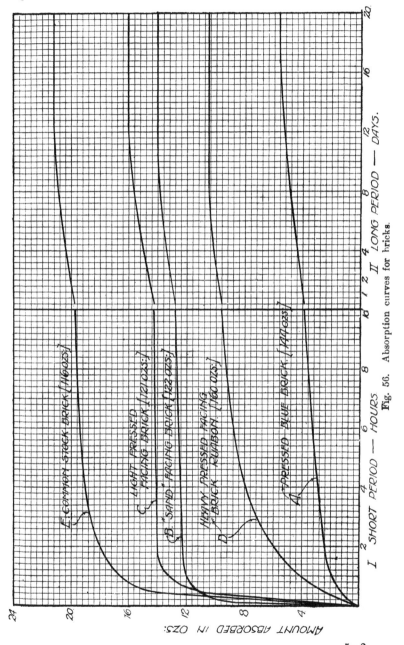

Fig. 56. Absorption curves for bricks.

not been shown in the curves given, which may therefore be considered as average curves.

It should be particularly noted that with the more porous bricks (*B* and *C*) the greater part of the water is absorbed in the first two hours. With the dense blue brick (*A*), the heavy facing brick (*D*) and the well-burnt stock brick (*E*) the rate of absorption is more gradual and falls off regularly until the point of saturation is reached. (See Problems V, 1 and 2.)

Surface Absorption. For roofing or facing the outer walls of buildings, materials specially prepared to throw off water are generally used, such as slates, tiles, facing bricks, cement rendering, etc. The ability of these materials to resist the penetration of water cannot be fairly tested by total immersion, since all the

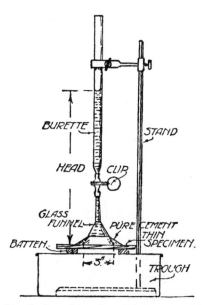

Fig. 57.   Surface absorption of facing materials.

faces may not be prepared for exposure, e.g. the top and bottom faces of a facing brick would not be exposed and with cement rendering only the trowelled face would be exposed. Partial immersion of the face to be tested in a shallow tray may form a fair test, but the following method is an interesting variation which may be easily applied to a number of materials.

Experiment 28.   To test the surface absorption of various facing materials.   The apparatus is shown in fig. 57.   A glass or metal funnel is secured to the face of the specimen with pure cement (preferably water-proofed).   Thin specimens are supported over the trough, while thick speci-mens stand in the trough.   The funnel is first filled with water and then connected to a burette—also full—as shown.   As soon as the connections are made the first reading should be taken and then repeated at intervals, as with the experiments just described.   (The level in the burette should be made up from time to time so as to keep the "head" fairly uniform.)

To compare the results obtained with various materials, the area covered by the funnel and the head should be kept the same and the comparison may then be made by drawing a curve for each material showing the varying rates of absorption for this area and head.   It is more useful, however, to reduce the amounts so as to show *cubic inches absorbed per square inch of area exposed* as it is then possible to utilise the term employed in measuring rainfall and speak of "inches of water" absorbed in a stated time. (See also Problems V, 6 and 7.)

Typical curves are given in fig. 58.   Generally they show that water is absorbed rapidly at first until, with thin and porous specimens, the water begins to "sweat" or drop from the other surfaces of the specimen, the rate then becomes fairly steady and the test need not be carried further.   When water passes *through* a material it is described as "permeation" to distinguish it from "absorption."

If we wish to consider the behaviour of facing materials during prolonged rain-storms it is evidently the first part of the curves which will be of greatest value.

The curves given for facing bricks should be examined along with the graphs of total absorption for the same bricks, when the value of the smooth and denser face of the pressed brick should be at once apparent.   The same lettering is used on each curve and the examination of curves *B*, *C* and *D* in each of the figures will emphasise the point just mentioned.

As compared with common tiles, slates are practically non-absorbent (total absorption on immersion 0·5 to 1 per cent.), hence the above test cannot add much to our knowledge concerning them.

Porosity and Drying.   It must by no means be assumed that the only property possessed by porous materials is that of absorbing water.   It is not difficult to show that porous materials will, under suitable conditions, get rid of surplus moisture much more readily than non-porous materials.   It is this fact which makes it possible to use comparatively porous materials for facing buildings, since the exposure to water during rain-storms is never of long duration and is usually followed by comparatively dry

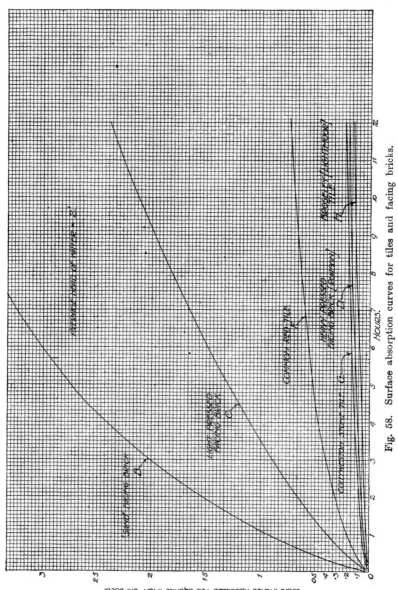

Fig. 58.   Surface absorption curves for tiles and facing bricks.

weather, during which periods the absorbed water evaporates. Hence, so long as a wall is sufficiently thick or the face is isolated from the main portion of the wall, as in "hollow-walls," no trouble need arise from absorbed water. In this connection it should be noted that *many mortars are very porous* (see p. 60), thus trouble more frequently arises from water absorbed and transmitted through the joints than through the bricks.

Experiment 29. To compare the drying powers of bricks (or stones). Take samples of the bricks to be tested, obtain their weight when dry and then immerse them for say 24 hours. At the end of this period take the bricks from the water, wipe them dry, weigh them and tabulate the increase in weight. Stand the bricks in a room free from draughts and having a fairly steady temperature. Repeat the weighings at intervals of a day until *no further*

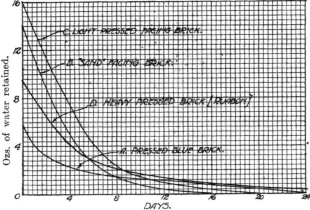

Fig. 59. Drying curves for bricks.

decrease takes place, and tabulate the times and the excess of weight over the original weight when dry. With the values obtained draw curves for each of the specimens similar to that shown in fig. 59.

Typical curves for four types of bricks are given and should be read in conjunction with the absorption curves for the same bricks in fig. 56. It will be noticed that the porous bricks get rid of nearly three times as much moisture as the dense blue brick and in less time. It is sometimes stated that "a good brick should absorb water slowly and give it up readily," but these graphs tend to show that this is an impossible requirement and that no such brick has yet been produced.

Capillarity. So far we have dealt with the possibility of dampness being caused by the absorption of water through walls or roofs; the most frequent cause of damp houses, however, is the water which rises in the walls of a house built upon a damp site. This rise is due to a phenomenon known as *capillarity* and, although it may not be simply explained, the following considerations should help to make the nature of this phenomenon clear.

Surface Tension.   If a soap bubble be blown it assumes as we know a spherical form and if the pipe, by which the bubble was blown, be left open the bubble will close down upon the pipe until it stretches across the opening like a flat skin.   The bubble in fact acts in every way like a bladder of *stretched skin*. If a clean glass be carefully filled with water it will be found to be possible to run water in until its level is actually above the rim of the glass, the water being held apparently by the tension of the surface of the water.   In this, as in other cases, it may be shown that such a *state of tension* actually exists on the free surfaces of all liquids; this is known as *surface tension*.   This tension or pull is due to the *cohesion* existing between the molecules of water, and although the actual force exerted is very small its effect is clearly seen in the soapy film forming the soap bubble.

In the simple experiment with a glass of water described above it would appear that the "stretched skin" to which we have referred adhered to the rim of the glass; this force of *adhesion* coming into play between the molecules of a liquid and the molecules of a solid when they are brought infinitely close together.   If this force exceeds the surface tension of the liquid, the liquid will adhere to the solid—in common language it will "wet the solid."   Thus water will wet glass if it is clean but not if it is greasy, the attraction between water and grease being less than between water and water; therefore we usually say that grease repels water.

Capillary Attraction.   If a clean glass plate be held vertically in water as in fig. 60 A, the water will be drawn up the sides and form a meniscus.

If two plates are used and brought very close together, the pull acting on each side of the water between the plates, will be sufficient to raise it above the level of the water outside the plates, see fig. 60 B.   The height "h" to which the liquid is drawn will be found to increase as the distance between the plates is diminished. This latter effect may be shown in a graphic way by allowing the plates to touch along one vertical edge, when the surface of the liquid will follow a curve somewhat as *ABC* in fig. 61.

If glass tubes of fine bore be used instead of plates the same effects may be noted, see fig. 62.   It was in tubes of very fine bore—capillary tubes—that this phenomenon was first noticed, hence it is generally referred to as *capillary attraction* or *capillarity*.

Mercury, unlike water, will not adhere to or "wet" clean glass, owing to the fact that its surface tension is considerably greater than the molecular attraction between mercury and glass, hence its meniscus takes the reverse form to that taken by water, see *A* and *B*, fig. 63. When a capillary tube is pushed down into

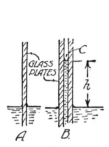

Fig. 60. Capillary attraction.

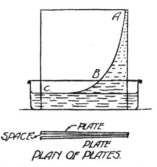

Fig. 61. Capillarity between plates.

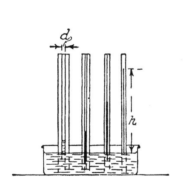

Fig. 62. Capillarity in tubes.

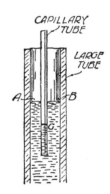

Fig. 63. Capillary attraction in mercury.

mercury the surface of the mercury in the tube is depressed as at *C*, fig. 63.

Capillarity in Walling Materials.   In examining porous bricks and stones it may be noted that the pores are of small dimensions and frequently continuous.   Hence we may expect that the pores of such materials will act in every respect like capillary tubes.

Experiment 30.   To show and compare capillarity in bricks.   Place the brick to be tested in about a $\frac{1}{2}$ inch of water, as shown in fig. 64, and note the time which elapses between the placing of the brick in water and the appearance of dampness on the top of the brick.   The presence of moisture on the top of the brick may be shown (a) by its condensation inside a bell-jar secured to the top of the brick with some plastic substance or standing on a rubber washer, or (b) by placing some anhydrous copper sulphate on the top of the brick and covering it with a watch-glass secured to the brick so as to be air-tight. (The substance mentioned is white but turns blue on contact with water.)

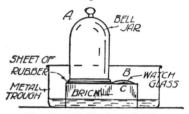

Fig. 64.   Capillarity in bricks.

Various bricks should be tested in this way.   With very porous bricks, such as rubbers, the water will rise very rapidly and will be *visible* on the top of the brick in an hour or two.   A very much longer period will be necessary with other bricks, and blue bricks will not usually give any result at all.

The Prevention of Capillarity in Walls.   Capillary action can only take place in materials which are porous; hence materials which are practically non-porous, since they prevent this action taking place, are used to prevent the upward passage of water in walls.   Horizontal layers of these materials are laid right across the walls at not less than 6″ from the ground level and when so used, are known as **damp proof courses.**

Materials commonly used are sheet lead, natural asphalte laid on hot, bituminous felt sheeting, and blue bricks, glazed stoneware, or two courses of slates laid in 1 to 1 cement mortar.   These materials will be dealt with more fully in the next volume.

Experiment 31.   A simple test of the effectiveness of various damp proof courses and mortars.   Prepare, from rubber bricks, some bricks half the usual size and build a series of small square piers similar to that shown in fig. 65, using a 3 to 1 mortar (porous). Erect the piers on small boards, so that they may be moved about, and let them be exactly alike with the exception of the joint AB.   Into AB build in each pier one of the D.P. courses or mortars to be tested.   Each pier should be placed in about 2 inches of water—made up from time to time—and the tests completed as explained in Experiment 30. If a course of blue bricks (clinkers may be used to represent the blue bricks) be laid in one of the piers it is possible to show that unless an *impervious mortar*

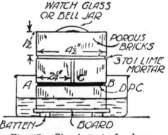

Fig. 65.   Simple test of a damp proof course.

is used the impervious bricks will fail to prevent the passage of moisture.

Capillary Grooves. If a capillary tube has a bulb blown a short distance from one end, see C fig. 66, and the end B be immersed in water, the water will not rise further than the bulb owing to the sudden increase in internal dimensions. This is the principle adopted in the formation of **capillary grooves** and two examples are illustrated in figs. 67 and 68.

In fig. 67 the surfaces of the bottom rail of the sash and the sill are seen to come very close together; if during a rain-storm

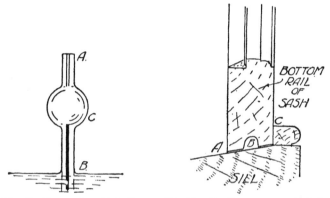

Fig. 66.   Capillary tube with bulb.   Fig. 67.   Capillary groove at window sill.

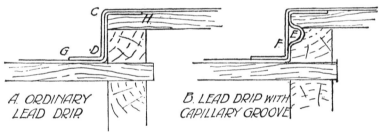

Fig. 68.   Capillary groove in lead drips.

water lodges at A it will be drawn between these two surfaces by capillary attraction and eventually emerge inside the window at C. By running a groove along the underside of the sash rail a large space is formed at B and the capillary action is thus prevented.

In fig. 68 A an ordinary lead drip is shown; if water stand at G it will be drawn by capillary attraction between the two sheets of lead, and if this continues for some time the water may eventually find its way out at H and cause a troublesome leak. To prevent this a groove is run in the front of the drip and the lead dressed into it, the overlying sheet is then dressed straight down forming a large space between the sheets as at E, fig. 68 B; this, as we have seen, will prevent the water rising higher than F.

PROBLEMS V

1. Using the values shown on fig. 56 calculate the percentage amount of absorption after 10 hours' immersion for each of the bricks shown.

2. From the same figure calculate the percentage amount of *maximum* absorption.

3. Calculate the amount of water which would be absorbed by, (a) 1000 common bricks and (b) 1000 light facing bricks, if they were immersed in water for (say) 2 hours before use in hot dry weather. (10 lbs. = 1 gallon.)

4. Assuming that all the pores have been filled with water in the pressed blue brick (A) and the "sand" brick B, after total immersion for 3 weeks, calculate the "percentage voids" in each of the bricks mentioned using the values given in fig. 56. Take each brick to measure $9'' \times 4\frac{3}{8}'' \times 3''$.

5. To show that the assumption made in the last question is not a good one the following experiment was carried out. (a) A piece of limestone measuring $3'' \times 2'' \times 1\frac{1}{2}''$ and weighing 10·5 ozs. was immersed in water for 3 weeks and increased in weight to 11·3 ozs. (b) An exactly similar piece was placed in water in a closed vessel in which the pressure was reduced with an air-pump. After an hour's immersion the weight had increased from 10·5 ozs. to 11·8 ozs.
Calculate the percentage voids occupied by water in each case.

6. In Experiment 28, with a funnel having an internal diameter of 2·25 inches, the water in the burette fell in 1 hour from 92·6 cubic cms. to 30·1 cubic cms. with a sand brick specimen; reduce these values to show "cubic inches absorbed per sq. inch."

7. Using the same values calculate "the number of cubic cms. absorbed per sq. cm." and show that in both cases it represents the *same depth* of water which has been absorbed in a stated time.

8. If the total surface of any of the bricks tested in Experiment 28 be calculated and the total surface absorption *over this area* be found for (say) the first 6 hours, it gives an increase in weight far greater than is actually obtained by total immersion as in Experiment 27. How may this be explained?

9. The dry weight of a portion of brick is 1·5 lbs. The volume is 0·0125 cu. ft. Given that the actual density of the brick material is 166 lbs. per cu. ft., calculate the pore space of the brick.

10. Write a short account of the porosity of building materials, noting in particular the advantages and disadvantages which may arise from this characteristic when the materials are used in certain items of building construction.

CHAPTER VI

THE MEASUREMENT OF FORCE. EFFECTS OF FORCE ON MATERIALS. FORCES AT A POINT

The Measurement of Force. We have already defined **Force** as *that which changes or tends to change a body's state of rest or of uniform motion in a straight line* (see p. 1); this definition forms the basis of a system of measuring forces dependent on the consideration of the motion imparted to a body by a given force acting upon it.

As our study of Mechanics, however, is confined almost exclusively to that branch of it known as Statics, which deals with forces acting upon *bodies which remain at rest,* it will be sufficient for our purpose to show how a system of units for the measurement of *statical forces* may be built up from the statement, that *any two forces will be equal in magnitude if when applied to the same particle but in exactly opposite directions the particle remains at rest;* if the forces be not equal the particle will move in the direction of the greater force.

We have seen that what is known as the "attraction of gravity" acts upon all bodies and that "the weight of a body" is the *force* with which it is attracted to the earth (see p. 2).

Thus we adopt *a force equal to the weight of one pound* (or one gramme) as the *unit of force* in the **gravitational** system of force units, and an upward force which is just able to balance the downward pull of a 1 lb. weight will be "*a force of one pound.*"

Experiment 32. To show how a spring may be used as a "force-measurer." In the piece of apparatus shown in fig. 69 a small scale pan is suspended from a spiral spring, a cork is attached as shown through which is thrust a needle which moves over a paper scale,

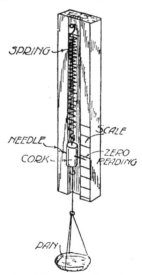

Fig. 69.   Graduation of a spring to measure force.

(a piece of $\frac{1}{10}''$ squared paper will do). Note the position taken up by the needle with no load on the pan, call this "zero." Add a suitable weight and note the *extension*. Remove the weight and note that the needle returns to zero. Now take a number of weights and after each is placed on the pan note the position of the needle and tabulate corresponding values as set out below. *Do not overload the spring.*

Readings for a spring made from $\frac{1}{32}''$ wire and of $\frac{5}{16}''$ mean diameter.

Weights on pan (ozs.)	Reading on scale (inches)	Extension in inches
0	1·80	0
2	2·06	·26
4	2·35	·55
6	2·61	·81
8	2·85	1·05
10	3·11	1·31

Even a casual reading of the figures set out in the first and third columns will bring out the fact that there is a definite relation between the *forces*, due to the weights on the pan, and the *extensions* of the spring, the increase in every case being *directly proportional* to the amount added or, in other words, we have "*equal extensions for equal increases of loading.*" If the figures be used to plot a graph as shown in fig. 70 this relation will be brought

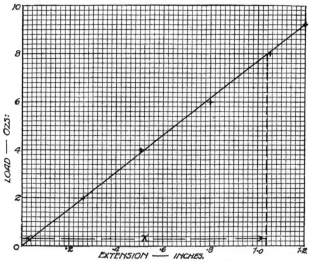

Fig. 70.   Relation between load and extension of a spring.

out more forcibly as the points plotted will be found to lie approximately on a straight line.   The graph thus obtained may then be
utilised to construct a scale, marked in ozs., which may be permanently fixed on the apparatus, when it will be available for measuring
other forces.   The distance **X**, representing the extension for 8 ozs.,
should be found from the graph and divided into 8 equal parts
to represent ounces.   In fig. 71 the *spring is being used to measure*

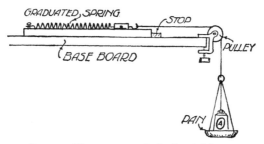

Fig. 71.   Measurement of a horizontal force.

a horizontal pull which, as we shall see presently, is *transmitted* from
the weight in the pan and along the cord; we are thus able to
convert the *downward acting force* due to weight into one acting
in any desired direction.

The principle just described for graduating a spring is the one
underlying the construction of the ordinary *spring-balance*, and
such a balance may be used in all the succeeding experiments to
measure forces.

Experiment 33.   To show how a "pulling force" may be transmitted.
Arrange a piece of apparatus as shown in fig. 72 in which the pull in the

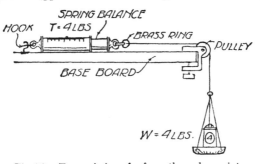

Fig. 72.   Transmission of a force through a point.

horizontal part of the cord is measured by means of the spring-balance.   The
weight of the scale pan will effect the balance, and the reading when the pan is
empty should be taken as zero. The pulley should be as easy running as possible.

(a) *Transmission through a point and along a chain or cord.* Consider any *particle* in the vertical part of the cord; since it remains in equilibrium the upward pull of the cord at that *point* must be equal in magnitude to the downward force due to the weight. Thus we may think of the force being transmitted from point to point along the chain. This applies to all parts of the cord and the balance will show experimentally that the pull in the horizontal part is equal to that in the vertical part of the chain, the **pulley**

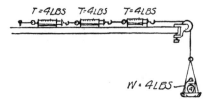

Fig. 73. Transmission of a force along a cord.

not introducing any new force into the cord but merely serving to change its direction. If we take the small brass ring in fig. 72 to represent a particular point, then the force acting in the cord is *transmitted through this point* to the balance.

That *the pull is the same at all points along the cord* may be shown by inserting a number of light spring-balances as shown in fig. 73, when each balance will register a pull T equal to the weight on the pan.

(b) *Transmission through a rigid body.* For our purpose we may consider a **Rigid Body** to be one which does not alter appreciably in shape or size under the action of forces applied to it.

The rigid body may, in this experiment, take the form of a sheet of stout cardboard of irregular outline as shown in fig. 74. To support its weight and

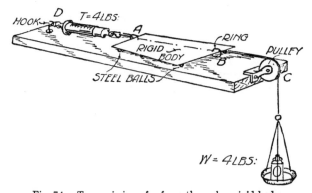

Fig. 74. Transmission of a force through a rigid body.

reduce friction between it and the surface of the board it may be supported on steel balls as shown. By trial it will be found that the body will only come to rest when A and B lie on the straight line $DABC$, formed by the portions of string on either side; this is an important fact and will be referred to later. When at rest the balance will register a pull equal to the weight in the pan, the pull evidently having been transmitted *through* the rigid body.

The Effects of Force on Materials. Terms. In dealing with forces and their effects upon structures various terms will be used which it will be convenient to illustrate as described in the following experiment.

Experiment 34. To illustrate the terms compression, tension, shear, stress, strain and elasticity.

On the pan of a weighing machine place a block of rubber as shown in fig. 75. On the rubber place a wood block equal in size to the end of the rubber, note what the balance registers and take this as "zero." Place any convenient weight on the rubber and note that, as shown by the balance, a force equal to this weight is *transmitted through* the rubber. By measurement show that the height of the rubber under load is less than when free, it has

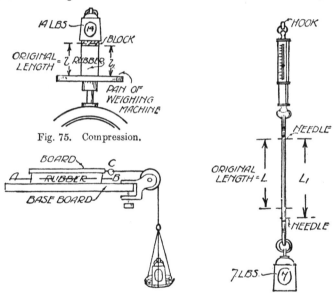

Fig. 75. Compression.

Fig. 77. Shear.   Fig. 76. Tension.

obviously been *compressed* by the weight and we say that the rubber is now subjected to a total force of **compression** of 14 lbs. (say).

Similarly a rubber cord may be used to suspend a weight as shown in fig. 76 when the cord will be found to *lengthen* and is said to be subjected to a total force of **tension** of 7 lbs. (say).

If to the base board shown in fig. 77 a piece of rubber be suitably secured with another board fixed above the rubber, a cord may be fastened at C and the upper board subjected to a pull of say 14 lbs. This force will evidently tend to make the upper layers of rubber slide or *shear* over the lower layers of the rubber, and the rubber is said to be subjected to a total **shearing** force of 14 lbs.

We have seen how the rubber alters in shape and size when subjected to a load, this *alteration in shape* is known as **strain,** and *the resistance set up in the material owing to the strain* is known as **stress.** Thus a tensile force will produce a tensile stress and the strain will be one of elongation. A compressive force will produce a compressive stress and the strain will be one of shortening.

Each of the forces mentioned above has been uniformly distributed over a certain area; for instance the force of 14 lbs. in the first case was distributed over the area of the section of the block of rubber. On p. 22 in comparing pressures we found the amount or intensity of pressure acting on a unit area for each case, similarly with stresses. Given the total force acting uniformly over a known area, we have, that the "intensity of stress," the "stress per unit area" or merely the "stress" $= \dfrac{\text{total force}}{\text{area}}$.

When the whole of the strain disappears on the removal of the stress a body is said to be *perfectly elastic* and the property is known as that of **elasticity.**

No known materials are perfectly elastic but within certain limits many are practically so and in this respect act like the spring which was tested in Experiment 32.

Experiment 35. **To ascertain how a rubber cord acts under gradually increasing loads.** Arrange a piece of apparatus as shown in fig. 78 in which a scale pan is suspended from a hook by means of a rubber cord of square or circular section. Put a small load on the pan so as to straighten the cord and take this as *zero load*. Near the ends of the cord insert two needles and measure the distance between them. Now add weights to the pan and after each increase in load ascertain the distance between the needles and tabulate the values as shown below.

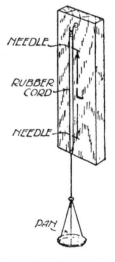

Test of a rubber cord of square section, $\frac{1}{4}'' \times \frac{1}{4}''$.

Load on pan (ozs.)	Length between needles (ins.)	Extension over length at zero
0 ozs.	9·8 ins.	0 ins.
2 ,,	9·97 ,,	0·17 ,,
4 ,,	10·12 ,,	0·32 ,,
8 ,,	10·4 ,,	0·6 ,,
12 ,,	10·7 ,,	0·9 ,,
16 ,,	11·0 ,,	1·2 ,,
20 ,,	11·4 ,,	1·6 ,,

Fig. 78. Elasticity of a rubber cord.

From inspection of these values it will be noted that approxi-

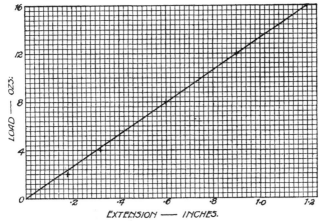

Fig. 79.   Relation between load and extension of a rubber cord.

mately the same relation holds as with the spring, that is we have "equal extensions for equal loads," and the relation may be shown as before by plotting these points on squared paper when it will be found that (approximately) a straight line passes through the points obtained.

Now remove the weights and note whether the rubber returns to its original length.   In the case of rubber which has not been overstrained it will do this *if sufficient time is allowed.*

Experiment 36.   To ascertain whether iron wire possesses the property of elasticity.   Since the increases of length will be very small great care in measuring is necessary in dealing with this material.   The piece of wire used should be as long as possible and if the apparatus shown in fig. 80 is used the wire may be carried right up to the ceiling.   The *extensions* are measured by means of a vernier reading to $\frac{1}{1000}''$ and the *length* is measured from the point of support of the wire to the point at which the vernier is attached.   The method of reading and of tabulating the values is the same as in the last experiment.   Fig. 81 shows a graph drawn from values obtained on a wire ·05″ diameter and of a length of 7 ft.   It shows, for this material, the direct proportion which exists between load and extension within the limits taken.

Action and Reaction.   Referring again to the loaded block on the scale pan in fig. 75 we saw that a force of 14 lbs. was transmitted through the rubber to the pan of the balance; evidently to support this

Fig. 80.
Elasticity of
iron wire

6—2

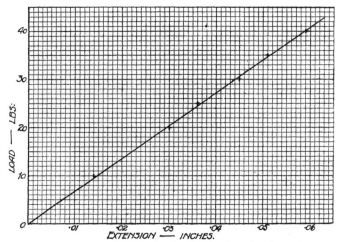

Fig. 81.   Relation between load and extension of an iron wire.

the balance must exert an equal force upwards as is shown in fig. 82. Thus both above and below the block there is a force of 14 lbs. acting and, if the rubber is able to resist crushing, it is evidently capable of supplying two equal outward acting forces to balance the forces applied to the block, see fig. 82.

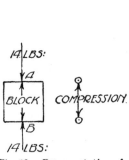

Fig. 82.   Representation of a body in compression.

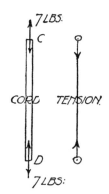

Fig. 83.   Representation of a body in tension.

Similarly with the rubber cord in fig. 76 to resist the pulls of 7 lbs. at the upper and lower ends the material of the cord must supply two inward acting forces of equal magnitude, see fig. 83. Hence to represent a body in *compression* we may place two outward pointing arrow-heads and for a body in *tension* two inward pointing arrows as shown in figs. 82 and 83. The most important fact to note here, however, is that the action between two forces which keep a point in equilibrium, as at *A, B, C* or *D,* is mutual and if one force be termed the action the other which balances it is known as the re-action. *Action and reaction are always equal and opposite.* Thus if a beam press upon a wall with a force of 5 tons the wall must evidently supply an upward acting force of 5 tons to support it, which we may speak of as the "supporting force" or the **reaction.** Again when a load is suspended from a hook the supporting force supplied by the hook is equal to the downward pull of the load.

Forces acting through a point. It will be convenient for us to commence our study of the statical side of building mechanics by considering the relations which exist between forces acting *through* or *at a point* and whose combined action is such that any small particle situated at that point will be kept *at rest* or in a state of *equilibrium.* Our present discussion will be confined to forces acting in one plane—*coplanar forces.*

Experiment 37. To investigate the case where two forces act at a point both along the same straight line. For this experiment prepare a wire frame, made and secured at one end to a spring-balance as shown in fig. 84. This is placed in the middle of a large board and the ring of the balance passed over a hook in the board as shown in fig. 85. To represent the case of two forces acting in the *same direction,* two fine cords, with hooks at both ends, are passed over pulleys, arranged *slightly out of line,* hooked to one end of the frame and weighted with unequal weights as shown in fig. 85.

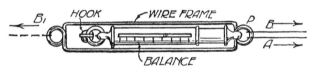

Fig. 84.   Wire frame for Experiment 37.

It ought to be clear that with the cords arranged as described we have two unequal forces acting at the point *P* (represented by the small ring as before) and both pulling in the same direction (see fig. 84). The spring-balance will evidently register the total effect due to these forces. If the forces *A* and *B* be 5 lbs. and 3 lbs. respectively the balance will register 8 lbs.—*the sum of the two forces.* Now take the cord with the smaller weight and arrange it to pull in the opposite direction to force *A,* as shown at B_1, figs. 84 and 85. The balance will still register the total effect due to these forces but this will now be only 2 lbs. Evidently to get the total effect of two forces acting in opposite directions we must *subtract* the smaller from the larger and the result will give the force acting *in the direction of the larger.*

We could represent these forces and their addition or sub-traction *graphically,* by taking say $\frac{1}{2}$ *inch to represent a* 1 *lb. force,*

when a line 2½ inches long would represent 5 lbs. Where the
forces were to be *added* we would have to add lines representing

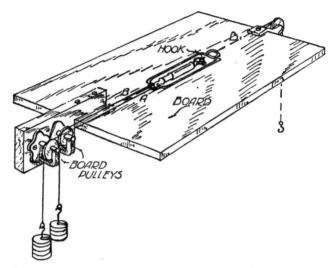

Fig. 85. Two forces acting in the same straight line.

3 and 5 lbs. and would obtain the sum—8 lbs.—acting in the same
direction, see fig. 86 *A*. In the second case the *smaller* force is
reversed in direction and the *subtraction* of this graphically is
shown at fig. 86 *B*. If we were
to call all forces acting in the
direction of the larger force *positive*
forces and all forces acting in the
opposite direction *negative* and
prefix the usual + and − signs,
then we might say that in all such
cases the "resulting force" or the
resultant would be obtained by
adding the forces *algebraically*
(that is, taking regard to their
signs).

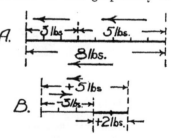

Fig. 86. Graphical addition and
subtraction of forces.

Since the *point P* does not move under the action of this
resultant (that is, after the spring ceases to extend) evidently the
spring of the balance supplies another force which, since it is able
to keep *P* from moving, must be *equal and opposite to the resultant*
(see p. 77); this force is known as the balancing force or **equilibrant.**

The Specification and Representation of a Force. Before proceeding further it will be necessary to add to what has already been said respecting the graphical representation of a force.

Any given force is completely defined if we know :—

The *point* at which it acts (if any);
The *direction* in which it acts;
The *magnitude* of the force.

All these conditions may be represented graphically or by drawing, since we may :—

Choose a *point* to represent that at which the force acts;
Draw a *line* through that point to show the direction of the force;
Mark off a length on the line to a suitable scale to represent the *magnitude* of the force.

(*Note.* The term **sense** is frequently used to indicate how a force acts along a given line and is taken to refer to the small arrow-heads placed on the line of action of the force. No difficulty need arise, however, if " direction" is understood to refer to both the "line of action" and what we have just called "sense." In fact it is difficult to think of "direction" otherwise.)

Inclined Forces. Arrange a horizontal board with pulleys and balance as shown in fig. 87. Attach various weights to *A* and *B* and note that in every case *a single force*, as supplied by the balance, is able to balance two inclined forces, although in each

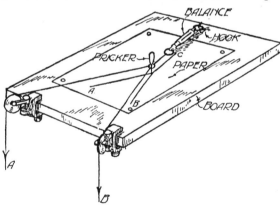

Fig. 87.   Two inclined forces acting at a point.

case the amount registered by the balance *will be less than the numerical sum of the two forces A and B,* in fact no simple relation between the three forces will be apparent and further investigation is necessary.

Experiment 38.   **To find the relations existing between three forces which keep a point in equilibrium.**   Attach any suitable weights to the cords *A* and *B* and, when the point *O* has come to rest, place a sheet of paper beneath the cords as shown in fig. 87.   With the aid of a fine pricker prick off two points immediately beneath each cord so that on the removal of the sheet the directions of the forces *OA*, *OB* and *OC* may be marked, see fig. 88. Note the reading of the balance and mark on each line the corresponding force.

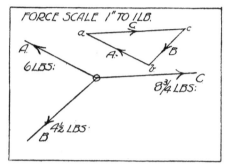

Fig. 88.   The triangle of forces.

Select a suitable force scale, say 1″ to represent 1 lb., and anywhere on the sheet set off the line *cb* to represent in *direction* and *magnitude* the force *B*. From the end *b* similarly set off *ba* to represent force *A* in magnitude and direction.   Join *ac*.   If the work has been done carefully, *ac* will be parallel to *OC* and will represent the force *OC* (8¾ lbs.).   Note that we took the forces in *clockwise* order—moving round *O* as with the hands of the clock—and that the arrow marks on the completed triangle *follow round*.   You will find that the same results are obtained no matter what three forces are taken *so long as the point O is in a state of equilibrium when acted upon by them.*

The results of this experiment lead directly to the following statement of the conditions under which three forces may keep a point in equilibrium.

The Triangle of Forces.   If three forces acting at a point are in equilibrium, then any triangle whose sides are parallel to the directions of the forces will have the lengths of these sides proportional to the magnitudes of the forces.
The converse of the Triangle of Forces is equally true.

Resultant of two Inclined Forces.   Referring once more to fig. 88 it may be noted that the force *C* is such that it just balances the effects of forces *A* and *B* on point *O*, in other words *C* is the *equilibrant* of *A* and *B*; it is represented in fig. 88 by the line *ac*—note "*the line a* (to) *c*"—and from what was said on p. 86 it should be clear that were we to *reverse the direction* of this force and speak of force *ca*—"*c* (to) *a*"—the line would then represent

the *resultant of forces A and B,* and would be such that it alone
could replace these two forces, see fig. 89.

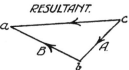

We may now define a resultant more
fully.

The resultant *of two or more forces is
that single force which can replace these
forces and which would by itself produce
the same effect as the two or more forces
acting together.*

Fig. 89.   The resultant of
two inclined forces.

The equilibrant *of any number of forces is equal and opposite
to the resultant of those forces and is such that when acting together
with those forces it produces equilibrium.*

Applications of the Triangle of Forces.   Numerous cases
occur in the design of a building where it is necessary to ascertain
the forces which are likely to act in various parts of the structure.
Various methods are adopted to discover what these forces are
but in the case of *framed structures,* such as iron roofs, the method
almost universally adopted is to apply the principle of the Triangle
of Forces and its accompanying principle the Polygon of Forces
(see p. 91).   The complete problems so treated are too difficult
for introduction at this stage, but the simple application given
below should be readily understood and will lead the way to fuller
treatment at a later stage.

Experiment 39.   To ascertain the forces acting in the jib and tie of a
jib crane.   The apparatus shown in fig. 90 represents a model of a type of
crane used by builders and stone-masons, the force acting in the *jib* is measured
by a compression balance whilst the forces in the *tie* at the top and the *stays*
at the back are measured by tension balances.   Load the hook with any suitable
weight, say 7 lbs., and adjust the base of the apparatus until the post is vertical
(compare with the plumb-line shown).   For the present we shall consider
only the forces acting at the top of the jib; these are three in number, the load
acting vertically downwards, the force acting along the tie and the force
acting along the jib.   Of these forces only the first is fully defined in direction
and amount.   Before we can obtain the unknown facts about the other two
forces by drawing we must first set down lines on a sheet of paper showing
the angles between the lines along which the forces act.   Measure from the
point where tie, jib and chain meet to the points where the plumb-line inter-
sects the centre line of the tie and of the jib and draw a **frame diagram** to
scale, see fig. 91.   The direction of the pull in the chain will be parallel to the
plumb-line.
      To any convenient *force scale* set down *ca* parallel to the chain and of a
length representing 7 lbs.

Bow's Notation.   It will be convenient for us to adopt in future a special
method of lettering the diagrams known as Bow's Notation.   To each
space between the lines of action of the forces on the frame diagram a capital
letter is assigned, thus we have lettered the space between the chain and the
jib as *A,* between the jib and the tie as *B* and the space outside from the tie

to the chain as C.   Each force may now be referred to by means of the letters standing on each side of its line of action.   For reasons which will appear later these letters should be read in a definite order *round* the point O and it will be convenient to read them always in a *clockwise direction*, thus the three

Fig. 90.   Experimental jib crane.

forces will be: in chain, force CA; in the jib, force AB; in tie, force BC. On the completed triangle of forces which we will in future describe as the *force diagram*—the letters will be used in the *same order* for each force, but small letters will be used, thus *ca* represents the force CA, etc.

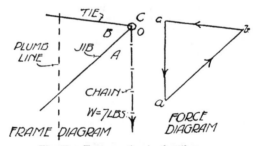

Fig. 91.   Forces acting in the jib crane.

To complete the triangle draw a line *ab* through *a* and parallel to the jib. Similarly draw *cb* parallel to the tie, its intersection with the line *ab* at *b* completes the triangle.   Now put on the *sense* marks, *ca* acts downwards and may be marked at once, the other sense marks must *follow round*.   The information thus obtained enables us to say whether the forces are acting towards O or away from it. The force a (to) b evidently acts up the jib towards O and the force b (to) c acts away from O, in other words the jib is in a state of *compression* and the amount of the force is 9·4 lbs., found by measuring ab, whilst the tie is in *tension* and the force one of 7 lbs., found by measuring bc.

To test these values. Read the balances in jib and tie. Remove the weight from the hook and read them again. Subtract these latter (due to the weight of the apparatus) from the former, giving the forces acting in jib and tie respectively due to the weight on the hook. These values should verify those obtained graphically.

Experiment 40. To ascertain the relations existing between more than three forces keeping a point in equilibrium. It will be convenient to arrange this experiment on a vertical board as shown in fig. 92, where five forces are shown keeping the point P in equilibrium. The relative directions of the forces may be obtained by pricking through on to a sheet of paper as already described or the angles between them may be measured by means of a circular protractor, see fig. 92. Obtain the frame diagram as shown in

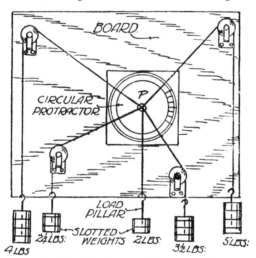

Fig. 92. Five forces acting at a point.

fig. 93, mark on the sense and magnitude of each force and letter the spaces as already described. Starting with any of the forces proceed to draw the force diagram to a suitable scale, drawing in order say ab, bc, cd and de to represent the corresponding forces, see fig. 94. Now draw ea and note that the end of this line comes either very near to or coincides with the point a, from which we started. Were there no experimental errors, the last line would with the lines representing the other forces form a *closed polygon*.

This fact leads to the following statement of the **Polygon of Forces. If any number of forces acting at a point are in equilibrium then a closed polygon may be drawn whose sides shall represent these forces in magnitude and direction.**

The converse of this statement is also important.

Resultant and Equilibrant of more than Three Forces. If *any one* of the forces keeping *P*, fig. 92, in equilibrium were removed then evidently the point would cease to be in a state of equilibrium, hence *we may regard any one of the forces as the* **equilibrant** *of the rest.* If its sense were reversed, it would represent the **resultant** of the other forces. Thus, in figs. 93 and 94, force

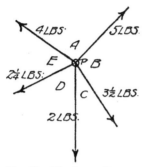
Fig. 93.   The frame diagram.

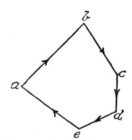
Fig. 94.   The force diagram.

ab might be described as the *equilibrant* of forces *BC, CD, DE* and *EA*, whilst *ba* would be the *resultant* of the four forces. (Read again the definitions of Resultant and Equilibrant given on p. 89, after which some problems utilising the Polygon of Forces should be attempted, see p. 95 and also Problems VI, 6.)

The Parallelogram of Forces. On p. 89 we showed that it was possible to obtain the resultant of two inclined forces acting at a point by means of the Triangle of Forces. The same result may be obtained by means of what is known as the **Parallelogram of Forces.** This does not introduce any new experimental facts but is, so far as we are concerned, merely another graphical method of solution *based upon the same experimental results.*

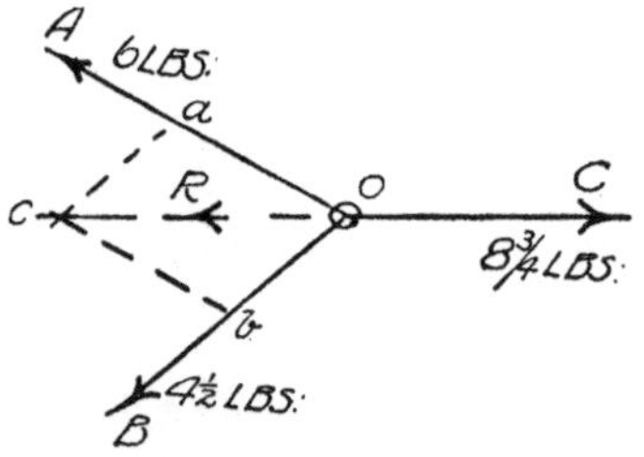

Let fig. 95 represent the three forces *A*, *B* and *C* which kept the point *O* in equilibrium in Exper. 38. As already described the *resultant* of forces *A* and *B* must be a force equal to *C* (*equilibrant*) but acting in the opposite direction. On the line *OB* mark off *Ob* representing force *B* to any convenient scale and similarly mark off *Oa* representing force *A*. Draw *ac* parallel to

Fig. 95.   The parallelogram of forces.

OB and bc parallel to OA. Join Oc. Now it will be found that Oc and OC form one and the same straight line and also that the length of Oc represents a force of $8\frac{3}{4}$ lbs. to scale. Evidently Oc *represents the resultant of forces A and B.* Note that figure $Oacb$ is a parallelogram.

The following statement of the **Parallelogram of Forces** should be carefully memorised. **If two forces acting at a point be represented in magnitude and direction by the adjacent sides of a parallelogram drawn *from* (*or to*) that point, then their resultant will be represented by the diagonal of the parallelogram drawn from (or to) that point.**

An additional experiment to verify this is unnecessary, but the following case where the two forces act at 90° to each other is important and may be experimentally investigated.

Experiment 41. To verify the parallelogram of forces for two forces acting at right angles to each other. This experiment may be arranged on a vertical board as shown in fig. 96 and the amounts on the load pillars should be varied until the angle between two of the cords is 90°. As

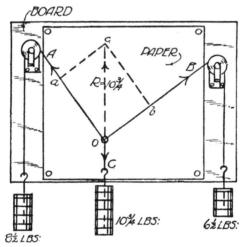

Fig. 96. The resultant of two forces acting at right angles.

before mark off on a sheet of paper the directions and magnitudes of the forces acting at O. Complete the parallelogram $Oacb$ as already described. It will be found that, allowing for experimental errors, the *resultant R* is opposite and equal to the force C—the equilibrant of the other two forces A and B.

Resolution of a Force. If, instead of finding a single force (the resultant) to replace two other forces, it is desired to replace a force *OC*, fig. 97, by two forces acting along *OA* and *OB*, the process of solution would evidently be the reverse of what we have been doing, that is, given the diagonal and the direction of two sides of the parallelogram to complete the figure. Using the values and angles just obtained set off *Oc* representing 10¾ lbs.—*the given force*. Complete the parallelogram by drawing *ca* and *cb* parallel to *OB* and *OA*. Then *Oa* and *Ob* will represent the two forces which, acting along these lines, would just *replace* force *C*.

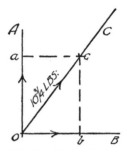

Fig. 97.   The resolution of a force.

This process is known as the *resolution of a force* and we are said to *resolve* force *C* into its *components* along the directions *OB* and *OA*. (The amounts of the components thus obtained should of course equal the values found in the last experiment, but other values may be taken and checked experimentally.)

Experimental Applications of the Polygon and Parallelogram of Forces. If the jib crane described in Experiment 39 be provided with a small pulley the load *W* may be suspended by a cord passing over this pulley, as shown in fig. 98, the other end being attached to a hook at some distance up the vertical post. Under

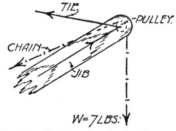

Fig. 98.   Forces acting in the jib crane with pulley.

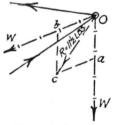

Fig. 99.   The frame diagram.

these conditions we evidently have *four forces* acting at *O*. The pull in the tie, the thrust in the jib and the pull in both portions of the "chain"; the pull in the two parts of the chain may be taken to be equal to the weight in each case (see p. 80).

On the frame diagram in fig. 99 these forces are represented by the solid and chain lines.

The problem is to obtain the forces acting in the tie and the jib. It may be completed in two ways.

(a) With the aid of the *Parallelogram of Forces* replace forces W and W by the single force R acting downwards from O. Redraw the frame diagram as shown in fig. 100 and complete by means of the Triangle of Forces; the force diagram *cab* gives force *ab* 13·8 lbs. and force *bc* 3¾ lbs. W was 7 lbs. and the value of R, 11½ lbs., was obtained from the parallelogram shown in dotted lines in fig. 99.

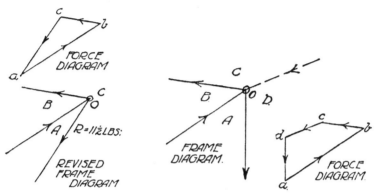

Fig. 100.   Solution by   Fig. 101.   Solution by polygon of forces.
   triangle of forces.

(b) The problem may also be solved by using the *Polygon of Forces.* Replace the force in the inclined part of the chain by an *equal force acting in the same direction* but *towards O*, instead of away from it, see fig. 101. Letter the spaces. To any convenient scale draw *cd* parallel to and representing force *CD*, draw *da* similarly. Next draw *ab* through *a* and *bc* through *c* parallel to the forces *AB* and *BC* respectively. The intersection *b* will complete the polygon and the forces may be measured and should give the same values as above.

Having found the forces in tie and jib graphically they should be checked by obtaining the readings of the balances as already described.

PROBLEMS VI

1. Calculate the stress in lbs. per square inch (a) in the rubber cord mentioned on p. 82 when the load was 20 ozs., (b) in the wire mentioned on p. 83 when the load was 30 lbs.

2. A square brick pier with footings (square) and concrete (square) is shown in fig. *A*. If the pier carries a central load of 22 tons calculate the stress in tons per square foot on (a) the pier, (b) on top of the concrete, and (c) on the ground beneath the concrete. (The weight of the pier, etc., may be neglected.)

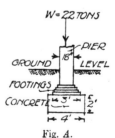

Fig. *A*.

3. Calculate the tensile *breaking stress* in tons per sq. inch for (*a*) a piece of deal $\frac{1}{2}'' \times \frac{1}{2}''$ in cross section which requires 2795 lbs. to *pull* it apart, and (*b*) the compressive breaking stress of the same timber if a block $1\frac{1}{2}'' \times 1\frac{1}{2}''$ in cross section requires 15,200 lbs. to crush it.

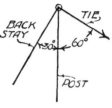

Fig. *B*.

4. If an experimental crane similar to that shown in fig. 90 has a single back stay instead of two stays, find the force acting in (*a*) the stay and (*b*) the vertical post, when the angles between the various members are as shown in fig. *B* and the pull in the tie is 8 lbs.

5. A pulley is suspended from the centre of a rope fixed at two points 12 ft. apart. The pulley is used for lifting stone. If the rope sags 1 ft., see fig. *C*, when a load of 5 cwts. is being lifted what is the force acting in the rope?

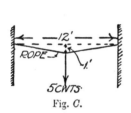

Fig. *C*.

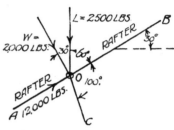

Fig. *D*.

6. Fig. *D* shows two external forces *L* and *W* acting at a joint *O* in a roof truss. The force in the lower part of the rafter is 12,000 lbs. Find the magnitude and sense of the forces acting in members *OB* and *OC*.

7. Fig. *E* shows a rafter inclined at 40° to the horizontal and exerting an inclined thrust upon the wall of 5 cwts.

Resolve this force into two component forces, (*a*) one tending to push the wall over and acting horizontally, and (*b*) one force acting vertically downwards on the wall.

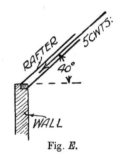

Fig. *E*.

8. A piece of iron wire, 7 ft. long, was loaded with gradually increasing loads, and the increases in length with the corresponding loads tabulated as below:—

Load ... lbs.	0	10	20	25	30	35	40
Extension ... ins.	0	·014	·03	·037	·045	·051	·059

Plot these points on squared paper, and see whether a straight line graph may be drawn to pass approximately through the points.

From this graph find the total extension and the extension per inch of length of the wire when the load was 38 lbs.

CHAPTER VII

FORCES ON RIGID BODIES. PARALLEL FORCES.
REACTIONS OF BEAMS

So far we have dealt only with forces acting at a point or upon a body of very small dimensions and it is now necessary for us to deal with forces acting upon bodies of more extended size. In every case we shall consider these to be *rigid bodies* (see p. 80) and shall treat of their equilibrium when acted upon by forces acting along parallel lines—*parallel forces*—and also by forces acting along lines inclined to each other.

Experiment 42. To find the magnitude of the equilibrant of two parallel forces. We shall consider these forces to act upon a rigid body represented in this case by a light rod supported horizontally on rollers so that its weight may be neglected, see fig. 102.

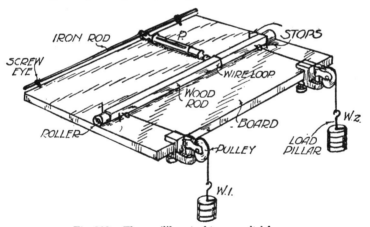

Fig. 102. The equilibrant of two parallel forces.

(a) Let the two parallel forces act in the *same direction* along two cords passing over pulleys and weighted as shown in fig. 102. The equilibrant is supplied by the pull of a spring-balance which is so mounted that its *position* may be varied at will. Stops are provided to prevent undue movement of the rod.

With two suitable loads on the load-pillars adjust the position of the spring balance until the rod will stand away from the stops. When this is possible the forces W_1 and W_2, see fig. 103, are evidently balanced by P, the pull of the balance. Vary the positions and amounts of the forces and also of the equilibrant and note that in each case (i) the amount of the equilibrant is equal to the sum of the two forces or Equilibrant $= W_1 + W_2$, (ii) the position of the equilibrant is nearer to the larger force, and (iii) when the two forces are equal P pulls at a point halfway between A and B.

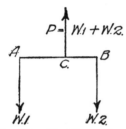

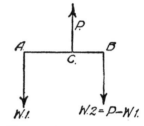

Fig. 103.   Equilibrant of two
like parallel forces.

Fig. 104.   Equilibrant of two
unlike parallel forces.

(b) Next let the two forces act in *opposite directions* and be represented by the force W_1 and by the pull in the balance P, see fig. 104, W_2 is then the equilibrant and will be found (i) to be equal to the difference between the two forces or Equilibrant $= P - W_1$, and (ii) the position of the equilibrant is outside of the larger force.

When parallel forces act in the same direction (have the same sense) they are known as *like forces* and *unlike forces* when they act in opposite directions.

Centre of Gravity. Any body of extended size may be considered to consist of a number of smaller portions each of which has weight or is acted upon by gravity. Since gravitational forces are vertical forces we may consider that for such a single body they are *like parallel forces*. Utilising the information gained in the last experiment it must evidently be possible to find *a single equilibrant* which would balance a large number of like parallel forces, such as would act upon a single body as explained above; since for any two of the forces a *resultant* could be found— equal and opposite to the equilibrant—which could then be combined with another of the forces and the process repeated until the resultant of *all* the forces had been found. This resultant would be equal in magnitude to the *total weight* of the body. As we shall show presently it is possible to find the point at which this resultant force may be considered to act. This point is called the **Centre of Gravity** (c.g.) and for any rigid body *is a point fixed in or near the body at which the weight of the body may be considered to act.*

If a body be suspended at its c.g. it has no tendency to rotate.

Consider the case of a rod of uniform section; from experience we know that it is possible to find a point in the length of the rod about which it would balance, see fig. 105.

Let us suppose that the uniform rod AB in fig. 105 is divided into an even number of equal portions of weight w and that the total weight of the rod is W. Working in from each end we have that for the two outer forces the *resultant* equals $2w$ and acts half-way between them (at the centre C); similarly with the other pairs

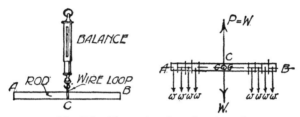

Fig. 105. The centre of gravity of a rod.

of forces. Proceeding thus we have that the total resultant is W and acts in the vertical line through C. Suspending the rod at this point from a spring-balance it should register W and the rod should remain horizontal. The c.g. of the rod actually lies at the intersection of the centre line AB with the vertical line through C.

Experiment 43. To find the c.g. of any irregular plane figure. We have seen that the weight of a body may be considered as acting at its c.g. If the body be suspended from any other point so that it may *swing freely*, the only two forces acting upon the body are its weight acting *vertically* downwards at its c.g. and the force supplied by the point of suspension, since these two forces keep the body in equilibrium they must evidently act in opposite directions along the same straight line (a vertical line), see p. 85. This fact gives us a very convenient method of finding experimentally the c.g. of irregular sheets *of uniform thickness* in cardboard or metal.

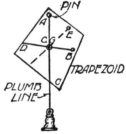

Fig. 106. Finding the centre of gravity by suspension.

The body is suspended from any convenient point A as shown in fig. 106. From what we have already said the c.g. will lie on a vertical line dropped from A, such a line AC should be marked on the figure by means of a plumb-line. Next suspend the figure from any other point B and similarly mark another line BD. Since the c.g. lies on both AC and BD *it must evidently lie at their intersection.* Finally test the correctness of the position found for the c.g. by suspending from some other point, as E, or from the c.g. itself. Repeat the experiment with any of the figures shown in fig. 107.

The following additional points should be noted:

(1) If the figure possesses an *axis of symmetry* the c.g. will lie on this line See both the T section, the rectangle and the cast iron girder section.

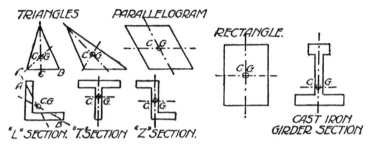

Fig. 107.   The c.g.s of plane figures.

(2) If it possesses two axes of symmetry then the c.g. lies at their intersection.   See rectangle and parallelogram.

(3) The c.g. may lie outside the figure.   See the L section.

(4) The c.g. of a triangle lies at the intersection of two *medians* (lines drawn from the corners of the triangle to the middle of the opposite sides).

(5) A graphical construction for the c.g. of a trapezoid is shown in fig. 108. *a* and *b* are the lengths of the parallel sides respectively.

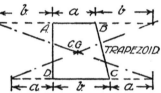

Fig. 108.   The c.g. of a trapezoid.

Moments.   In carrying out Experiment 42 we noted that to obtain equilibrium the *position* of the balance was quite as important as the *amount* of the pull and also that considerable adjustment was necessary before equilibrium was obtained, the forces at the ends tending *to turn the rod* first one way and then the other.   In the experiment referred to we considered only the *amounts* of the forces, in the following experiment we shall consider the effect of both *forces* and *distances*.

Experiment 44.   To find the conditions of equilibrium for two (or more) **parallel forces acting on a rod pivoted at its centre.**   Take a rod pivoted at its centre so that when unloaded it hangs horizontally, see fig. 109. Evidently when so suspended the c.g. of the rod lies immediately beneath P and the effect of the weight of the rod may be disregarded.   A stand suitable for this and other experiments is shown in fig. 110 and the suspension of the rod is shown in detail in the section given in fig. 109.

By means of wire loops and load-pillars put two unequal loads W_1 and W_2 on the rod and adjust their positions until the rod balances in a horizontal

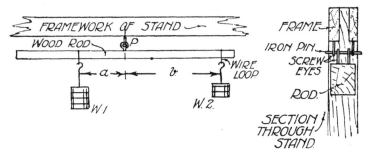

Fig. 109. The equilibrium of two like parallel forces.

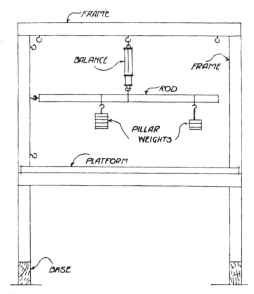

Fig. 110. Framed stand for mechanics experiments.

position. Measure a and b. Repeat with other weights and tabulate the results as shown below.

Exp. no.	W_1	W_2	a	b	$W_1 \times a$	$W_2 \times b$
1	3 lbs.	5 lbs.	15 ins.	9 ins.	45	45
2	7 ,,	4 ,,	6 ,,	10·5 ,,	42	42
3	2½ ,,	6½ ,,	12 ,,	4·6 ,,	30	29·9
4	1 ,,	3 ,,	14 ,,	4·65 ,,	14	13·8

NOTE. (a) In each case the product of W_1 by a is equalled by the product of W_2 by b.

(b) W_1 tended to turn the rod about P in a direction opposite to that of the hands of a clock or *anti-clockwise*, while W_2 tended to turn it in a *clockwise* direction.

(c) In obtaining the product W_1 by a we multiplied units of weight by units of length and the new units thus obtained we speak of as pound-inches (lb. ins.), pound-feet (lb. ft.) or gramme-centimetres (gm. cms.) according to the units of weight and length used.

When a *force* acting on a body causes or tends to cause the body to *turn round* some point at which it is pivoted, we obtain a measure of "the turning tendency of the force" by *multiplying the force by its distance from the point, measured at right angles to the line of action of the force*; this product is known as the **moment of the force about** P and may be either clockwise or anti-clockwise. (The moment of F equals $F \times d$ and is anti-clockwise, see fig. 111.)

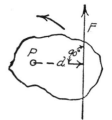

Fig. 111. The moment of a force.

In the experiment just carried out it was noted that for equilibrium, with two forces about a point, the *clockwise moment equalled the anti-clockwise moment* and, if the experiment were repeated with more than two forces, it would be found that the *sum* of all the clockwise moments would equal the *sum* of all the anti-clockwise moments, in every case where equilibrium was obtained. If we speak of the clockwise moments as being *positive* (+) and the anti-clockwise moments as being *negative* (−) we may then make the general statement that:—*if a pivoted body is in equilibrium when acted upon by a number of forces then the algebraic sum of the moments of the forces about the pivot will be zero*. E.g. in Experiment 44, $(W_2 \times b) - (W_1 \times a)$ should equal zero in each case. Taking the values on the second line we have:

$$(4 \times 10·5) - (7 \times 6)$$
$$= 42 - 42 = 0.$$

At present we are dealing only with parallel forces but in Experiment 47 we shall show that the above statement applies also to inclined forces.

Experiment 45. To test the statement just made in the case of several forces acting on a pivoted rod. Any convenient weights may be taken but the arrangement shown in fig. 112 is interesting because an upward pull (as measured by the balance) is applied at one end. Adjust the weights until equilibrium in a horizontal position is obtained then measure the distances and note the amounts of the weights W_1 and W_2 and the pull T as registered by the balance.

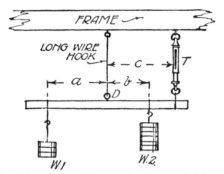

Fig. 112. The equilibrium of unlike parallel forces.

Then, if the statement we have just made is applicable here, we have, considering clockwise and anti-clockwise moments:

$$(W_2 \times b) - (W_1 \times a) - (T \times c) = 0.$$

In the experiment illustrated in fig. 112, $W_1 = 3$ lbs., $W_2 = 6$ lbs., $T = 1\cdot8$ lbs., $a = 8$ ins., $b = 7$ ins. and $c = 10$ ins. Hence

$$(6 \times 7) - (3 \times 8) - (10 \times 1\cdot8)$$
$$= 42 - 24 - 18$$
$$= 0$$

which verifies the statement for this experiment.

Experiment 46. To find the c.g. of a rod by moments. Take a rod pivoted at P near one end as shown in fig. 113. Weigh the rod and let its weight be W_R (say 1 lb.). Now suspend the rod at P as already described, hang a weight to the left of P and adjust its position until the rod hangs horizontally. The rod is evidently now in equilibrium under the action of two forces, W_1 acting at a distance a from P and W_R, the weight of the rod, acting at an unknown distance (say x ins.) to the right of P.

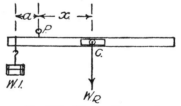

Fig. 113. Finding the c.g. of a rod by moments.

Since the rod is in equilibrium the algebraic sum of the moments must equal zero. Let W_1 be 3 lbs. and a be 5″, then

$$(W_R \times x) - (W_1 \times a) = 0,$$

i.e. $$\hspace{3em} (1 \times x) - (3 \times 5) = 0,$$

or $$\hspace{4em} x - 15 = 0,$$

$$\hspace{4em} \therefore \ x = 15 \text{ ins.}$$

Gum a piece of paper to the side of the rod at C and mark the exact position of the c.g. thus obtained.

A number of experiments may now be arranged with the point P situated anywhere on the rod (e.g. at the end, see fig. 110) when the weight of the rod, W_R, acting at the c.g. may be included as one of the forces. Fig. 114 illustrates such an experiment.

The Principle of Moments. If the rod shown in fig. 114 were suspended at P from a spring-balance the amount of the supporting force at P could be ascertained. We should then know both the position and the magnitude of *all* the forces keep-

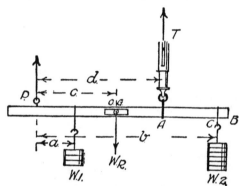

Fig. 114. The equilibrium of a body acted upon by a number of parallel forces.

ing the rod in equilibrium. It is then simply a matter of calculation to show that if we take the algebraic sum of the moments of the forces *about any point* (either in or out of the rod) the result will be zero. (*Note.* If the point be taken in the line of action of one of the forces the moment of that force about that point will evidently be zero, since $F \times 0 = 0$.)

We are now in a position to state what is known as the **Principle of Moments**, which we have so far verified for parallel forces and which we shall presently proceed to verify for inclined forces.

If a body is in equilibrium under the action of a number of forces acting in one plane, then the algebraic sum of the moments of the forces about any point in the plane is zero.

Experiment **47.** Equilibrium of a pivoted body under forces inclined to each other. Take a rod pivoted at the end and support it, as shown in fig. 115, by means of a cord and spring balance. Suspend from the C.G. a weight and let the total force acting at this point be equal to W (including the weight of the rod). Then evidently the rod is in equilibrium under the action of the vertical force W acting at C, the pull T in the cord and a supporting force acting through P. Consider moments of these forces about P. Note the reading of T (5·3 lbs.) and the distance b (measured from P at right angles to the direction of this cord, say 18 inches); also measure the distance a from P to the vertical cord (say 11·9 inches) and let $W = 8$ lbs.

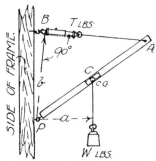

Fig. 115. The equilibrium of a body under three non-parallel forces.

Then

$$(W \times a) - (T \times b) + (P \times 0)$$
$$= (8 \times 11\cdot9) - (5\cdot3 \times 18)$$
$$= 95\cdot2 - 95\cdot4 = 0 \text{ (approx.)}.$$

This verifies the Principle of Moments for this case of inclined forces. (See also Problems VII, 3.)

An experiment may be arranged, similar to that given below (Experiment 48), in which the body may be kept in equilibrium by *more than three forces* and the above Principle verified for this case.

Experiment **48.** To find the conditions of equilibrium of three non-parallel forces, not acting at a point, which keep a body in equilibrium.

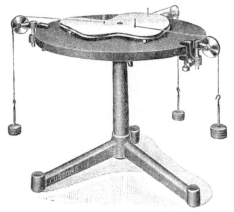

Fig. 116. The equilibrium of three forces not acting at a point.

Cut out an irregular figure from stout cardboard and support this horizontally on steel balls as has already been described, see fig. 116. Attach three cords at any convenient points and to each of these apply a load in the manner shown; adjust the weights until the body takes up a convenient position on the table. Note the amounts of the forces and obtain their directions; this may be done either by marking the lines on the body itself or by pricking them on to a sheet of paper laid on the table. Let fig. 117 represent the body and

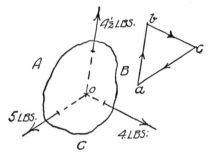

Fig. 117.   Three forces acting on a rigid body.

the forces. Produce the lines of action of the forces and note that *they are concurrent*, i.e. all intersect in the point O; see whether a triangle of forces can be drawn having its sides parallel to and proportional to these forces, (see triangle *abc*, fig. 117).

The following statement of the facts verified in this experiment is important.

When a body is kept in equilibrium under three non-parallel forces acting in one plane, then the lines of action of these forces will meet at a point and a force triangle may be drawn the sides of which will be proportional to these three forces.

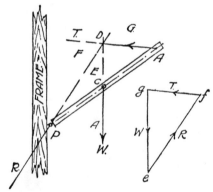

Fig. 118.   Finding the unknown force.

Applying this statement to the case of the pivoted rod used in Experiment 47 it becomes possible for us to ascertain the direction and magnitude of the force R (the reaction) acting at P.

Reproduce the outline of the apparatus to scale, see fig. 118. Produce WC to intersect AD at D. Join D to P and produce. Then R evidently acts in the line DP *since the three forces must be concurrent.*

Suppose that only the weight W is fully defined and we require to find the magnitude and direction of both R and T. To any convenient scale draw the force triangle *gef*, after lettering the spaces as shown. The sense of W being known the sense of both R and T "follow round," R evidently acts upwards toward P and the tie is in tension. The magnitude of T and W may be checked experimentally.

We shall now proceed to consider a number of simple problems which may be solved by aid of the principles discussed in the preceding pages.

Example. *A crowbar, cranked at the end as shown in fig. 119, is to be used for raising one end of a girder 20 ft. long and weighing 10 cwts. Find what* vertical *force applied at the end of the crowbar will just be sufficient to raise the girder. The horizontal distances a and b are 64 inches and 4 inches respectively.*

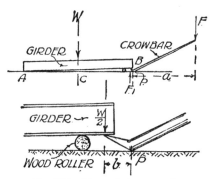

Fig. 119. Example in moments.

Since the weight of the uniform girder may be considered as acting at the centre of its length we may calculate the upraising force necessary at B. Calling this force F_1 and taking moments about A we have

$$(W \times 10) - (F_1 \times 20) = 0,$$
or
$$(10 \times 10) - (F_1 \times 20) = 0,$$
or
$$100 - 20F_1 = 0,$$
i.e.
$$20F_1 = 100,$$
or
$$F_1 = 5 \text{ cwts.},$$

or half the weight of the girder, as might have been expected.

Now consider the crowbar as a rod pivoted at P and in a state of equilibrium under the action of two vertical forces equal to F_1 and to F respectively.

Then   clockwise moments = anti-clockwise moments,

or $F \times a = F_1 \times b,$

i.e. $F \times 64 = 5 \times 4,$

or $F = \frac{20}{64}$ cwts.

$$= \cdot 3125 \text{ cwts.}$$
$$= 35 \text{ lbs.}$$ $\bigg\}$ *Ans.*

Example. *Suppose that a straight crowbar be used to raise the same girder, see fig. 120, the total length of the crowbar being 68 inches and the force F applied at right angles to the length of the bar. If the horizontal distance between P and B is 4 inches find the magnitude of the force necessary to raise the girder.*

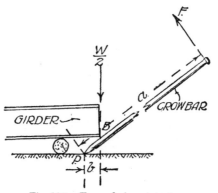

Fig. 120.   Example in moments.

Consider the bar as pivoted at P, it is in equilibrium under the force F and the vertical force $\dfrac{W}{2}$, therefore the algebraic sum of these moments should be zero, then

$$\left(\frac{W}{2} \times b \right) - (F \times a) = 0,$$

i.e. $(5 \times 4) - (F \times 68) = 0,$

or $68F = 20,$

$\therefore \quad F = \frac{20}{68}$ cwts.

$$= \cdot 294 \text{ cwts.}$$
$$= 33 \text{ lbs.}$$ $\bigg\}$ *Ans.*

The Reactions of Beams. In referring to the forces which act so as to support loaded beams we generally speak of the "supporting forces" as the **reactions**. We will now proceed to ascertain the reactions for a number of simple cases of loading and to describe how the results may be verified experimentally.

Example. *A beam of span L ft. is loaded at the centre with a weight of W tons. Find its reactions.*

The sketch given in fig. 121 represents the beam under the conditions of loading stated. Since a certain length of the beam "bears" upon the wall at each end, we shall usually consider the "span" to refer to the distance between the centres of the "bearings," these are marked with arrow-heads at A and B in fig. 121. The reaction at A we will speak of as "R_A," similarly the reaction at B will be "R_B."

Either by experiment (see Experiment 49) or by calculation (see p. 107) it is easy to show that each wall takes half the load and hence that $R_A = R_B = \dfrac{W}{2}$; and further that $W = R_A + R_B$. That *the sum of the reactions equals the total load* follows from the fact

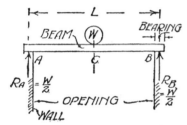

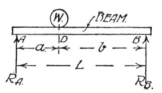

Fig. 121. A beam loaded at the centre.　　　Fig. 122. A beam loaded out of the centre.

that the downward acting forces are balanced by two upward acting forces, so that the total amounts must be equal. This affords a useful check of calculated reactions.

If W were the weight of the beam we could still consider it as acting at the centre, since the beam is of uniform section; hence *half the weight of the beam is taken by each wall.* In the following examples we do not again refer to the weight of the beam, the amounts to be added to the reactions, where this weight is to be considered, being easily calculated.

Example. *A beam of span L ft. is loaded at* a *feet from A with a load of W tons, find the reactions, fig.* 122.

The beam is in equilibrium under the action of three parallel forces R_A, R_B and W. To obtain the reaction at B take moments about A. Since R_A acts through point A its moment about this point will be zero, (see p. 104).

Then $(W \times a) - (R_B \times L) + (R_A \times 0) = 0,$

i.e. $R_B \times L = W \times a,$

or $R_B = \dfrac{W \times a}{L}.$

Similarly $R_A = \dfrac{W \times b}{L}.$

Putting these results into words we have:

$$\text{Reaction at one side} = \frac{\textbf{Load} \times \textbf{distance from opposite side}}{\textbf{Span}}.$$

This formula may be applied to all cases of simply supported beams of *single spans* provided that each load is considered individually.

Experiment 49. **To verify by experiment the results of the last two examples.** The experiment may be conveniently arranged as shown in fig. 123. The supporting forces are supplied by two spring-balances, these are suspended from small brass chains so that an adjustment may be readily made to keep the beam horizontal. The rod is placed in wire loops and it

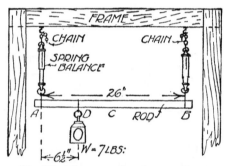

Fig. 123. Beam reactions by experiment.

should be first noted that *the weight of the rod affects each balance equally* (take these readings as zero in all the experiments). Now place a weight of 7 lbs. at the *centre* of the beam and note that each balance registers $3\frac{1}{2}$ lbs. (additional to that already shown). Now place the weight out of the centre and note that the balances are unequally affected. Measure the distances AB and AD, let them be $26''$ and $6\frac{1}{2}''$ respectively. Then by calculation we have

$$R_B = \frac{W \times 6\frac{1}{2}}{26} = \frac{7 \times 6\frac{1}{2}}{26} = \frac{7}{4} = 1\tfrac{3}{4} \text{ lbs.}$$

Similarly $$R_A = \frac{W \times 19\frac{1}{2}}{26} = 5\tfrac{1}{4} \text{ lbs.}$$

And $$R_A + R_B = 5\tfrac{1}{4} + 1\tfrac{3}{4} = 7 \text{ lbs.} = W.$$

Take the readings of the balances (above "zero") and see whether they verify this.

Repeat the experiment with a number of loads, noting that the total reaction at each side will be the sum of the reactions due to each individual load.

Concentrated Loads and Uniformly Distributed Loads. Each of the loads which we have so far considered has been taken as acting *at a point* in the length of the beam; in actual practice such "point loads" or **concentrated loads** very rarely occur. If a column or a post rests upon a beam, it can be treated as a concentrated load, though it may actually be spread over 6 ins. or a foot of the length of the beam. More frequently, however, we have to consider loads such as are due to brick walls, partitions and floors coming upon beams, and since the effect of these loads is distributed along the length of the beam we speak of them as **distributed loads.** If the distribution is uniform from point to point, that is if, say, each foot of length carries an equal weight, then we speak of this as a *uniformly distributed load* and we specify its amount as so many "lbs. per inch run" or so many "tons per foot run" according to the units used.

With a uniformly distributed load we may, *so far as the reactions are concerned,* consider it as a concentrated load of equal total amount acting at its C.G.—the centre of its length in this case. This we have already done in considering the weight of the beam in the example on p. 109.

Example. *A beam AB, fig. 124 (the weight of which may be disregarded) has a span of 25 ft. and is loaded with a uniformly distributed load of ½ ton per foot from a point 4 ft. from A for a length of 10 ft.; a concentrated load of 2 tons acts at 6 ft. from B. Find the total reactions at each support.*

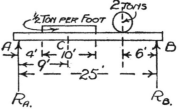

Fig. 124. A beam with concentrated and distributed loads.

(*a*) Consider the reactions due to the concentrated load,

$$R_A = \frac{2 \times 6}{25} = \frac{12}{25} = \cdot 48 \ ton \quad \text{and} \quad R_B = 2 - \cdot 48 = 1 \cdot 52 \ tons.$$

(*b*) Consider the reactions due to the distributed load.

Its total value $= 10 \times \frac{1}{2} = 5$ tons, and it may be considered as acting at its centre point C which is 9 ft. away from A.

Then
$$R_B = \frac{5 \times 9}{25} = \frac{9}{5} = 1 \cdot 8 \ tons,$$

and
$$R_A = 5 - 1 \cdot 8 = 3 \cdot 2 \ tons.$$

(c) The *total reactions* may now be obtained by addition.

Total reaction at A = ·48 + 3·2

= 3·68 tons,

Total reaction at B = 1·52 + 1·8

= 3·32 tons.

Experiment 50. To verify by experiment the result of the last example. To represent the distributed load small cast iron weights, of say 1 lb. each, are used which fit over the beam, see fig. 125. The arrangement of rod and balances is the same as in the last experiment; inches of span are taken to represent feet and each pound weight represents a ton. The five small weights are spread out equally over the ten inches. The readings of the balances should check the reactions already calculated, reading lbs. for tons.

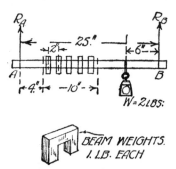

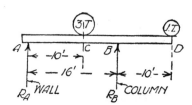

Fig. 125. Experimental determination of reactions with concentrated and distributed loads.

Fig. 126. The reactions of a cantilever.

Cantilevers. Where one end of a beam runs beyond the support, see fig. 126, or where it simply projects from a wall and is suitably secured at the other end, we refer to the overhanging portion as a **cantilever**. Where the beam simply *rests* on its supports as shown in fig. 126 we may calculate the reactions at A and B by the principle of moments (*but not by the formula given on p.* 110).

Example. *A beam 26 ft. long rests on a wall at A and a column at B, the distance between the centre lines of which is 16 ft., fig.* 126. *The overhanging end has a 1 ton load at its extremity and another concentrated load of 3 tons acting at C, 10 ft. from A. Find R_A and R_B.*

(a) Take moments about A, then

$$(R_A \times 0) + (3 \times 10) + (1 \times 26) - (R_B \times 16) = 0,$$

i.e.
$$30 + 26 - 16R_B = 0,$$

or
$$16R_B = 56,$$

$$\therefore R_B = \tfrac{56}{16} = 3\tfrac{1}{2} \text{ tons.}$$

(b)　Take moments about B, then
$$(R_B \times 0) + (R_A \times 16) + (1 \times 10) - (3 \times 6) = 0,$$
i.e.　　　　　　$16R_A + 10 - 18 = 0,$
cr　　　　　　$16R_A = 8,$
$$R_A = \tfrac{1}{2} \text{ ton.}$$
(c)　Then　　　　$R_A + R_B = 3\tfrac{1}{2} + \tfrac{1}{2}$
$$= 4 \text{ tons} = \text{total load.}$$

Experiment 51. To verify by experiment the results of the last example. The arrangement of the rod, balances and weights is shown in fig. 127; the procedure is exactly the same as in the preceding experiments.

If the weight at the overhanging end were increased the reaction at A would act downwards, giving a negative result in the calculations above; this could be measured experimentally by attaching a scale pan at A and putting in weights until the balance was restored. In practice the downward reaction is supplied by the weight of the wall above the beam or by a long bolt running down into the wall beneath (see Problems VII, 8).

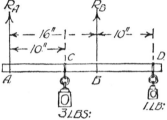

Fig. 127.　Cantilever reactions by experiment.

Experiment 52. To ascertain the forces acting in a simple roof truss and to draw a complete force diagram. The following experiment, though somewhat long, is useful and interesting since it affords an opportunity of revising the information given in this and the preceding chapter and also of illustrating still further the possibilities of its application to practical problems.

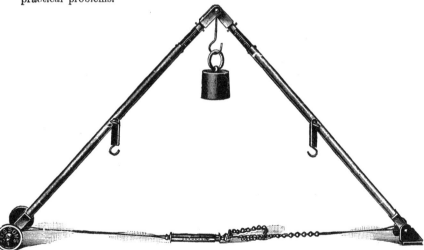

Fig. 128.　Experimental roof truss.

The truss to be considered is of quite a simple type consisting merely of two rafters and a horizontal tie. The only load considered is that coming upon the ridge. In its experimental form the truss is shown in fig. 128. All joints are pin-joints, the force in the tie is measured by a spring-balance. The tie may be altered in length by means of a chain; this also alters the pitch of the roof. The forces in the rafters are measured by compression balances. The load is represented by a weight suspended from the apex or "ridge." In order to give the spring-balance in the tie freedom to extend, when the load is put on, the left-hand joint runs on two wheels, the other end is fixed.

Put any convenient load, say 14 lbs., on the truss and take the readings of the three balances (deducting in each case the readings when no load was on except the weight of the parts of the truss itself). Measure carefully the distances between the joints of the truss (after loading) and to any convenient scale draw the frame diagram shown in fig. 129.

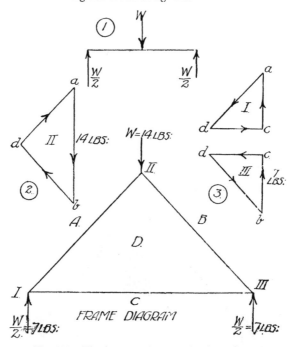

Fig. 129.   The forces acting in a simple roof truss.

Forces external to the truss. So far we only know the force W, acting *vertically* at the ridge as shown in fig. 129. If we consider the truss as a *rigid body* and note that it is symmetrical, the case may be treated as a beam loaded with W at the centre, see fig. 129 (1), when each reaction equals $\frac{W}{2}$ and acts vertically. Draw the lines of action of these external forces as shown and letter the *spaces* between them as A, B and C, see fig. 129.

Forces in the members of the truss. Letter the one remaining space inside the truss, *D*. Consider the forces at the top joint II. *W* acts downwards and equals 14 lbs. Remembering to take the letters in *clockwise order* draw the force triangle *abd* for joint II as already described, see fig. 129 (2). Similarly draw the force triangles for joints I and III, remembering that both *BC* and *CA* act vertically upwards, see fig. 129 (3).

From these separate triangles we may now read off the forces acting in the various members of the truss and also ascertain whether they are tensile or compressive forces. To obtain the senses of the forces at any joint read the large letters round the joint *in clockwise order* and follow the small letters on the corresponding force triangle in the same order.

Consider the force in the left-hand rafter at the top joint. The triangle should be read "*a–b–d–a*," when the direction of the line "*d* (to) *a*" shows that the force *DA* acts *towards* the joint and the rafter is in compression. In this way it will be found that both rafters are in compression and the tie in tension. Compare the values found graphically with those found experimentally.

(With the above truss and those of a more complicated design it is possible to combine the force triangle (or polygon) for each joint so as to produce a complete **force diagram** for the whole truss. This will be fully explained in Vol. II.)

Experiment 53. To obtain the forces acting in a roof truss with unequal pitches. If it is possible to alter the length of one of the rafters of the truss shown in fig. 129 it may be arranged as an unsymmetrical truss as shown in fig. 130. The reactions may be found experimentally by

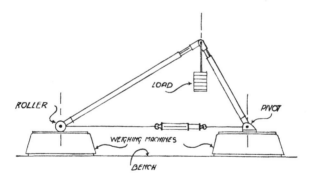

Fig. 130. Experimental truss with unequal pitches.

supporting each side of the truss on the table of a small weighing machine as shown, due allowance being made for the weight of the truss itself.

Graphically the forces acting in the members of the truss may be found as already explained for the symmetrical truss. The reactions may be calculated by considering the truss to be a beam with a concentrated load *W* out of the centre (see Problems VII, 11).

PROBLEMS VII

1. A retaining wall is 15 ft. high, 3 ft. thick at the top, 6 ft. thick at the bottom with a vertical back. Calculate the weight of one foot of this wall, given that the material of which it is constructed weighs 135 lbs. per cubic ft. Find the position of the c.g. of this section of the wall.

2. In the experiment illustrated in fig. 114, if $W_1 = 3$ lbs., $W_2 = 6$ lbs., $W_R = 1$ lb., $a = 8''$, $b = 28''$, $c = 15''$ and $d = 24''$, find T such that the rod will balance about P. What is then the supporting force at P?

3. An experiment is arranged as shown in fig. A. For the given forces and distances find (by moments) the stress in the tie. (Draw the positions to scale first.)

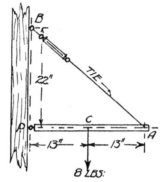

Fig. A.

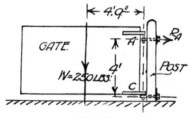

Fig. B.

4. Find also the amount and direction of the reaction at P in fig. A.

5. A gate which weighs 250 lbs. is suspended from a post at points A and C as shown in fig. B. At A the pivot fixed to the gate rotates in an eye-bolt fixed to the post; the eye-bolt cannot, however, take any part of the *weight* of the gate, in other words the reaction at the point can only be *horizontal*. At C the pivot has shoulders which rest upon the eye-bolt, the reaction here may therefore act in any direction. Given that the weight of the gate may be taken as acting 4 ft. 9 ins. from the axis of the pivots, find (a) the pull on the bolt at A, and (b) the direction and amount of the reaction at C.

6. Fig. *C* shows a brick wall temporarily supported by shoring, consisting of a horizontal needle and two dead shores. If the load to be carried is estimated to be 3½ tons, calculate the forces acting in the shores.

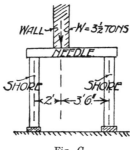

Fig. *C*.

7. A girder which weighs 45 lbs. per foot run is loaded as shown in fig. *D*. Calculate the total reactions at *A* and *B*.

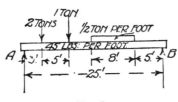

Fig. *D*.

8. A gallery is carried by a cantilever which rests on two walls as shown, fig. *E*. The loading consists of a uniform load of ½ ton per foot from *A* to *C* and a load of 1 ton at *E* 12 ft. from *A*. Calculate the reaction at *B* and the necessary holding-down force *F* at *A*.

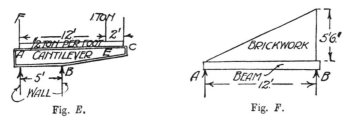

Fig. *E*.　　　　　　　　　Fig. *F*.

9. The brickwork of a small gable is carried by a beam as shown in fig. *F*. If the brickwork is 9″ thick and weighs 112 lbs. per cubic foot, calculate (*a*) the total weight carried by the beam, and (*b*) the reactions at *A* and *B* due to this weight. (Find the c.g. of the triangle and take the weight as acting at this point.)

10. Fig. *G* shows the outline of a king-post roof truss with the external loads and reactions. Find the forces acting in the members of the truss at each of the joints; span 20 ft.

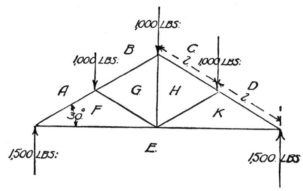

Fig. *G.*

11. Find the reactions and stresses in the members of the experimental truss shown in fig. 130 if one rafter slopes at 30° and the other at 60° to the horizon and the load at the ridge is 20 lbs. Span 30″.

12. The weight of a main wall of a building is carried by cantilevers (see Fig. *H*). The load comes on at *A*, and at *B* the cantilever rests upon a block carried by a large concrete slab. For the sizes shown calculate the load upon the block at *B*. The end of the cantilever at *C* is held down by the weight of another portion of the building.

The shape of the foundation slab is as shown in the figure. In order that the load may be evenly distributed, the block *B* must be over the c.g. of the slab area.

Draw the slab to a scale of $\frac{1}{8}''$ to a foot and find the c.g. graphically.

NOTE. The treatment of building mechanics is continued in chapter XVII.

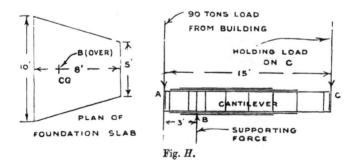

Fig. *H.*

CHAPTER VIII

TEMPERATURE AND HEAT. EXPANSION AND CONTRAC-
TION OF BUILDING MATERIALS DUE TO TEMPERATURE
CHANGES

Temperature and Heat. It is a fact of common experience
that, if two bodies at different temperatures be placed in contact,
then the hotter body will show a fall in temperature and the
other a rise in temperature until, if the circumstances allow, the
temperatures of the two bodies be equal. These changes in temperature are evidently due to the transference of heat from one
body to the other.

There is thus a certain analogy between the flow of water and
the flow of heat. If two reservoirs, in one of which the water is
at a higher level than in the other, be connected by a pipe, water
will flow from one to the other until the levels in the two reservoirs
are the same. Similarly we may think of heat as *flowing* between
bodies at different temperatures and, as we shall see later, if we
choose suitable units it is possible to calculate the *quantity of
heat* present in a body at any moment and also the quantity
passing from one body to another.

Summing up, we may say that **temperature** marks "heat
level" or "degree of hotness" and *difference in temperature is
the condition of flow of heat.*

For the present we shall confine ourselves to a brief examination
of the simpler methods of measuring temperature and of some of
the effects on materials and construction arising from changes
in temperature.

THE MEASUREMENT OF TEMPERATURE

The Thermometer. The construction of all the simpler
types of thermometers is based upon the fact that most substances
expand when their temperature rises and contract when it falls.
With solids the changes are extremely small and therefore difficult
of measurement; liquids usually expand much more than solids for

a given change in temperature and for this reason—apart from others—form very suitable thermometric substances. With gases the changes are comparatively great but, since the volume of gases is readily affected by changes of pressure and elaborate precautions are necessary to maintain a uniform pressure, gas thermometers are not available for elementary work.

The construction of the ordinary thermometer is shown in fig. 131. It consists essentially of a tube of very fine bore ending at the bottom in a relatively large bulb with thin walls. For reasons which we need not enter into here, mercury is generally used in thermometers intended to measure temperatures which are not extreme.

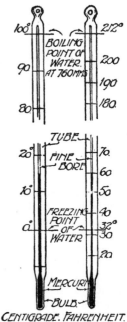

Fig. 131.   The graduation of thermometers.

The Graduation of Thermometers. In order that the readings of thermometers may be strictly comparable it is necessary that some agreed system of marking be adopted. Three well-known methods of graduation are the Centigrade, the Fahrenheit and the Réaumur; the first two only are of interest to us. All these scales are alike in one respect, viz., that two points on each scale correspond to two exactly equal temperatures which are known as the *fixed points*. The two temperatures chosen are those of melting ice and of the steam from boiling water (at standard pressure). As we shall see later we can—with proper precautions—be sure of obtaining two perfectly definite and fixed temperatures under these conditions, hence the reason for their selection.

The scales differ, however, in respect to the numbering of these points.

Fig. 131 shows two exactly similar thermometers placed alongside each other, the one marked out in Centigrade degrees and the other in Fahrenheit degrees.

The "freezing point" temperature on the Centigrade scale is marked 0° (zero) and the "boiling point" temperature 100°. On the Fahrenheit scale these are 32° and 212° respectively. The distance between these two points is divided in the one case into 100 Centigrade degrees and in the other case into 180 (212 − 32)

Fahrenheit degrees. Since the total change of temperature is in each case the same we have that 100 Centigrade divisions correspond to 180 divisions on the Fahrenheit scale.

Equivalent Temperatures on the two scales. From what we have just said it follows that one division on the Centigrade scale corresponds to $\frac{180}{100}$ or $\frac{9}{5}$ths of a Fahrenheit division and, remembering that zero on the Centigrade scale marks the same temperature as 32° F., we have, if C and F stand for corresponding temperatures on the two scales,

$$F = \tfrac{9}{5}C + 32.$$

This expression will enable us to convert from one scale to the other. It is also convenient to construct a graph to this equation, when equivalent temperatures may be read off at once.

The divisions below 0° C. or 0° F. should be prefixed with a minus sign, $-10°$ C. being 10 centigrade degrees below the centigrade zero (0° C.). (See Problems VIII, 1 and 2.)

Example. *To find the Fahrenheit reading for 15° C.*
$$\begin{aligned} F &= \tfrac{9}{5}C + 32 \\ &= \tfrac{9}{5} \times 15 + 32 \\ &= 27 + 32 \\ &= 59° \text{ F.} \end{aligned}$$

Example. *To find the Centigrade reading for 86° F.*
$$F = \tfrac{9}{5}C + 32,$$
i.e. $$86 = \tfrac{9}{5}C + 32,$$
or $$86 - 32 = \tfrac{9}{5}C,$$
$$\therefore \; C = 54 \times \tfrac{5}{9} = 30° \text{ C.}$$

EFFECTS OF HEAT ON MATERIALS

Expansion of Solids. We have already mentioned the fact that most bodies expand with a rise in temperature and contract with a decrease in temperature. Owing to the variations in temperature which take place from day to day, it is important that we should be able to realise the full effect of these changes in size in so far as they affect building materials and construction.

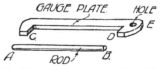

Fig. 132. The expansion of a solid.

Fig. 132 shows a cylindrical metal rod so prepared that it just fits between the jaws of the gauge plate CD and of such diameter

that it just fits the hole at *E*, at ordinary temperatures. If the
rod be strongly heated for several minutes on a gas furnace it will
be found to have increased in length, and also in its other dimensions, to such an extent that it will neither pass between *C* and *D*
nor enter the hole *E*. On cooling it will pass as before.

In carrying out the above experiment it should be noted that
the increases were so slight as to be undetected by the eye, hence
where the *length* of a solid greatly exceeds the other dimensions
it is only the *linear expansion* which we need consider, the other
increases being relatively much smaller. As this is the case with
such parts of buildings as beams, girders, tie rods and hot water
pipes, we shall now proceed to investigate the amount of linear
expansion for several materials and explain how the knowledge
thus obtained may be applied to actual problems.

When we wish to consider the effect of expansion in two directions—say
on the *area* of a flat plate—we speak of *superficial expansion*.   The total
effect of expansion on a solid is, as we have seen, to increase *all* its dimensions,
hence it increases in *volume* and we refer to this as *cubical expansion*.

Coefficient of Linear Expansion. If we ascertain the amount
of expansion which takes place in a given length of rod for a
given rise of temperature we may, by dividing the expansion by
the length of the rod and also by the rise in temperature, obtain

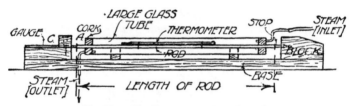

Fig. 133.   The linear expansion of a rod.

*the amount of expansion which takes place in a unit length of the
substance when the temperature rises by one degree.* This value for
each material is known as the *coefficient of linear expansion* and
is of great importance in all calculations concerning expansion.
Expressed concisely we have:

Coefficient of Linear Expansion

$$= \frac{\text{Increase in Length}}{\text{Original length}^1 \times \text{Rise in temperature}}.$$

Units. For measuring the rise in temperature either the
Centigrade or the Fahrenheit scale may be used, and it must
always be definitely stated which is employed. For the sake of

---

[1] Strictly, length at 0° C.

uniformity we shall use the Centigrade scale; the values of the coefficients given on p. 130 correspond to this scale. For the measurement of length and increase in length any units may be used, but it must be understood that the coefficients refer to *unit length,* for example if the coefficient of linear expansion for a material is $\frac{1}{10000}$ and the length taken is 1 inch, then for a rise of temperature of *one degree* the length will increase to $1\frac{1}{10000}$ inches, similarly for 1 foot it would increase to $1\frac{1}{10000}$ feet, etc. If the length is 13 inches or 13 feet then the final length will be $13\frac{13}{10000}$ ins. or $13\frac{13}{10000}$ ft. respectively, *each unit length having increased by an amount equal to the coefficient.*

Experiment 54. To find the coefficient of linear expansion for iron, and for other substances. Since the relative amount by which the length of a rod increases is very small special care is necessary in measuring this increase. Two methods are usually available for use with simple apparatus; (1) the actual increase may be multiplied by means of a lever to such an extent as to cause the visible movement of a pointer over a fixed scale; (2) the increase may be measured directly by means of a micrometer screw or by a straight vernier. The latter method will be adopted here as, assuming that the vernier is capable of measuring the increases, the work of calculation is

Fig. 134. Measuring the extensions with a "depth gauge."

much simplified. The piece of apparatus shown in fig. 133 will be found to give readings of sufficient accuracy for our purpose, while its construction is simple and straightforward. The rod, which should be about 25 to 30 ins. long, is enclosed in a stout glass tube or *steam jacket,* through this tube steam is passed from a small tin boiler. At one end the rod rests against a fixed stop whilst at A it touches the end of a "depth gauge," see fig. 134, the frame of which is clamped securely down to the base board at C. A thermometer is secured alongside of the rod by means of two rubber rings.

In conducting the experiment the length of the rod is first carefully measured; the rod is then inserted in the tube with the thermometer. After allowing the rod and thermometer time to take the same temperature as that of the room, the gauge is brought right up to the rod and a reading taken; the temperature is read at the same time. Steam is now passed through and when it has issued at the end A for several minutes—during which time the thermometer will have remained steady at or about 100° C.—the gauge is again read. The calculations are then as follows:

Coefficient of Linear Expansion of Iron

        Initial temperature of rod = 19° C.

        Final   ,,   ,,   = 100° C.

        ∴ **Rise in temperature = 81° C.**

Initial length of rod = 67·4 cms.
First reading of gauge = 2·58 ,,
Second ,, ,, = 2·52 ,,
∴ Increase in length = ·06 ,,

∴ Coefficient of linear expansion $= \dfrac{\text{Increase in length}}{\text{Initial length} \times \text{rise in temperature}}$

$$= \dfrac{0 \cdot 06}{67 \cdot 4 \times 81}$$

$$= \cdot 00001\text{I}.$$

Proceeding in a similar way the reader may find the coefficients for brass, copper, lead, zinc. Average values for a number of materials are given on p. 130. (See Problems VIII, 3, 4, 5 and 6.)

Force accompanying Expansion or Contraction and its Effect upon Construction. Although the alteration in the length of a rod due to change of temperature is so small it may be easily shown that, in the case of materials like iron, steel and brass, a very considerable amount of force would have to be exerted to prevent this expansion taking place when a bar is heated or to prevent contraction taking place when it is cooled.

Experiment 55. To show the force exerted by an iron bar in contracting after being heated. The usual form of apparatus used is shown in fig. 135. A strong base with two uprights is made in cast iron, a round bar of iron AB is provided with screw and nut D at one end and a hole C at the other, this bar rests in slots at the top of each upright. To carry out the experiment the bar is strongly heated and then dropped into the slots. A small cast iron bar is passed through the hole at C and bears upon each side of the slot at that end; the nut D is then tightened up *by hand only.* As the bar cools it contracts, putting a gradually increasing load on the small bar at C which it eventually breaks in two.

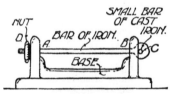

Fig. 135.   The force exerted by a rod of iron on cooling.

Effects on Construction. The force which we are now discussing is one which requires careful consideration in the design of buildings, wherever there occur long uninterrupted pieces of material of any kind, especially if considerable variations in temperature are expected. Long concrete walls, long lengths of piping in hot-water systems, long lengths of iron piping exposed to the sun, leadwork on roofs, are all cases where special precautions—usually the provision of some form of expansion joint—must be taken to allow expansion and contraction to take place freely without rupturing the material or damaging the building.

Long girders and iron roof trusses of large span are usually fixed
at the ends by bolts passing through *slotted holes* or are provided
at one end with special roller bearings which permit of these
variations taking place.

It is not, however, only as a destructive force that expansion
affects building; it may serve a useful purpose as the following
examples show.

It sometimes happens that from various causes the walls of
buildings bulge outwards; where it would have been too costly to
rebuild or not possible for other reasons, the following method has
been occasionally adopted for pulling in the walls so as to make
them approximately correct again. A large and strong bar is passed
through the building from wall to wall and, being screwed at each
end, a nut is put on outside of each wall and bears upon strong
iron plates which in their turn bear upon the bulged part of the
wall. The bar is now heated at several points by means of large
braziers and, as the bar expands, the nuts are tightened up so as
to take a bearing on the plates. The sources of heat are then
removed and as the bar cools and contracts the force exerted is
sufficient to draw the walls in; the process is repeated until the
bulge in the wall is corrected.

When riveting is carried out on plates, girders, columns or
tanks the rivets are usually "driven" when in a "white-hot"
condition; on cooling they contract and hold the plates together
with great force.

Calorifiers—which are cylindrical metal vessels in which water
is heated by the passage of steam through coiled pipes—frequently
have an automatic control (thermostat) to the steam, which is
worked by the expansion and contraction taking place in the
length of the calorifier with the rise and fall of the temperature
of the water inside. (See Problems VIII, 8.)

Unequal Expansion. When two pieces of different materials,
which have unequal coefficients of
expansion, are rigidly fastened together and subjected to change in
temperature, since one material will
contract or expand more than the
other, the forces produced usually
distort the pieces and may even
fracture one of them.

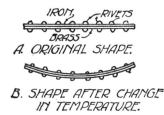

B. SHAPE AFTER CHANGE
IN TEMPERATURE.

Fig. 136. Unequal expansion.

**Experiment 56. To show the effect
of unequal expansion.** The apparatus
consists of a strip of brass and a strip of
iron riveted together at frequent intervals, see fig. 136 A. The coefficients
of linear expansion for these materials are respectively ·000011 and ·000019,

that is in the ratio of 11 to 19. If the strips be heated (or cooled) *equally*, either by means of a small gas furnace or by plunging into a hot liquid, they will take up the shape shown at *B*; the explanation being that the expanded length of the brass is greater than that of the iron. Cooling below the normal temperature would cause the strips to bend in the opposite direction.

Experiment 57. To show the effect of fixing sheet lead at both edges. When sheet lead or sheet zinc is used to cover flat or sloping roof surfaces it is exposed to considerable variations in temperature, which result in comparatively large alterations in size, this coupled with the fact that for both materials the coefficient of linear expansion is high (lead, ·000029, zinc, ·000029, as compared with iron, ·000011), necessitates special precautions being taken so as to prevent buckling or rupture. (Since the sheets are usually

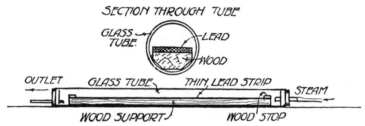

Fig. 137. The fixing of sheet lead.

laid on wood boarding this is partly a case of *unequal expansion,* the coefficient of linear expansion for wood being only about one-fifth that for lead or zinc.) To carry out the experiment a *thin* strip of lead is secured at each end to a piece of wood as shown in fig. 137, the whole being of such a size as to pass inside the glass tube used in Experiment 54; steam is then passed through the tube as before, when the lead will be seen to buckle and rise from the surface of the wood. If one end of the lead strip be left free no buckling will occur.

In laying the lead sheets the joints are so made that the sheets are comparatively free to move on at least two adjacent edges.

Walls are sometimes finished with thin "glass" or "vitreous" tiles which are secured to a cement rendering on the wall. To prevent cracking by unequal expansion the tiles are backed with an elastic material, covered with coarse sand to give a key to the cement.

The "crazing" of the glaze on ordinary tiles is due to the unequal expansion of the glaze and the body of the tile in cooling after burning.

In building "fire brickwork" for furnaces and flues to withstand high temperatures, it is important that the mortar used should, as near as is possible, have the same coefficient of expansion as the bricks, otherwise the joints are soon destroyed.

In this connection it is interesting to note, that where large expansion occurs in brickwork, the brickwork—being in units not very strongly held together—cannot return to its original length or shape unless drawn in by iron bands, which contract on cooling; such bands are to be seen on circular brick kilns. (See Problems VIII, 7.)

When washing coppers are built into an angle of a scullery and the brickwork finished to a quadrant plan, trouble is frequently experienced with the brickwork over the fire opening. The explanation is the same as above; on being heated the brickwork expands, but is unable to return to its original shape on cooling. Though the actual movement is exceedingly small, the process is repeated every time the fire is used and the accumulated effects soon become noticeable.

Unequal Heating. The buckling of columns and girders which takes place so frequently when a fire occurs in steel-framed buildings, is partly due to *unequal heating*; one side of a girder may be intensely hot while the other side is at a much lower temperature—either owing to some protection or to water being played on it from a fireman's hose.

Expansion of Liquids. In dealing with the expansion of liquids it is obvious that we can only think of their *cubical expansion* and further, experiments upon their expansibility can only be carried out when they are contained in suitable vessels. Since the containing vessel itself will be affected by changes of temperature considerable difficulty is experienced in obtaining the *real expansion* of the liquid. Since, however, the expansion of liquids is usually so much greater than for solids the effect of the expansion of the vessel may for all ordinary purposes be neglected.

Except in the case of water, the expansion of liquids is of no great importance to students of building, hence we do not propose to give any experimental methods for ascertaining the coefficients of liquid expansion; a list of such coefficients is given on p. 130 and this should be studied together with the problems given which utilise these coefficients. (See Problems VIII, 8 and 9.)

The Peculiar Expansion of Water. As will be apparent from the list just mentioned liquids vary considerably in expansibility. Another fact, which the list of coefficients does not show, is that the coefficients vary according to the range of temperatures over which the effect is observed. Water is no exception to this rule. Between 4° C. and 100° C. it increases in bulk by about 4·5 per cent., three-quarters of this expansion, however, takes place between 50° and 100° (see Probs. VIII, 11). In high pressure hot-water systems, in which the water is contained in a closed system of pipes, special provision has to be made to allow for this expansion.

It is, however, in respect to its peculiar variation in volume at low temperatures that water is unique. *From 4° C. (or 39·2° F.) an increase in volume of the water takes place whether the temperature rises or falls.* It follows that a given mass of water occupies the least space at 4° C., in other words water will reach its greatest density at that temperature.

Experiment 58. To demonstrate the peculiar variation in volume of water at low temperatures. If a flask be fitted up, as shown in fig. 138, with a long tube of fine bore passing through the cork and filled with water, the variations in volume may be noted at low temperatures by placing the flask in a suitable freezing mixture. The temperature of the water in the flask will steadily fall to 0° C.—changing to ice if the experiment is continued— and the temperature of greatest density will be shown by noting the temperature at the point when the water in the tube is at its lowest level. Owing, however, to the changes taking place in the volume of the flask the temperature of greatest density would not apparently be 4° C. but some other and higher temperature. It is possible, however, to counteract the effect of these changes in the volume of the flask.

Mercury is a liquid with a much higher coefficient of cubical expansion than glass. If the correct amount of mercury be taken and placed in the flask its contraction will just equal the contraction in volume of the flask as the temperature falls ; e.g. if the volume of the flask contract by 1 c.c. then the volume of the mercury in the flask contracts by the same amount *and the volume of the flask above the mercury will remain constant.*

The coefficients of expansion for mercury and glass are ·000182 and ·0000237 respectively, thus the expansion (or contraction) of 1 c.c. of mercury

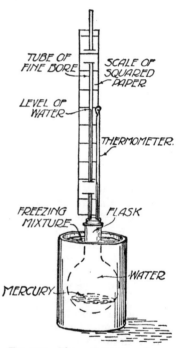

Fig. 138.   The variation in volume of water at low temperatures.

will equal the expansion (or contraction) of $\dfrac{·000182}{·0000237}$ or 7·7 c.c.s of the glass flask

(volume). Hence $\dfrac{1}{7·7}$ of the volume of the flask should be filled with mercury. (See Problems VIII, 9.)

Adopting this precaution the flask should be filled up with water above the mercury and placed in a strong jar, see fig. 138. Pack the space between the flask and the sides of the jar with alternate layers of broken ice and of salt, put in in the proportions of 3 parts of ice to 1 part of salt by weight. Now watch the level of the water in the tube and the temperature of the water in the flask, as the temperature falls towards 4° C. the level will fall also; from 4° C. on to 0° C. the water will show a slight rise. In order to get good results a tube of very fine bore should be used. If the volume of flask and tube was found, it would be possible with the exercise of sufficient care to calculate the exact changes in volume taking place, but probably the accuracy required to get reasonably good results is beyond the reader at this stage. (See Problems VIII, 10.)

The Expansion of Gases. While it is not our intention at this stage to investigate with any degree of fullness the effect of heat upon gases, it will serve to complete our discussion of the effect of heat upon various substances if we briefly state that, as with liquids and solids, gases expand when heated and contract when cooled. The amount of expansion is very much greater even than for liquids and a remarkable feature is that, over a considerable range of temperature and for all gases, the coefficient of cubical expansion is practically the same and equal to $\frac{1}{273}$ or ·00366. What is known as **Charles' Law** states this as follows:—*that all gases expand about $\frac{1}{273}$ of their original volume at 0° C. for every rise in temperature equal to one Centigrade degree, the pressure remaining constant.*

The Effect of Expansion on the Density of Liquids and Gases. Since, as we have seen, Density $= \dfrac{\text{Mass}}{\text{Volume}}$ it will be evident that if we increase the *volume* of a body, whilst its *mass* remains constant, a *decrease in density* must follow. This fact makes it necessary in accurate work to state the temperature at which the density of a liquid is found. (See Problems VIII, 11.)

It is, however, in the formation of what are known as convection currents in water and in air that this alteration of density with temperature is of the most importance to us. It will be obvious from what we have already done that in a boiler or other vessel containing water to which heat is applied, the heated portions of water, being of less density, will tend to rise to the surface of the water and give place to the colder and heavier portions.

With gases this same alteration of density takes place with change in temperature, and although the effect of pressure upon the volume (see Boyle's Law) complicates the issue, it is upon this change and the resulting air currents that many systems of ventilation depend for their success. The up-draught in a chimney flue is due to the lessened density of the heated air and gases passing from the fire, and the higher the temperature of the gases and the longer the heat is retained by the gases the more powerful will be the draught. These questions will be more fully discussed in the succeeding volume, but sufficient has been said to indicate the importance of a correct understanding of the effect of heat upon the density of liquids and gases.

Coefficients of Expansion (Centigrade Scale).

Linear Expansion		Cubical Expansion	
Substance	Coefficient		
Cast Iron	·0000106		
Wrought Iron ...	·0000114		
Steel	·0000105 to ·0000116	(This may be obtained for any solid by multiplying the linear coefficient by 3)	
Brass	·0000185		
Copper	·0000168		
Lead	·0000292		
Zinc	·0000291	Air	·00367
Glass	·0000079	Water (about 20° C.)	·00045
Cement and Concrete	·000010 to ·000014	Alcohol	·00108
Marble	·0000014 to ·0000035	Turpentine ...	·00105
Portland Stone ...	·000003	Glycerine	·00053
Sandstone ...	·000007 to ·000012	Mercury	·000182
Slate	·000006 to ·00001	Glass	·0000237
Brick	·000010 (?)		

	Along grain	Across grain
Yellow Deal ...	·000005	·000034
Oak	·000005	·000054

PROBLEMS VIII

1. Calculate the equivalent Fahrenheit temperature of: (a) 1100° C., the temperature of vitrification of some clays, and (b) 227° C., the melting point temperature of plumber's solder.

2. Draw a graph showing the relation between temperatures on the Centigrade and Fahrenheit scales, reading up to 200° C. and down to −20° C. Obtain from it the equivalent temperature of (a) 159° C., the boiling point temperature of turpentine, and (b) −10° C., the freezing point temperature of the same liquid.

3. Calculate the increase in length of a sheet of lead 10 ft. long for a change of temperature of 35 Centigrade degrees. Coefficient of expansion ·0000292.

4. Using a coefficient of ·000011 find increase in length of a steel truss of 70 ft. span when the temperature rises from 32° F. to 80° F. (convert to Centigrade degrees).

5. In an experiment similar to that described on p. 123, the following values were obtained:

Original temperature of brass rod = 16° C.
Final   ,,   ,,   ,,   = 100° C.
Original length of rod   = 58 cms.
First reading of vernier   = 2·73 cms.
Second   ,,   ,,   = 2·64 cms.

Obtain from these values the coefficient of expansion for the brass rod.

6. If the coefficient of expansion for zinc on the Centigrade scale is ·0000291, what would be the coefficient to use with the Fahrenheit scale of temperatures?

7. Calculate the increase in (a) circumference and (b) diameter, of an iron hoop binding a kiln of 25 ft. diameter (coefficient of expansion of the iron being ·0000114), if the temperature rise from 10° C. to 55° C.

8. One form of "thermostat," for controlling the supply of steam (or gas) to a calorifier, consists of a long closed tube filled with mercury, one end of the tube having a flexible covering the movement of which controls the steam- (or gas-) valve.
Given that the coefficient of expansion for mercury is ·000182, calculate the increase in volume of the mercury contained in a tube 10″ long and 1″ internal diameter, when the temperature rises from 15° C. to 90° C.

9. A glass flask to be used in Experiment 58 has a volume of 280 c.c.s and the glass has a coefficient of cubical expansion of ·000025. Calculate the amount of mercury necessary to just counterbalance the expansion of the flask (coefficient for mercury = ·000182).

10. If the flask in the last question holds—above the mercury—241 c.c.s of water up to a certain mark in the tube, calculate the percentage increase in volume of the water in the flask, if on heating the flask the water rises in the tube by 14·08 cms. The bore of the tube is 0·2 cms. in diameter.

11. If the density of water at 39·2° F. is 62·425 lbs. per cubic ft. (maximum), at 70° F. is 62·313 and at 212° F. is 59·64, calculate the volume occupied by a body of water at each of these temperatures if at 39·2° F. it occupied 1 cubic foot. What are the percentage increases?

12. What are the reasons for (a) covering steam pipes with asbestos or similar material; (b) enclosing steel girders and columns in concrete or terra-cotta; (c) laying felt beneath the slating on roofs? What is the special property possessed, in this case, by each of the covering materials mentioned?

CHAPTER IX

In the early part of the preceding chapter we discussed briefly the methods of measuring temperature changes. We shall now proceed to investigate the methods which are available for the measurement of *the quantity of heat in a body* as distinct from *the temperature of the body* (see p. 119).

Quantity of Heat in a Body.

Experiment 59. To show that the quantity of heat in a body varies with (*a*) its temperature, (*b*) its mass, and (*c*) the substance. For this experiment several equal-sized tins or *calorimeters* (see p. 133) are required; they should be filled to equal depths with water and placed on one side so that they may all take the temperature of the room. This temperature should be found for each vessel at the commencement of each experiment.

(*a*) Take two pieces of iron of *equal weight*, place one in a vessel containing boiling water (100° C.) and the other in one containing water maintained at about 60° C. After a few minutes, when the two pieces of iron may be considered to have taken the temperature of the two bodies of water, take them out and drop them into two of the vessels already mentioned in which two thermometers have been placed. Note in each case the initial temperature of the water and also the final highest temperature which the thermometer indicates, stirring the water meanwhile.

(*b*) Repeat the experiment with two unequal-sized pieces of iron, *both heated in boiling water*.

(*c*) Finally obtain the result when a piece of lead and a piece of iron, of *equal weights*, are heated in boiling water and dropped into separate vessels. The results obtained in such an experiment are given below:

Copper calorimeters were used containing in each case 150 gms. of water. Initial temperature in each case 16° C.

(*a*) Weight of iron in each case = 89 gms.

    (i) Piece heated to 100° C.

                 Initial temperature of water = 16° C.
                 Final   ,,   ,,   = 22·8° C.
                 Rise in temperature   = 6·8° **C.**

    (ii) Piece heated to 60° C.

                 Rise in temperature   = 3·6° **C.**

(b)   Both pieces heated to 100° C.
     (i)   Piece weighing 89 gms. (see above).
         Rise in temperature=6·8° C.
     (ii)   Piece weighing 45 gms.
         Rise in temperature=3·2° C.
(c)   Both pieces heated to 100° C. and both weighed 89 gms.
     (i)   **Rise in temperature for iron=6·8° C.**
     (ii)   ,,   ,,   ,,   lead=**2° C.**

The Unit Quantity of Heat.   The careful perusal of the data obtained in the above experiment should enable the reader to see that the amount of heat contained in any body depends upon three things, (a) the temperature of the body, (b) the weight of the body, and (c) the kind of matter of which the body consists.   Hence any unit devised to measure quantity of heat must conform to these facts.   A standard substance (water) is chosen, so that the definition of the unit is only concerned with the amount of heat required to raise a definite weight of water through a definite temperature.

The calorie, which is the unit used almost exclusively for scientific purposes, is **the quantity of heat given out (or taken in) by 1 gram of water when its temperature falls (or rises) by 1 Centigrade degree.**

The British Thermal Unit (B.T.U.) is the unit largely employed by heating and mechanical engineers, and is *the quantity of heat required to raise 1 lb. of water through 1 Fahrenheit degree.*

A new unit, finding considerable favour in this country, uses the Centigrade degree and the 1 lb. of water.

The Calorimeter.   To obtain greater accuracy in experiments upon heat the piece of apparatus shown in fig. 139 is generally used; it is designed to prevent undue loss of heat during the experiment.   A small highly polished copper vessel (already used in Exper. 59) rests on a cork or asbestos pad placed at the bottom of a larger vessel, also of copper.   The space between the two is packed with cotton wool or other non-conducting material and the water is placed in the inner vessel.   A thermometer may be held in the liquid by means of a burette stand as shown. A stirrer is usually supplied which consists of a copper ring with a long wire handle; when the hot body is placed with the cold water in the

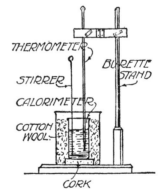

Fig. 139.   The calorimeter.

calorimeter the stirrer is moved up and down so as to obtain uniformity of temperature throughout the body of water.

Equality of Heat lost and gained. The experiments given below are based upon the fact that if loss of heat be prevented during the experiment then, when two bodies at different temperatures are placed in intimate contact, *the heat lost by the hotter body in falling to the final temperature equals the heat gained by the colder body in rising to the final temperature,* or

Heat lost by one body = **Heat gained** by the other body.

Experiment 6o. **To show the equality of heat gained and lost during the mixture of two bodies of water at different** temperatures. Place in a calorimeter a known quantity of cold water (find the weight as shown below). Allow the water, thermometer and calorimeter to take the temperature of the room. Note this temperature. Prepare and quickly pour in an approximately equal quantity of water heated to about 60° or 70° C. Note the temperature of the hot water just before pouring into the cold. Stir the mixture and note the rise in temperature. By weighing obtain the weight of hot water poured in. Set out the data as below.

Weight of calorimeter and cold water	= 152·04 gms.	(a)
„ „ and mixture	= 225·77 „	(b)
„ „	= 69·93 „	(c)
∴ Weight of cold water = (a) – (c)	= 82·11 „
and „ hot water = (b) – (a)	= 73·73 „
Final temperature of mixture	= 34·25° C.
Original „ cold water	= 17·25° C.
∴ *Rise in temperature of cold water*	= 17° C.
Final temperature of mixture	= 34·25° C.
Initial temperature of hot water	= 55·6° C.
∴ *Fall in temperature of hot water*	= 21·35° C.

Now *heat gained by "cold" water* = weight × rise in temperature
= 82·11 × 17
= *1396 calories.*

And *heat lost by "hot" water* = weight × fall in temperature
= 73·73 × 21·35
= *1574 calories.*

NOTE. As the results of this experiment at present stand it would appear that more heat has been given up by the hot water than has been gained by the cold; if, however, we remember that not only has the cold water been raised to a temperature of 34·25° C. but also the calorimeter, the thermometer and the stirrer, it will be obvious that, except for very slight losses in other ways, the whole of the apparent discrepancy may be accounted for.

It is convenient to ascertain *what amount of water would just absorb the same amount of heat as the calorimeter, etc.* in rising through a given temperature, this is known as the **water equi-**

valent of the calorimeter and its value is *added to the weight of cold water in the calorimeter.* With this correction the experiment may be repeated with other amounts of water and other temperatures, when the heat lost will be found to equal the heat gained.

Experiment 61. To find the water equivalent of the calorimeter, etc. Proceed exactly as in the last experiment (or the same values may be taken) and supplement the calculation as below.

Heat lost by hot water ... ... = 1574 calories
„ gained by cold water ... ... = 1396 „
∴ Difference = heat gained by calorimeter etc. = 178 „

Hence calorimeter, etc., required 178 cals. to raise it by 17° C. and would require $\frac{178}{17}$ = 10·47 cals. to raise it by 1° C.

Water Equivalent (w.E.) = 10·47 grams (see Exps. 62 and 63).

Capacity for Heat. Referring to the two experiments just completed it will be noticed that although the calorimeter weighed nearly 70 grams, yet the amount of heat which it required to raise it through 17° C. would only have raised 10·47 gms. of water through the same range. It will be evident from this that bulk for bulk water has a much greater *capacity for heat* than copper (compare also iron and lead in Experiment 59). As we have seen, 1 gram of water requires 1 calorie to raise it through 1 Centigrade degree; if then we ascertain the amount of heat (in calories) required to raise 1 gram of any other substance through 1 Centigrade degree we might prepare a list showing the *relative* capacities for heat of various substances, in which the value for water would be 1 and for the other substance some other number. Remembering the terms *relative density* and *specific gravity* the meaning of the terms *Relative Capacity for Heat* or *Specific Heat* should not be difficult to understand. The latter term is more commonly used and we have that:—Specific Heat

$$= \frac{\text{amount of heat required to raise } g \text{ grams of a substance through } 1° \text{ C.}}{\text{amount of heat required to raise } g \text{ grams of water through } 1° \text{ C.}}$$

or, since g grams of water would require g calories, we have that:—

The Specific Heat of a substance is the number of calories required to raise the temperature of 1 gram of the substance through 1 Centigrade degree.

Further, if m be the mass of a body of which the relative capacity is s then $m \times s \times t$ *calories* will be absorbed or given out when the body has its temperature raised or lowered by $t°$ C.

Experiment 62. To find the specific heat of a solid. To carry out this experiment a small piece (or pieces) of the solid is heated to a known temperature in some form of "heater," see fig. 140. The one shown consists of a large test tube fitting loosely into a flask in which water is kept boiling, the temperature of the solid being obtained by means of the thermometer shown. A calorimeter is prepared as already described and the temperature of the cold water read. The heated solid is then dropped in, care being taken to see that no condensed steam drops from the heater into the calorimeter. The final temperature is obtained as before.

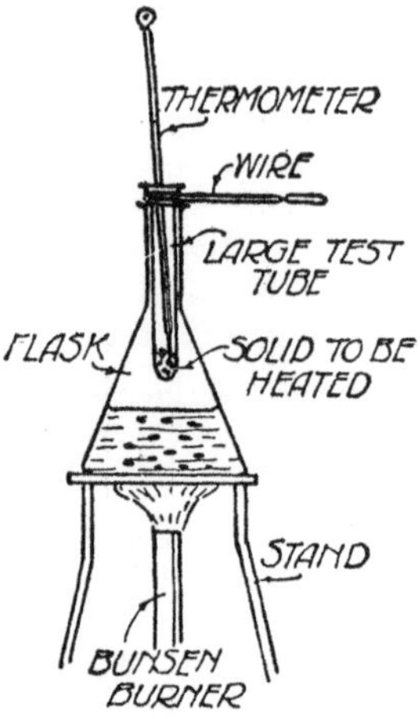

To find the specific heat of iron.

Weigh of calorimeter and water

	= 101·73 gms.
,,	= 69·93 ,,
∴ Weight of water	= 31·8 ,,
Water equivalent	= 10·47 ,,
∴ Total equivalent weight of water	= 42·27 ,,
Weight of iron (iron nails)	= 46·1 ,,
Initial temperature of iron	= 98·5° C.
Final ,, ,,	= 26·0° C.
∴ *Fall in temperature*	= 72·5° C.
Initial temperature of water	= 17·3° C.
Final ,, ,,	= 26·0° C.
∴ *Rise in temperature*	= 8·7° C.

Fig. 140. A heater for small solids.

Now Heat lost = Heat gained.

But *heat lost by solid* = weight × fall in temperature × specific heat (*s*)
= 46·1 × 72·5 × *s*,

and *heat gained by water* = weight × rise in temperature
= 42·27 × 8·7.

But these are equal,

$$\therefore \ 46{\cdot}1 \times 72{\cdot}5 \times s = 42{\cdot}27 \times 8{\cdot}7,$$

or $\qquad$ Specific Heat of iron $= s = \dfrac{42{\cdot}27 \times 8{\cdot}7}{46{\cdot}1 \times 72{\cdot}5} = 0{\cdot}11.$

Other substances may be dealt with in a similar way; a list of the specific heats of various substances is given on p. 145.

To find the Specific Heat of a Liquid. Proceed exactly as in the last experiment, except that the liquid to be tested must take the place of the water in the calorimeter and the value of the specific heat for the solid must be known.

Experiment 63. To find the specific heat of turpentine.

Specific heat of iron (assumed known) =	0·109
Weight of iron taken	= 52·4 gms.
Weight of calorimeter and turpentine	= 104 83 ,,
,, ,,	= 69·93 ,,
∴ Weight of turpentine	= 34·9 ,,

Water equivalent ...   . $= 10\cdot47$ gms.

Initial temperature of iron   ...   . $= 99°$ C.

Final   „   „   ...   . $= 32\cdot75°$ C.

∴ Fall in temperature   ...   . $= 66\cdot25°$ C.

Initial temperature of turpentine (and calorimeter) $= 17\cdot5°$ C.

Final   „   „   „ („   „) $= 32\cdot75°$ C.

∴ Rise in temperature   ...   . $= 15\cdot25°$ C.

Then Heat lost = Heat gained.

But **heat lost**   = weight of iron × fall in temperature × specific heat

                       $= 52\cdot4 \times 66\cdot25 \times \cdot109$

                       $= 378\cdot4$ calories,

and **heat gained**   = weight of turpentine × specific heat (s) × rise in temperature + water equivalent × rise in temperature

                       $= 34\cdot9 \times s \times 15\cdot25 + 10\cdot47 \times 15\cdot25$

                       $= 532\cdot5 \times s + 159\cdot8;$

hence $532\cdot5 \times s + 159\cdot8 = 378\cdot4,$

or   **Specific Heat of turpentine** $= s = \dfrac{378\cdot4 - 159\cdot8}{532\cdot5} = \dfrac{218\cdot6}{532\cdot5}$

                       $= \cdot411.$

The high Specific Heat of Water. The high capacity of water for heat should now be apparent (see list of specific heats on p. 145), and it is this property which more than any other makes water such a valuable medium for storing and transporting heat. Owing to its high specific heat it requires more heat to raise it through a given range of temperature than any other liquid and, conversely, *weight for weight it will give up more heat than any other liquid* in cooling through the same range of temperature. Hence its use in the various hot-water heating systems, wherein the heat is first stored in the water by heating in a boiler and the heated water is then conveyed—either mechanically or by reason of its own lessened density—to other parts of the building, where it gives up its heat, finally returning once more to the boiler to be reheated. It will be apparent that, owing to its high specific heat, a much smaller amount of water would have to be *transported* to a distant point on a building, to yield up a given amount of heat, than of any other liquid, the advantages in lessened cost and size of pipes being obvious.

CHANGE OF STATE. MELTING AND BOILING

So far we have considered only two of the changes which heat may effect in a body, (*a*) alteration in temperature, and (*b*) alteration in size. Another and very important change, which may be effected under certain conditions, is *change of state,* a change which has reference to the existence of a substance as a solid, a liquid or a gas. These changes may be simply illustrated by placing some pieces of ice in a calorimeter and noting the temperature-changes by means of a thermometer. A very gentle heat should be applied at first, when it will be noted that whilst the ice is melting the thermometer will register a *steady temperature of 0° C.* The **water** formed may then be heated more rapidly and a steady rise in temperature will be noted until the water commences to boil, when from this point until all the water has been converted into **steam** the thermometer will again *stand steady at 100° C.*

If it were possible to collect the steam and gradually abstract heat from it by cooling, these phenomena would take place in the reverse order, the temperature remaining steady at 100° C. whilst the steam was being converted into water and, if the cooling process be continued sufficiently far, the thermometer would again register a steady temperature of 0° C. whilst the water was being converted into ice.

With but few exceptions all pure elementary substances exhibit this phenomenon of a steady temperature on changing from one state to another. Since the heat absorbed or given out during these periods does not effect any change in temperature it must evidently be utilised in effecting the *change of state.* The heat used up in this way is termed **the latent** (or "hidden") **heat.** It may be shown that the amount of heat absorbed or given out in this way is a perfectly definite amount for any particular substance; for example when 1 gm. of ice at 0° C. is converted into water at 0° C., *80 calories* are used up and this is known as the *latent heat of ice,* and again when 1 gm. of water at 100° C. is converted into steam at 100° C. *536 calories* are necessary and this gives us the *latent heat of vaporisation of water.*

Melting Point. The fact, that the temperature at which melting—or solidification—takes place is a perfectly definite one for most pure substances, provides us with a very powerful means of identifying substances and also of testing their purity since, as we shall see presently, the addition of other substances usually affects the melting point temperature. Two methods of ascertaining the melting point are given below, the first being only applicable for small quantities and for comparatively low temperatures.

Experiment 64. To find the melting point of naphthalene. Prepare a small tube with one end closed, as
shown in fig. 141, into this put some of the
substance to be tested and secure the tube
to a thermometer by means of two rubber
bands. Now suspend the whole in a beaker
of water and apply heat by means of a
bunsen, stirring the water continuously. In
carrying out this experiment for the first time
note *roughly* the temperature at which the
wax appears to melt, then repeat the experiment heating the water rapidly until the
temperature is just below that of melting,
after which the heat should only be applied
gently and the temperature of melting noted
more carefully. Repeat the experiment and
take an average of the results. Obtain also
in this way the melting point of paraffin wax
and sulphur.

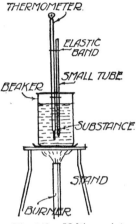

Fig. 141. Melting point
temperature.

If the melting point of the substance is
above the boiling point temperature of water
(100° C.) then some other liquid with a higher
boiling point must be used in the beaker
(see list of boiling points, p. 145).

Melting Point from a curve of cooling. If a solid be
converted by heating into a liquid and then allowed to cool
we have seen that the temperature of the liquid will continue
to fall until the "temperature of solidification" be reached, when
it will remain steady until all the liquid has been converted once
more into a solid. If the temperatures of this substance be taken
at stated intervals and a graph be drawn showing the relation
between time intervals and temperatures, then the period during
which the temperature remained steady—the temperature of
melting—will be indicated by the line of the graph running parallel
to the "time" axis, see fig. 143. We thus have a most interesting
and instructive method of obtaining the melting point. The circumstances of the experiment must, however, be such that the substance loses heat at a steady rate, this will easily be arranged for
by conducting the experiment in a room free from draughts and
away from other sources of heat.

Experiment 65. To find the melting point of paraffin wax from a
curve of cooling. Place some of the wax in a large test tube as shown in
fig. 142. Heat the wax to a temperature somewhat above the melting point,
say to about 75°. Remove the source of heat and take readings of the
temperature at one minute intervals and continue them beyond the point at
which the wax solidifies. Now plot the values thus obtained on squared
paper and through the points draw as smooth a curve as possible. The curve
will be similar to that shown in fig. 143, from which the melting point may be
readily obtained. (See also Problems IX, 6.)

A similar curve obtained for tin is shown in fig. 146, curve *A*. Since the temperatures are much higher in this case the apparatus shown in fig. 144 should be used.

Substances without definite Melting Points. There are some substances—of which lead, glass, wrought iron, clay, pitch and solder are familiar examples—which have no definite melting point temperature, but which pass through a plastic or viscous state before finally becoming liquid, the temperature not remaining steady in the interval. This property may be of great value in working up these materials for constructive purposes, enabling us to roll, hammer and weld wrought iron, to weld pieces of glass together, to "draw" or squirt lead piping and to "wipe" soldered joints.

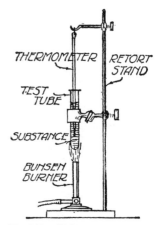

Fig. 142.   Melting point temperature by a curve of cooling.

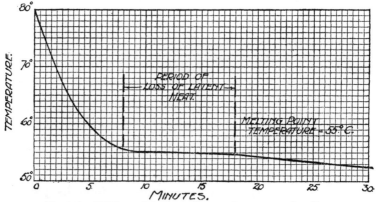

Fig. 143.   Melting point of paraffin wax from curve of cooling.

The **Melting of Solder.** A curve of cooling for a solder consisting of 1 part of tin to 1½ parts of lead ("Plumber's solder" has 1 part of tin to 2 parts of lead), is shown in curve *B*, fig. 146.

This curve is interesting because it shows definitely the period during which the solder may be worked. That portion of the curve reaching from *E* to *D* corresponds to the period during which some of the lead in the solder separates out as solid lead;

the curve from D to C corresponds to the solidification of that portion of the solder still remaining liquid and is peculiar in that it takes on the form of a "latent heat" curve as for a pure substance.

During the whole of the period from E to C the solder is in a pasty condition and may be worked or "wiped" round a joint.

The two curves shown on fig. 146 are also of interest as illustrating the striking effect which the mixing of two metals may have upon the *melting point temperature.* Lead has a melting point of 327° C. and tin 232° C., while the particular alloy of lead and tin mentioned above commences to melt at 175° C. and is completely melted at 220° C. (See also Problems IX, 7.)

With many other substances the addition of foreign substances affects their melting points, hence the melting point temperature may be utilised as a refined test of the *purity* of many

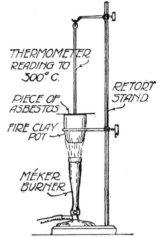

Fig. 144.　Melting point temperature from a curve of cooling [high temperatures].

materials.　(The presence of salt may lower the freezing point of water to $-9°$ C.)

The softening period which precedes the melting of clays is sometimes utilised to *measure the maximum temperature reached* (ranging from 1000 to 1300° C.) in brick and tile kilns.　Fig. 145 shows a set of what are known as "Seger Cones"; they consist of slender cones of clay mixtures of known melting points, these bend over when the temperature of softening is reached. By taking a series, of slightly differing fusibilities, the

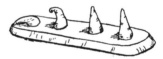

Fig. 145. Seger fusible cones

temperature reached in the kiln may be gauged by noting which cones have collapsed and which have not.

Change in Volume accompanying Melting or Solidification. Most substances *shrink on solidifying,* or in other words they expand on melting.　Lead is one instance of a substance which acts in this way and it is for this reason that it is not a satisfactory "casting metal."　To obtain "sharp" and dense castings in lead, either pressure must be applied or some other substance must be added to produce an alloy which does expand on solidifying. *Type-metal* consists of 5 parts lead and 1 part antimony and possesses this property.

Cast iron, water and a few other substances expand on solidifying. (*Note.* This expansion must not be confused with the expansion due to heating alone.)

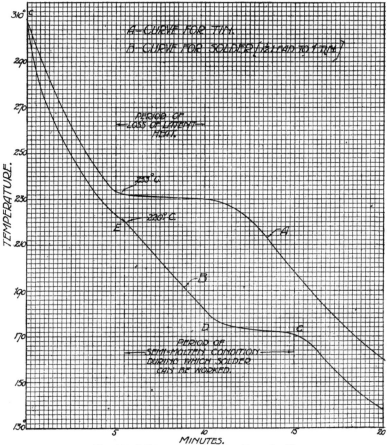

Fig. 146. Curves of cooling for tin and solder.

Expansion of Water on Freezing. It is common knowledge that ice floats on water and from this fact alone might be deduced the statement that *water expands on freezing,* since its reduced density in that state must be due to increased volume. In round numbers the density of ice is to the density of water as 11 : 12 and, since the volume of 1 gm. of water at 0° C. is slightly over 1 c.c. and of 1 gm. of ice at 0° C. is slightly over 1·09 c.c.s, the increase in volume is approximately 9 per cent.

To this increase in volume is due the bursting of water pipes in frosty weather, since the expansion in volume of the ice formed from the water in the pipes exerts enormous pressure, sufficient to fracture strong iron pipes. The simplest remedies are (a) to empty the pipes when frosts are likely to occur, (b) to keep the water in the pipes moving slowly, or (c) to so protect the pipes with some non-conducting material that the temperature of the water cannot fall to freezing point.

In the weathering of stones, bricks and other facing materials it is probable that the freezing of absorbed water and the consequent disruption of the exposed faces has much to do with the gradual decay of such materials.

Experiment 66. To show the change in volume which occurs when ice melts. Fit up a wide-necked flask with a long tube as shown in fig. 147. Fill the flask about half-full with broken ice, then fill up completely with coloured water and insert the stopper, so that the water rises well up the tube. Watch the level of the water in the tube and note that it rapidly falls as the ice continues to melt, showing that *the water takes up less space than the ice from which it is being formed.*

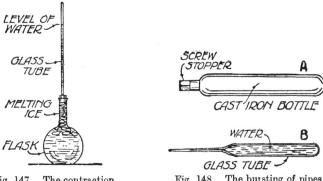

Fig. 147. The contraction of ice on melting.　　Fig. 148. The bursting of pipes by freezing water.

Experiment 67. To demonstrate the bursting of pipes by freezing water. Cast iron bottles may be obtained for this experiment, see fig. 148 *A*, these are filled with water and the screw stopper inserted. The whole is then placed in a freezing mixture (see p. 128) and left for some time. On taking the bottle out, the water will be found to have been converted into ice and to have fractured the bottle. If these bottles are not available, take some glass tubing of about 3 or 4 mms. internal diameter, close up one end and draw out the other to a capillary tube, see fig. 148 *B*, by alternately heating and cooling fill the tube with water and then seal up the open end. These may then be placed in the freezing mixture as described for the cast iron bottle.

BOILING.

Boiling Point. When dealing with melting point temperature we saw that it was a perfectly definite temperature for most substances and also, that such temperature was affected by the addition of foreign substances. The same remarks would apply to boiling point temperatures and it is for this reason that the boiling point of a liquid may furnish us either with a means of identifying that liquid or of testing its purity. (Salt raises the temperature of boiling water to 104° C.)

Experiment 68. To ascertain the boiling point of turpentine. The boiling point of good turpentine should be about 165° C. The test is carried out in some form of *hypsometer*; fig. 149 shows one which may be readily fitted up. The bulb of the thermometer is suspended in the vapour coming from the turpentine and is thus not affected by hot currents in the liquid during boiling. The vapour should be free to issue from the side tube. If only a small quantity of the liquid is available then the test should be carried out in the piece of apparatus shown in fig. 149 *A* and *B*. The bent tube is closed at the end of the short limb, some of the liquid is introduced and, by alter-

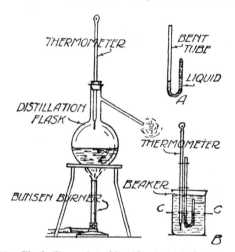

Fig. 149.   The boiling point of liquids at atmospheric pressure.

nately heating and cooling, is made to stand at a higher level in the short limb than it does in the other. The tube is attached to a thermometer and the whole immersed in a liquid having a higher boiling point than the one to be tested; the temperature is gradually raised by heating, the liquid in the beaker being stirred meanwhile. When the level of the liquid in the short limb falls and takes up the same level *C–C* in both limbs the boiling point of the liquid in the tube has been reached and the temperature may be noted. It should be remarked that when the levels are the same in both limbs of the tube the pressure on each surface must be the same and *equal to atmospheric pressure.*

Effect of Pressure on the Boiling Point. So far we have not considered the effect of pressure upon either melting point or the boiling point temperatures. The former are affected but slightly but in the case of the latter the effects are very considerable, increase of pressure raising and decrease of pressure lowering the boiling point temperatures. This is important in dealing with hot water or steam heating systems, where the fluid is under pressure, but we propose to leave the consideration of it to be dealt with in the succeeding volume. It should, however, be noted that, when ascertaining boiling point temperatures, the vapour coming from the liquid must not be confined so that the pressure may be increased. Strictly they should be ascertained for *standard pressure*.

Heat Constants for Materials (Centigrade Scale).

Substance	Specific Heat	Melting Point	Boiling Point
Water	1	0	100
Cast Iron	·114	1200	—
Wrought Iron ...	·109	2000	—
Brass	·092	1000	—
Copper	·094	1085	—
Lead	·031	327	—
Zinc	·094	419	—
Glass	·117	1100	—
Marble	·22	—	—
Granite	·2	—	—
Ether	·53	− 113	35
Paraffin Wax (hard)	55	52 to 56	—
Alcohol	·55	− 130	78
Naphthalene ...	32	79·9	—
Sulphur	·17	115	—
Mercury	·033	− 38·9	357
Turpentine ...	·41	− 10	159
Glycerine	·58	− 17	290

PROBLEMS IX

1. In an experiment on the mixing of two bodies of water at differing temperatures, 54 gms. of water at 70° C. are mixed with 57 gms. of water at 16° C. Calculate the final temperature of the mixture, if there be no heat losses.

2. In the above experiment if the final temperature of the mixture be actually 39·9° C., what is the "water equivalent" for the calorimeter, etc.?

3.   A lump of copper weighing 28·5 gms. is heated to 99° C. and dropped
into 63 gms. of water (including "water equivalent") at 16° C. The final
temperature is 19·25° C. What is the specific heat of the copper?

4.   Using the value obtained in question 3 for the specific heat of copper,
calculate the specific heat of glycerine, if when the same piece of copper is
dropped into 57 grams of glycerine at 16° C., the final temperature is 21° C.
Take the water equivalent of the calorimeter, etc. as 10·4 gms. and the original
temperature of the copper as 99° C.

5.   To measure the temperature in a small laboratory furnace a piece of
iron weighing 35 grams was placed in the furnace for some time, until it had
taken the temperature of the furnace; it was then plunged into 110 gms.
of water at 15° C., the final temperature of the water being 44° C. What
was the temperature in the furnace?   Take the specific heat of iron as ·114.

6.   In an experiment to find the melting point of naphthalene by a curve
of cooling the following values were obtained:

Time in mins.	0	2	4	6	8	10	12	14	16	18	20
Temp. (° C.)	99	90	83·5	79·5	79	79	78·5	77	75	71	68

Plot a curve and obtain from it the desired melting point temperature.

7.   The table below gives the temperatures at which a series of lead-tin
alloys become completely molten (corresponding to the temperature at E in
Fig. 146). Plot these points on squared paper. (Note. The points are really on
two separate curves, the one to the left, in which there is an excess of tin, and
the one to the right, on which there is an excess of lead.)
From the graph obtain (a) the upper melting point for plumber's solder
(2 of lead and 1 of tin), (b) the percentage of lead to give the lowest melting
point. (General note. This graph is of great practical importance in any attempt
to understand the action taking place when solder is melted. Thus, if a horizontal
line is drawn through the lowest point on the curve (183° C.), it is easy to
demonstrate by experiment that, for any particular alloy, the vertical distance
between the two graphs represents on the graph the range of temperature
during which the alloy is in a plastic condition.)

Percentage of lead	0	10	20	30	50	60	80	100
Temp. of melting (° C.)	232	219	205	193	218	244	300	327

8.   If 50 gallons of water at a temperature of 200° F. are drawn from a tank
and replaced by water at 55° F., find the total original volume of water if the
final temperature of the water in the tank is 110° F.

9.   Gas is now almost universally sold by the "Therm." A therm is the
quantity of heat represented by 100,000 British Thermal Units.
If the calorific value of a town gas is 4·75 therms per 1000 cu. ft. and the gas
is sold at 4s. 2d. per 1000 cu. ft., calculate the cost of heating 60 gallons of
water in a gas heated from an initial temperature of 50° F. to a final temperature
of 194° F. (You may assume that there is no loss of heat in the process. Take
the weight of a gallon of water as 10 lbs.)

CHAPTER X

Physical Changes. In the preceding chapters we have noted the effects of both heat and mechanical force upon various substances. We have seen how heat may convert a solid into a liquid or into a gas, how most substances expand when heated and contract when cooled and also how materials may be compressed, crushed or elongated by the application of force. It should be noted, however, that all such changes are merely changes of shape or of the physical condition of the substances considered and hence are known as **physical changes.** They may be recognised by the fact that although they may involve alterations in the physical properties of the substances *no new substances are formed.*

Further, the changes—like expansion or contraction—may only be temporary, the substance returning to its original condition on the removal of the special circumstances producing these changes.

Chemical Changes. We have now to consider another kind of change which is known to affect materials and which, in its results, may be much more far-reaching than any of the changes mentioned above. The changes of which we now speak are characterised by *the formation of new substances,* with properties entirely different from those possessed by the original substances taking part in these changes. These are known as **chemical changes** and result from chemical actions of which familiar examples are:—the rusting of iron, the drying of paints, the setting of lime, the decay of wood and, to some extent, the weathering of building stones.

Signs of Chemical Action. It is not always easy to distinguish between physical and chemical actions, but in the great majority of cases there are certain signs which enable us to decide whether chemical action is taking place. Briefly they are:

(1) The formation of new substances;

(2) Changes in temperature whilst the action is taking place;

(3)   Changes of weight in the substances taking part in the action, and

(4)   The permanency of the changes.

While it must be clearly understood that all these facts may be noted in any chemical change, one or other of them may be more strikingly shown in some one particular change than in another. The following simple experiment will serve to emphasise each of the points mentioned above.

Experiment 69. To illustrate signs of chemical action. If a small piece of limestone be heated at a high temperature, as explained on p. 184, (a small piece may be held in the bunsen flame by means of a piece of wire) a *new substance*—"lime"—will be produced. The difference between the lime and the limestone may be shown by dropping some water on each; no change will be observed in the limestone, whereas with the lime a fresh chemical action will commence—"slaking"—steam being given off and the lime splitting up into many pieces. If, *whilst slaking is proceeding*, a thermometer is inserted into one of the cracks of the lime, a rapid *rise in temperature* will be noted.

The change in temperature accompanying chemical action need not necessarily be a rise in temperature, while in some cases the alteration in temperature is so slight as to be unnoticed unless special means are adopted to detect it. (When water is added to cement there is a rise in temperature denoting chemical action; if no such rise takes place it is a sign that the cement is inert and useless.)

Changes in Weight. In both the examples of chemical action given above changes of weight may be easily detected by weighing; the lime will be found to weigh less than the limestone from which it is formed (see Problems X), while if the slaked lime be dried in an oven (see p. 173), to drive off the surplus water, it will be found to have increased in weight as compared with the lime.

Thus we see that the change may be either a decrease or an increase in weight. We must be careful, however, not to assume that some matter has been destroyed in the first instance nor created in the second. As we shall see later a gas is driven off from the heated limestone and passes into the atmosphere, while in the second example the new substance is formed by the union of some of the water with the lime (see Problems X).

If it were possible to conduct these experiments in a closed vessel, so that nothing could be added to or taken from the contents of the vessel, no change in total weight could be detected and this fact may serve to introduce us to what is called *the law of the indestructibility of matter*, which simply states that matter cannot be created or destroyed although it may change its form.

Elements and Compounds. Chemical action may be divided into "chemical combination" and "chemical decomposition," the first referring to those actions in which two or more substances combine to form a new substance, known generally as a **chemical compound.** The second grouping refers to those actions in which a compound substance is split up by chemical action into two or more substances of a less complex nature. The production of lime from limestone is an illustration of chemical decomposition, while the slaking of lime is an illustration of chemical combination.

The process of decomposing compounds into simpler substances is known as *analysis,* while the building up of a new substance by the combination of two or more substances is called *synthesis.*

All substances which, up to the present, it has not been possible to decompose into simpler substances are known as **elements.** While there are tens of thousands of compounds known to the chemist, there are only about 80 elements at present known to exist. Some of these elements are of extremely rare occurrence, as may be judged from the fact that only some 20 of these elements go to make up about 99 per cent. of the earth's crust.

Examples of elements with which we already have an acquaintance are copper, lead, iron, mercury, tin and zinc.

Water, lime, rust and limestone are examples of compounds.

Compounds and Mixtures. Such materials as mortar, concrete and granite we cannot describe as either elements or compounds, they are really "mixtures of compounds," containing such separate "compounds" as sand, lime, quartz, felspar and mica, which do not chemically combine to form the materials mentioned.

It is important that a careful distinction should be drawn between a chemical compound and what is usually referred to as a "mechanical mixture."

A chemical compound is a substance of perfectly definite and unvarying composition, with properties of its own which may be totally unlike those of the elements from which it was formed. Usually a compound can only be split up into its constituent elements by chemical means.

A mechanical mixture is characterised by (a) the properties of the mixture are intermediate between those of the substances of which it is made up, (b) the properties of the different substances of which it is composed remain unchanged in the mixture, (c) the proportions in which the substances are present may be varied at will, and (d) the ingredients of the mixture may be separated by mechanical or physical means, such as crushing, hand-picking, sieving, solution or distillation. Some of these methods have already been described and others will be discussed later.

Experiment 70. To illustrate the difference between a mechanical mixture and a chemical compound. Mix together in a mortar about 5 gms. of iron filings and 3 gms. of powdered sulphur.

The colour of the mixture is intermediate between the black iron and the yellow sulphur. Small pieces of iron can be easily detected amongst the sulphur and may be readily removed by drawing a magnet over a portion of the mixture. Further the sulphur could be removed by dissolving it out with a suitable liquid (carbon disulphide). Evidently we have a *mechanical mixture* of sulphur and iron.

Take a portion of the mixture, place it in a hard glass test tube and heat over a bunsen flame; after a while the mixture will begin to glow and give off fumes. When the action has ceased and the contents of the tube have cooled, knock them out on to a piece of paper and note any apparent changes. The substance thus produced is blackish-grey in colour and is porous, no separate pieces of iron can be detected or separated out with a magnet (but see p. 164) and it is unaffected by carbon disulphide.

We may thus conclude that this substance is a *chemical compound.*

AIR—A MIXTURE OF GASES

We shall now proceed to discuss with greater fullness the composition of two familiar substances—air and water. We shall find that they furnish us with an example of a typical mixture and of a typical compound.

The reader's attention is, in addition, drawn to the experimental methods and the apparatus used in this and the succeeding chapters, these should serve to familiarise him with the methods available for making elementary chemical investigations.

Experiment 71. To note what takes place when iron is exposed to moist air. Put some iron filings into a flat dish and weigh them, moisten them and place them on one side. If an oven is available (see p. 173) the dish may be placed in this, the water evaporated quickly and the filings moistened several times, giving a quicker result. After some time the iron will be found to be covered with red rust. If the dish and its contents are then dried in the oven, to expel all moisture, and once more weighed, a slight *gain in weight* will be noted over the original weight.

The question may now be asked as to how this gain in weight arises. The following experiment will help to explain this point.

Experiment 72. To note what takes place when iron rusts in air, in an enclosed space. Take a tube, closed at one end, about 18 to 20 inches long and ¾ inch in diameter, damp the inside of the tube and distribute as much fine iron filings over the sides as possible. Invert the tube and place in a tall jar of water as shown in fig. 150 A. After an hour or so the level of the water in the tube will be noticed to have risen and if the tube be left thus for several days the conditions will eventually be somewhat as shown in fig. 150 *A*. Raise the tube until the levels of the water outside and inside the tube are the same, see fig. 150 *B* (the pressure inside the tube will then be the same as outside—atmospheric pressure), and measure the lengths *L* and *l*. (Two tubes should be prepared in this way for use in Experiment 73.)

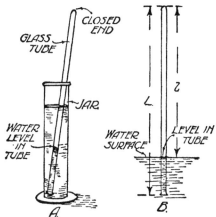

Fig. 150. The rusting of iron filings in a closed tube.

In considering what has taken place note that some only of the iron has rusted and that in so doing it has *either* used up some of the *air* in the tube **or** some *constituent part* of the air. Which? Since some of the iron is still unrusted it must be evident that, if it is the air itself which has been used up in this way, then the water will continue to rise until all the iron has rusted or all the air has been used up. But, if the tube be left in the water for an indefinite period, no further rise will be noted beyond a certain point. Thus we may dismiss the idea that the air has been used up by the rusting iron, the facts of the experiment pointing rather to it being a constituent part of the air which has been absorbed in this way, the action ceasing when no more of this constituent is present.

If the experiment has been carefully carried out *l* will be found to be about $\frac{4}{5}$ of *L*, so that we may conclude that *iron when it rusts combines with a substance which forms about ⅕ of the total volume of atmospheric air.*

Experiment 73. To test the properties of the residual gas in the tube of Experiment 72. Take one of the tubes from the water, first placing the finger over the open end of the tube. Note that, like air, the gas is colourless and that it has no smell. Into the second tube of the gas plunge a lighted taper and note that it is extinguished (compare with a tube of air). Hence we may say that this gas is colourless, without smell and that it does not support combustion nor is it inflammable.

This gas is called **nitrogen** and goes to make up approximately four-fifths of atmospheric air by volume; when obtained in the way we have just described the nitrogen is not pure, there being present slight traces of other gases which are found in air; the amounts of the gases are, however, so slight that we may omit their consideration for the present.

Aids to Chemical Action. If the iron filings in Experiment 71 had been enclosed in a bottle so as to exclude all moisture no rusting would have taken place, hence we see that *moisture* may be necessary before chemical action commences. Similarly we saw in Experiment 70 that *heat* was necessary to start the action which resulted in the iron and sulphur combining together.

These two simple illustrations should help us to realise that the *conditions* under which any given chemical action takes place may be quite as important as the substances concerned in that action.

Further while some actions will take place if sufficient time is allowed, *a change in the conditions* of the experiment may complete the action in a very brief space of time. For example if a piece of sheet lead be scraped so as to expose the bright metal beneath, this surface will rapidly tarnish and turn a dull grey, the lead combining with the same constituent of the air as did the rusting iron. Similarly with a piece of copper wire. If, however, a small quantity of the lead be melted in a crucible, this action will proceed much more rapidly on the exposed surface of the molten metal. If also a piece of the copper wire be heated in a bunsen flame it will be found on cooling to be covered with a black coating over the bright metal beneath.

The decay of timber will take place with great rapidity under certain conditions—generally the lack of ventilation and the presence of moisture with a gentle heat—and it is one of the objects of efficient construction to prevent these conditions arising where timber is used and so prevent decay.

It now remains for us to deal with the other constituent of air which, as we have seen, is absorbed when iron rusts and lead or copper tarnishes. This, as we shall presently see, is also a gas at ordinary temperatures, it is called **Oxygen** and forms approximately one-fifth of atmospheric air by volume.

Oxidation. The compounds formed when oxygen combines with another element are known as *oxides*; thus rust, the grey tarnish on the lead and the black coating to the copper were all oxides of the respective metals. The combination of a substance with oxygen is known as **oxidation.**

As we shall see later the *amount of oxygen* with which any

substance will combine may vary with the conditions existing during the change, so that most oxides may be again classified according to the amount of oxygen taken into chemical combination.

It will be of interest to point out here that the oxidation of the metals, of which we have already spoken, may not prove so destructive of their lasting qualities as is the case with iron. When iron rusts the scales of rust formed do not adhere to the parent metal beneath, but they fall away and thus expose fresh surfaces to the action of the moist air. With both lead and copper, however, the oxide *adheres* to the metal beneath and thus forms a protecting layer. It is largely to this fact that the lasting qualities of these metals, when used as roofing materials, are due. The oxide of zinc formed on the exposure of zinc sheets to moist air is also adherent, but this metal is peculiarly subject to attack in other ways, against which this coating of oxide is insufficient protection. Tin is unaffected by moist air and but for its high cost might replace lead, copper or zinc as roofing materials.

Oxygen from the air. No easy way is available whereby we may obtain oxygen *directly* from the air, as we did nitrogen, but we may obtain it *indirectly* in the manner described below.

We have mentioned the fact that the amount of oxygen which a metal takes up may be influenced by the *conditions* under which the oxidation takes place. Heat is one of the most potent of these conditions. If the heating of the lead mentioned on p. 152 were continued for some time and the surface scum removed so as to expose a fresh surface of molten lead, the whole of the lead would finally be converted into a yellowish oxide of lead— "litharge." If then the heating were continued over a number of hours at a higher temperature, and with a steady stream of air passing over the heated substance, more oxygen would enter into combination to form a red oxide of lead—"red lead."

Lastly, if some red lead were heated strongly it would yield up some of its oxygen and be once more converted to the litharge, and it ought to be possible for the reader to realise that the oxygen obtained in this way *originally formed part of the air.*

In the following experiment we shall use red oxide of mercury which on heating yields up *all* its oxygen leaving pure mercury behind.

When oxygen is removed from an oxide the process is known as "reduction."

Experiment 74. To obtain oxygen by heating an oxide. Support a hard glass test tube on a retort stand as shown in fig. 151 (but without any delivery tube) and into it place 2 or 3 gms. of red oxide of mercury. Heat gently at first and afterwards more strongly, when a gas—oxygen—will be given off whose presence may be detected as follows: Prepare some thin splinters of wood, light one and, after it has burnt down a little way, blow

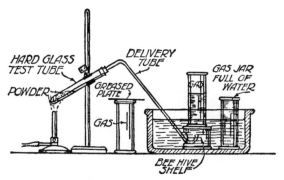

Fig. 151. The production of oxygen.

out the flame and push the glowing splinter into the test tube. It will immediately burst into flame once more and burn brilliantly. Little globules of mercury will form on the sides of the tube as the experiment proceeds.

Experiment 75. To prepare oxygen in quantity. Whilst the heating of red oxide of mercury provides us with a handy method of producing oxygen on a small scale, if larger quantities are required "oxygen powder" should be used; this gives large quantities of the gas easily and cheaply and consists of equal quantities of potassium chlorate and manganese dioxide. The oxygen is given off from the chlorate, the manganese dioxide remaining unaltered, but its presence has important effects in reducing the temperature at which the oxygen is given off and also in regularising the evolution of the gas.

The complete apparatus is shown in fig. 151. The gas is collected "over water," by placing "gas jars" full of water over the hole in the "bee-hive shelf," the gas passes through the hole displacing the water in the jar. The open end of the jar is covered with a greased plate before being removed from the water. This method is only suitable for gases which are insoluble or only slightly soluble in water. A number of jars of the gas may be collected and the tests already described carried out more carefully. For additional experiments with oxygen see Chap. xv.

From this and other experiments we may conclude that **oxygen** is a gas at ordinary temperature, that it is colourless, without smell and is not inflammable. Unlike nitrogen, however, it **supports combustion**; this is indeed its most striking characteristic and it may hence be described as the "active part of air," nitrogen forming the inactive part. Not only combustion but all forms of life would be "speeded up" were oxygen to form a greater part of the air than it does and, from this point of view, nitrogen apparently plays the part of a diluent only.

Is air a mixture or a compound? We may now summarise the results of our experiments with air. It evidently consists *chiefly* of two gases, oxygen and nitrogen, existing together in the proportions by volume of approximately 1 part of oxygen to 4 parts of nitrogen.

None of the facts which we have so far obtained enable us, however, to say whether air is a mixture or a compound formed of these gases. It will be convenient therefore to summarise below a number of facts which will enable us to decide this point.

(1) If 4 parts of nitrogen be mixed with 1 part of oxygen we have a mixture which acts in every way similarly to air, e.g. a candle will burn in it as in air.

(2) On mixing the gases no change of volume will be apparent nor will there be any change of temperature, in other words there are none of the usual signs of chemical change.

(3) Samples of air taken from various districts and from various parts of the earth's surface do not show absolute uniformity of composition (the *average* composition of air is given on p. 169). These variations though slight are not found in chemical compounds, which always have an unvarying composition.

(4) It is possible, though not easy, to separate the nitrogen and the oxygen by physical means—a thing which cannot be done with chemical compounds. One of the methods of physical separation mentioned on p. 150 was solution. (Explained more fully in Chap. XIII.) Now air is slightly soluble in water, see p. 176, but it is found that when so dissolved the ratio of the oxygen to the nitrogen is changed, these gases in fact acting as though they were separate and independent of each other.

Another gas, carbon dioxide, which is also soluble in water, see p. 170, does not act in this way but is dissolved or given off again from the water as carbon dioxide, showing unmistakably that it is a chemical compound (it is not an element like nitrogen or oxygen).

Taken together the above facts enable us to state that **air is a mechanical mixture of the gases nitrogen and oxygen** with traces of other gases present (see p. 169).

(For further experiments on air see Chapter XII.)

PROBLEMS X

1. How would you distinguish between physical and chemical changes? Describe two simple experiments illustrating the difference and give two examples of such changes from building.

2. Classify into chemical and physical actions the following: freezing water, rusting iron, the production of lime from limestone, expansion of an iron girder with change in temperature, the buckling of ironwork in a fire, the melting of lead, the tarnishing of lead on exposure to air.

3. Explain the difference between an element, a compound and a mixture, and give examples from building substances.

4. It may be shown that iron will not rust if kept in *dry* air. What then is the object of painting ironwork and what is the chief property which the paint must possess in order to fulfil this object?

5. Given that the density of nitrogen is 1·25 gms. per litre and of oxygen 1·43 gms. per litre, calculate the density of air if the proportion of nitrogen to oxygen by volume is as 4 : 1.

6. A piece of limestone weighing when dry 1·9 gms. was heated as described in Experiment 69, after which it was found to weigh 1·07 gms. (*a*) Calculate the percentage decrease in weight.

The lime was then slaked fully and dried, as described in the experiment, when it was found to weigh 1·33 gms. (*b*) Calculate the percentage increase in weight.

7. When magnesium is heated to a high temperature in air it combines with the oxygen forming a white ash, magnesium oxide or magnesia. The heating should be carried out in a porcelain crucible, with a lid on to retain the fine ash. In an experiment the following values were obtained:

Weight of crucible and lid   ...   . = 15·24 gms.

,,   ,,   ,, and magnesium wire = 15·96 ,,

,,   ,,   ,,   ,,   ,, oxide = 16·44 ,,

From these figures calculate the percentage increase in weight due to oxygen combining with the magnesium.

8. How would you explain that when limestone is heated in air it decreases in weight while magnesium, when similarly treated, gains in weight?

9. How would you proceed to show that air is neither an *element* nor a *chemical compound*?

10. Why is it necessary to remove the scales of rust, which may have formed on unprotected iron work, before proceeding to paint the iron work?

11. Compare the actions which take place when fresh surfaces of copper, iron, lead and zinc are exposed to the air.

12. Describe the characteristics of the gases nitrogen and oxygen. Describe how one of these gases may be produced in the laboratory.

CHAPTER XI

WATER—A COMPOUND

Proceeding now to the investigation of the composition of water we shall first—as with air—analyse it into the elements of which it consists and then discuss the question as to the nature of the combination in which those elements exist.

If iron be strongly heated in a current of air a black scale is formed, which may be shown to be an oxide of iron containing a smaller percentage of oxygen than the "red rust" with which we are already acquainted. This scale may be noted when a blacksmith is working up a piece of iron, it is also formed when iron heated to a high temperature is plunged into water. In the former case the oxygen is evidently obtained from the air but in the latter case it can only be obtained from the water, hence we are justified in assuming for the present *that the element oxygen is a constituent of water.*

We may now proceed in almost exactly the same way as we did with air and, by taking away the oxygen from the water, ascertain what element or elements remain.

Experiment 76. **The decomposition of water by heated iron.** The apparatus suitable for this experiment is shown in fig. 152. The iron, which is used in the form of iron filings or nails, is contained in an iron tube from 12 to 18 ins. long (if filings are used they must be spread out over the length of the tube so as not to choke it). The tube and its contents are heated to a red heat on a gas furnace, of which a simple type is shown. The water is used in the form of steam and is only allowed to pass into the tube and over the filings when they have been fully heated. The gas coming over is collected over water as shown. The gas coming over at first will be mixed with air from the apparatus and the collection should be delayed until all the air has been driven out. A simple test for the presence of air is given below. Do not let the gas come over too rapidly (regulate the flame under the boiler) and place the filled jars on one side mouth downwards, covering them with a greased plate as an extra precaution.

The gas in the jars should now be tested as follows: (1) Holding a jar of gas mouth downwards push a lighted taper right up into the jar. There will be a slight explosion at the mouth of the jar after which the gas will burn quietly with an almost colourless blue flame; the taper itself will be extinguished. (2) Place over the hole in the beehive shelf a jar only partly filled with water—the upper portion being filled with air—and complete the filling of the jar with gas. The jar will now contain a mixture of air and gas and if a lighted taper be put to the mouth of the jar the mixture will ignite with a

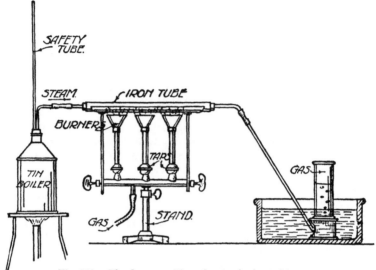

Fig. 152. The decomposition of water by heated iron.

loud report. (3) By holding a jar of air and one of the gas, as shown in fig. 153, the gas may be "poured" upwards into the jar of air, when it will displace the air. Test this by means of the taper.

NOTE. Since, as we have seen above, a mixture of this gas with air forms an explosive mixture, we may ascertain when gas only is coming from the generating apparatus by collecting test tubes of the gas from time to time and holding a lighted taper to the mouth. When the gas burns quietly it is free from air. (In any experiment in which this gas is to be ignited this should always be done, as otherwise a dangerous explosion may result.)

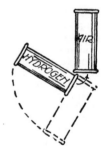

Fig. 153. "Pouring" hydrogen upwards.

The substance obtained from water as described above is the element **hydrogen**. As we have seen it exists in a free state as a gas at ordinary temperatures; like nitrogen and oxygen it is without colour or smell. It does not support combustion. It is differentiated from these two gases, however, by the fact that it will burn and also by reason of its extreme lightness. It is about 16 times less dense than oxygen and 14 times less dense than nitrogen and air.

In addition to the method stated above hydrogen may be

conveniently prepared by pouring dilute hydrochloric or sulphuric acid over zinc and collecting the gas over water; see
fig. 162 for a suitable form of apparatus.

The solution produced by pouring dilute hydrochloric acid
over zinc is the "killed spirits" of the plumber, being used in
soldering because of its powers of decomposing any oxide which
may form on the surfaces to be soldered.

We have now shown that both oxygen and hydrogen are present in water. Are they the only elements present? Evidently
this question would be answered in the affirmative if from oxygen
and hydrogen we could produce water.

Experiment 77. To find what results when dry hydrogen is passed
over heated copper oxide. (a) When air is passed over heated copper the
copper oxidises rapidly, turning black; the oxygen is absorbed from the air
and—if only a limited amount of air is used—nitrogen remains. To show
this experimentally a piece of apparatus may be arranged as shown in fig. 154.
The copper, which may either be used in the form of copper turnings or a roll
of copper gauze, is placed in a glass combustion tube which is heated over a
suitable form of burner such as that shown—a Ramsey burner. A current

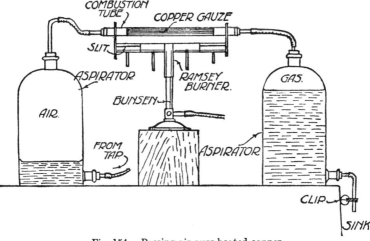

Fig. 154. Passing air over heated copper.

of air is then passed over the copper by means of two "aspirators" connected
to the tube. The aspirator on the left is at first full of air and the one on the
right full of water; when all is ready water flows into the first aspirator and
displaces the air. The water in the second aspirator is allowed to flow away
(but not quite so quickly) causing the air to pass over the copper gauze, and
the gas produced by the action in the tube enters the second aspirator. If
this gas be tested it will be found to be nitrogen. It will be noted that the
copper turns black as the experiment proceeds, copper oxide having been
formed.

(b) Disconnect the tube containing the copper oxide from the aspirators and connect it up to some form of hydrogen generator (see fig. 152 or fig. 162) so that a stream of dry hydrogen may be made to pass over the heated copper, see fig. 155. The hydrogen may be dried as described on p. 171. (Make sure that all air has been displaced from the apparatus before commencing to heat the tube.) The delivery tube discharges into a small flask, which is kept cool by a stream of running water as shown.

As the hydrogen continues to pass over the heated copper oxide a clear liquid will condense in the small flask. When sufficient liquid has been

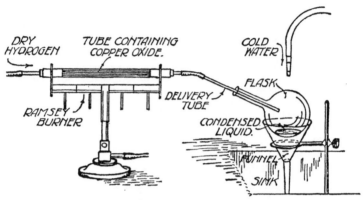

Fig. 155.   Passing hydrogen over heated copper oxide.

collected stop the action by removing the heat from the tube and allowing it to cool; finally stop the passage of the hydrogen by disconnecting from the generator.

Note that some at least of the copper has had the blackened surface removed and its natural colour once more restored. We may infer from this that the oxygen which went to form the black copper oxide has been removed—reduction—and that in all probability the liquid which has resulted from the action is a compound of the hydrogen and the oxygen.

Test the liquid in various ways. Its boiling point will be found to be 100° C. and its freezing point 0° C. It has neither colour, smell nor taste (compare with distilled water). Hence, so far as we are capable of investigating the matter, we may conclude that the liquid is **water**.

From the results of the preceding experiments we may now conclude that water consists of the elements oxygen and hydrogen. Whether they are chemically combined or not and what are the relative proportions in which they exist in water are questions remaining for us to settle.

The Synthesis of Water. While the experiment described below is not such as can be carried out by elementary students it is so instructive and so conclusive with regard to the points we have just mentioned that a full description has been included here, so that the reader, even if he cannot see the actual experiment carried out, may have an acquaintance with the results and so appreciate fully the arguments deduced from them.

The apparatus shown in fig. 156 is known as a "eudiometer" and consists of a specially strong U-tube in which it is possible to explode mixtures of gases. One branch is fitted at the top with a tap, near which two platinum points are sealed into the glass of the tube. By connecting these terminals to an electric battery and an induction coil, a spark may be made to pass across the small space between the points and thus ignite any explosive gases which may be enclosed in the tube. The "steam jacket" shown may be omitted in the first part of the experiment. A second tap is provided near the bottom of one of the tubes. The method of procedure is as follows:

Close the bottom tap, open the top one and fill both tubes with mercury, then close the top tap also. Now connect this end of the tube successively to vessels in which oxygen and hydrogen respectively are being generated and, by opening the top tap and adjusting the level of the mercury (by means of the bottom tap), allow about equal quantities of each gas to pass in. The exact volume of each gas at atmospheric pressure may be ascertained by adjusting the levels of the mercury until they are the same in each tube, *the pressure on the gas will then be equal to that of the atmosphere.* Do not let the mixture fill much more than half the length of the tube on one side.

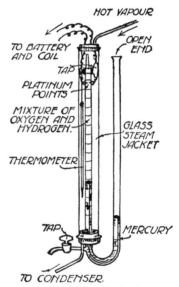

Fig. 156.   The synthesis of water.

Now run out some of the mercury until the conditions are somewhat as shown in fig. 156. Close the open end of the U-tube with the hand and pass a spark across the terminals as already described, when the gases will explode. Then adjust the levels of the mercury, by pouring fresh mercury in, and note that it reaches very nearly to the top of the closed tube before the levels are the same. In addition, small beads of moisture—water—will be observed on the inside of the tube.

Let us suppose that, as suggested, equal quantities by volume of the gases were taken, say two units of oxygen and two units of hydrogen. After the explosion it will be found that about one unit of a gas remains—in addition to the small drops of water. If this gas be collected in a tube and tested it will be found in this case to be oxygen—test with glowing splinter. Thus *two volumes of hydrogen have combined with one volume of oxygen.* The experiment may be repeated with other volumes of the gases when it will be found that this proportion always holds good, the surplus oxygen or hydrogen, as the case may be, always remaining over after each explosion. Evidently, if the explosion tube were filled with a mixture of two parts of hydrogen to one part of oxygen by volume, the whole of it would disappear, leaving only a small drop of water in its place. Such a mixture, however, results in a very forcible explosion which may shatter the tube.

We have now seen that the result of the explosion is to produce a small drop of water, which occupies very much less space than the original mixture of gases. That is, the combination of the gases has produced amongst other things a change from the gaseous to the liquid condition. Such a change of state frequently accompanies chemical action. Let us next compare the volume of the gases before explosion with the volume of the watery vapour formed after the explosion. Evidently, if the tube be kept at a temperature above 100° C., then the water formed after the explosion will remain in a gaseous condition—as steam. The temperature of the explosion tube may be so kept up by enclosing it in a larger tube, see fig. 156, through which passes the vapour of some liquid which boils at a higher temperature than 100° C. (turpentine, which boils at 159° C., may be used).

The experiment is conducted as already described and it is found that *two volumes of hydrogen combine with one volume of oxygen to form two volumes of water vapour at the same temperature,* i.e. there has been a change in volume on combination taking place.

Is water a chemical compound? We may now summarise the results of the foregoing experiment and see how far they go to assist us to decide whether water is a compound or not.

(1) A mixture of 2 parts of hydrogen and 1 part of oxygen did not form water but merely a mixture of the two gases.

(2) Heat, in the form of an electric spark, was necessary to make them combine which they did with great suddenness.

(3) The water vapour formed occupied only two-thirds of the volume occupied by the original mixture of gases.

The necessity for heat, the energy of the action and the change in volume may be taken together as signs of chemical action and we may conclude that water is a chemical compound, in which the elements oxygen and hydrogen are present in the ratio by volume of 1 to 2.

(The synthesis of water may be very simply illustrated by burning a jet of hydrogen in air, as described on p. 166, and collecting and testing the resulting liquid.)

Analysis of Water. Though it is not necessary to our argument, the following experiment will serve as an additional verification of the statement we have just made regarding the composition of water. It is an experiment which does not admit of a simple explanation, but the results are very striking and, where the necessary apparatus is available, it is not difficult to carry out. It is generally known as the "electrolysis of water," a current of electricity being passed through the water to decompose it into its elements.

Experiment 78. **To decompose water by electricity.** The water is contained in a glass trough as shown, fig. 157. To the two terminals on the base board are connected two wires which pass beneath the board, through the bottom of the trough, and are connected inside to two pieces of platinum foil as shown. Over these two "electrodes" stand two closed-end tubes, also filled with water. The water is slightly acidulated so that it may conduct the electricity better. When the terminals in the base board are connected

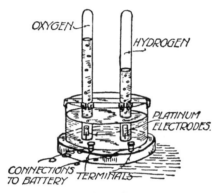

Fig. 157 The analysis of water.

to a 3- or 4-cell battery small bubbles of gas are seen to form on each electrode and, as the action goes on, these bubbles rise in the tubes and collect at the top. It will be found that the gas collects *twice* as rapidly in one tube as it does in the other. When sufficient gas has been collected in each tube it may be tested (see pp. 154 and 157). The tube containing the smaller quantity of gas will be found to contain oxygen. In the other tube there will be found to be exactly *twice* as much gas, which on testing will prove to be hydrogen.

The Definiteness of Chemical Combination. We have already stated, that one of the characteristics of a chemical compound is, that the elements going to make up the compound are always present *in definite and unvarying proportions* and the experiments just carried out should serve to emphasise this. We saw that when there was an excess of hydrogen (or oxygen) over the quantities required it was left unaffected after the formation of the water, the gases combining only in the stated proportions.

We have spoken of the relative proportions of these two elements *by volume*, exactly the same definiteness exists as regards *weight.* Oxygen being 16 times heavier than hydrogen, then the proportion—by weight—in which these elements should be present in water is as 8 is to 1. This may be shown to be so by experiment.

Similarly, in the experiment with sulphur and iron (see p. 150), if an excess of iron filings had been used, they would remain uncombined at the close of the experiment.

Thus we may say, that in the formation of chemical compounds the elements concerned always combine in definite proportions and also that, in any particular compound the same elements are present, united together in the same proportions.

(For further experiments with water see Chapter XIII.)

PROBLEMS XI

1. After reading the first paragraph in this chapter state what you think is the reason for the comparatively rapid destruction of iron fire bars and fire backs. Is the destruction of fire-clay " backs " (in fireplaces) due to the same cause?

2. Calculate the weight of a litre of (a) hydrogen, (b) oxygen, and (c) air, given that the density of hydrogen is ·00009 gms. per cubic centimetre and that oxygen is 16 times and air 14·3 times heavier than hydrogen.

3. From the densities of hydrogen and oxygen found in question 2, calculate the proportions *by weight* of these gases when combined to form water.

4. 20 c.cms. of hydrogen and 15 c.cms. of oxygen were mixed and exploded in a eudiometer. (a) How much gas is left and what does it consist of? (b) What would be the total volume of the gas and the water vapour formed if the temperature of the apparatus was kept at 105° C. say?

5. Using the densities found in question 2, calculate the weight of water formed from 1 litre of a mixture of 2 parts of hydrogen and 1 part of oxygen by volume.

6. Given that 1 gm. of water expands to 1700 c.cms. of steam at a temperature of 100° C., calculate the volume of hydrogen (at the same temperature) which could theoretically be obtained from 10 gms. of water as described in Experiment 76.

7. If the inside diameter of the aspirators in Experiment 77 is 15 cms. and the water rises 20 cms. in the aspirator containing air, calculate (a) the necessary fall in the other aspirator, and (b) the resulting volume of nitrogen, assuming that all the oxygen from the air has combined with the copper. (Assume that the final temperature and pressure are the same as at the commencement of the experiment.)

8. Using the values given in the last question, (a) calculate the gain in weight due to the combined oxygen (density as in question 2). Then (b) calculate the weight of the water formed if all the oxygen from the copper oxide combines with hydrogen as described in the second part of Experiment 77.

CHAPTER XII

THE NATURE AND PRODUCTS OF COMBUSTION. THE COMPOSITION OF THE ATMOSPHERE

In this and the succeeding chapters we propose to deal, in an elementary manner, with some problems which arise in the chemistry of building and building materials. This should serve to improve the reader's grip upon chemical methods and chemical knowledge and also prepare him for a fuller treatment of these problems in the succeeding volume.

The Nature of Combustion. When two or more gases combine chemically with the production of light and heat, *flame* is produced and marks the region where such combination is taking place.

Usually the temperature of the gases has to be raised, by the application of heat, in order to start the action and we are said to "ignite" the gases. The lowest temperature at which combustion commences is known as the "temperature of ignition." When combustion starts without outside aid it is described as "spontaneous combustion."

When a solid, such as wood, burns with the production of flame, part of the solid has been "volatilised" (converted into a gas or gases), combining with the oxygen of the air and producing the flame. If the solid be not volatilised, but heat and light be still produced, we have combustion but no flame (e.g. iron burning in oxygen, see p. 190).

It is important to realise that what we call combustion is essentially a chemical action (usually oxidation), hence it is possible to include under this head such actions as the rusting of iron and the decay of wood. These are examples of "slow combustion" without the production of light; the heat produced is so slight as to pass unnoticed unless very refined methods of observation are adopted.

In considering combustion we usually refer to "the thing which burns" or "the combustible" and "the supporter of combustion." Thus we speak of coal gas "burning in air." It is possible to show, however, that "air will burn in coal gas," and this fact should help to explain the nature of the action taking place.

Experiment 79. To explain the nature of combustion. Fit to one end of a chimney-glass a large cork, through which pass two pieces of tubing as shown in fig. 158. The centre piece should be not less than ¼ in. internal diameter. Connect the other tube to the gas supply, cover the top of the chimney with a card or with the hand and turn on the gas. Gas will presently issue from *A* and—when the chimney is full of gas—a light may be applied here and the gas will "burn in air." Now remove the card or hand from the top of the chimney. The upward flow of the gas will cause air to be drawn in at *A* carrying the flame up the tube and the "air will burn in an atmosphere of gas" at *B*. Place a piece of wire gauze over the top of the chimney and ignite the surplus gas coming through; once more we have "gas burning in air."

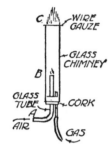

Fig. 158. The nature of combustion.

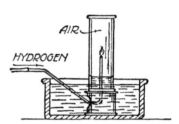

Fig. 159. Hydrogen burning in air.

The Products of Combustion in Air. If a jet of hydrogen be passed up into a gas jar, as shown in fig. 159, and ignited, the gas will continue to burn for a brief period, during which the water level will rise in the jar and a slight amount of moisture will collect on the sides of the jar. These facts go to show that the hydrogen has probably united with the oxygen in the air, forming **water**. (Actually—for several reasons—the flame expires before all the oxygen is used up, if it were not so the rising water would occupy one-fifth of the volume of the jar.) That water is actually produced in this way may be shown definitely by the following experiment.

Experiment 80. To show that water is produced when hydrogen burns in air. Allow the jet of hydrogen to burn in the enlarged end of a condensing tube, as shown in fig. 160. By passing water through the outer jacket of the condenser the inner tube is kept cool. As already suggested the

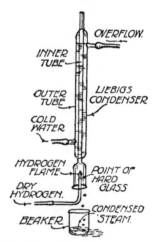

Fig. 160. Water from hydrogen burning in air.

hydrogen in burning unites with the oxygen of the air, forming steam which condenses on the sides of the cool tube. If the experiment be continued for a sufficient length of time the condensed vapour may be collected in a beaker and tested as already explained on p. 160.

If a jet of coal gas be treated in this way, water is similarly produced (since nearly 50 per cent. of hydrogen is present in this gas) and likewise for all "combustibles" which contain hydrogen.

When any compound is burned which contains the element "carbon," the carbon unites with the oxygen of the air to form a gaseous compound known as **carbon dioxide.** Coal, coal gas, oil, candles and wood all contain the element carbon, hence their combustion in air results in the production of this gas. We shall deal with the properties of carbon dioxide more fully at a later stage, but we may here state. that it possesses the characteristic property of turning lime water milky (see p. 178).

Experiment 81. To show that carbon dioxide is produced when coal gas is burnt in air. Lower a jet of coal gas into a jar of air, at the bottom of which a little lime water has been placed, and cover the mouth of the jar with a disc of asbestos, see fig. 161. The jet will burn for some little time and may then be withdrawn; close the top of the jar immediately and shake up the contents, the lime water will turn milky indicating the presence of carbon dioxide.

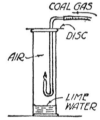

Fig. 161. The production of carbon dioxide when coal gas burns in air.

It would thus appear that with the substances mentioned the products of combustion include water and carbon dioxide. Other compounds are produced but these are of minor importance to us at present.

It may be further shown that in the case of "organic substances" (compounds of carbon, of which nearly all fuels and foods are examples), the "slow combustion" of decay and fermentation results also in the production of water and carbon dioxide. It is for this reason that we remove all vegetable soil from the site of a house or cover it up with "site concrete," the gases from decaying vegetation being thus kept from rising into the house.

Similarly with the breathing of human beings and of animals, the oxygen of the air is absorbed in the lungs and some of the waste products of the body pass into the air as carbon dioxide and water. As compared with ordinary air the breath contains nearly 100 times as much carbon dioxide.

The Bunsen Burner. Before leaving the subject of combustion it will be useful and interesting to deal briefly with the principle of the construction of the Bunsen burner, which is used so frequently in the laboratory as a source of heat and, in a slightly altered form, in domestic gas fires and stoves. In the ordinary bat-wing burner, the oil lamp and the candle we have a *luminous flame*. This luminosity is probably due to the incandescent particles of carbon; the temperature of the flame, however, is not high. In the Bunsen burner air is mixed with the gas before ignition, thus the combustion is more complete, the temperature is higher and the flame is *non-luminous* (there are other reasons for the non-luminosity).

In this burner the air is admitted by an air regulator near the bottom of the upright tube, see fig. 177; by turning this a greater or less supply of air may be admitted. When correctly adjusted the burner gives a blue flame which burns quietly. The point of lowest temperature is near the mouth of the tube (a cone of unburnt gas may be noted immediately over the mouth of the tube), while the highest temperature occurs about half-way up the flame and near to the outside (it may reach 1500° C. here). If too much air is admitted to the burner (or too little gas) the flame "strikes back."

In the ordinary form of Bunsen burner about 2 to 3 volumes of air mix with every volume of gas; a higher percentage of air produces an even more perfect combustion and hence a higher temperature. In the Méker burner (see fig. 172), the air is present in a higher ratio and the flame is prevented from "striking back" by a deep "grid." The action of this grid may be illustrated by using the apparatus shown in fig. 158. If when the gas is burning above the wire gauze, the gauze be lifted up from the top of the chimney, the gas will continue to burn above the gauze but will not pass to the inflammable gas beneath. This is explained by the fact that the wire of the gauze is able to conduct the heat away so rapidly as to keep the gas on the lower side of the gauze at a temperature below its ignition point.

The Composition of the Atmosphere

So far we have seen that air consists chiefly of a mixture of oxygen and nitrogen in the proportions (approx.) by volume of 1 : 4. Knowing that it is a mixture and recollecting the fact that gaseous matters of all kinds are continually being poured into it (some of which we have already mentioned), we may realise the truth of Robert Boyle's remark that "there is scarcely a more heterogeneous body in the world." It is remarkable however, that, except in confined places (like badly ventilated rooms), the power of "diffusion" (mixing of gases) and the dispersive powers of the wind are such that the composition of the air is *almost* uniform over the whole surface of the globe.

Disregarding the water vapour, the amount of which varies considerably, the *average* percentage composition of atmospheric air by volume may be stated in round figures as follows:

Nitrogen	78	per cent.
Oxygen	21	,,
Carbon dioxide	0·04	,,
Traces of other gases	0·96	,,

Carbon Dioxide in the Atmosphere. From the percentage composition of the atmosphere we see that about four volumes of carbon dioxide are present in every 10,000 volumes of air, and although this will appear to be an almost negligible amount, the presence of the gas may easily be detected by exposing a small dish filled with lime water. After a time the surface becomes covered with a white scum demonstrating the presence of this gas. Before proceeding to discuss the importance of this constituent of air, it will be convenient to explain how it may be produced in quantity and its properties examined more fully than has yet been possible.

Experiment 82. To prepare and test carbon dioxide. Place some pieces of marble (calcium carbonate) in a flask fitted up as shown in fig. 162. Cover the marble with water and pour strong hydrochloric acid down the funnel. Gas will be evolved fairly rapidly and may be collected over water, although it is to some extent soluble in water (see p. 170). Owing to the

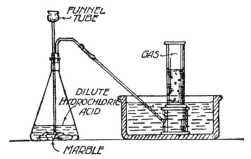

FUNNEL TUBE

GAS

DILUTE HYDROCHLORIC ACID

MARBLE

Fig. 162.   The production of carbon dioxide.

density of the gas (over 1½ times that of air) it is possible, however, to collect it in the manner shown in fig. 163 *A*, in which the gas flows from the tube to the bottom of the jar displacing the air. If a lighted taper be lowered into the jar it will be completely extinguished as soon as it reaches the gas (this may be used as a test to ascertain when the jars are full). The gas may be "poured" from jar to jar like water and its presence proved with the taper.

Thus we have learnt that this gas is heavier than air, that it
is colourless and that it neither
supports combustion nor burns
itself.

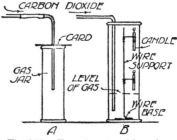

Fig. 163.   Experiments with carbon
dioxide.

A striking experiment may be
arranged to illustrate these properties
as shown in fig. 163 B.   In a large jar
a series of small candles is supported
at different levels on a stand and the
gas passed into the jar near the
bottom.   As the level of the gas rises
the candles are extinguished.

Owing to its density this gas
tends to collect at the bottoms
of wells, old mining shafts and
caves and, if its presence is suspected, the effect on a naked
light (unless explosive gases are likely to be present) is noted
before such places are entered.   The gas is not in itself particularly poisonous, and its fatal effects when present in large
quantities are probably due to the absence of oxygen.

Since the amount of carbon dioxide present in the air varies
to some extent with other and more important impurities and its
amount is fairly easily measured, the amount of carbon dioxide
present is usually taken as an indication of the efficiency of the
ventilation of buildings.   It is generally considered that the
amount present in such places should not be allowed to exceed
8 volumes per 10,000 volumes of air, or ·08 per cent.

Experiment 83. To show the solubility of carbon dioxide. The
solubility of carbon dioxide in water may be shown by passing the gas through
some water in a test tube.   On testing the water so treated it will be found
to give an *acid reaction*—turning blue litmus slightly red (see p. 192)—showing
that some of the gas has been dissolved uniting with the water to form a
weak acid—"carbonic acid."   Now let this water be boiled and once more
tested when it will be found to be *neutral* again, the carbon dioxide having
been driven off by boiling.

Vegetation and the Purity of the Atmosphere. We have
mentioned how that in *breathing*, animals use up the oxygen of
the air and give off carbon dioxide; plants also breathe and in so
doing also use up oxygen and give off carbon dioxide.   Considering the large quantities of carbon dioxide poured into the air in
this way and also from fires and the slow combustion of decay,
the question naturally arises as to how the amount of oxygen
is kept up and carbon dioxide reduced.   In this connection plants
perform an important function; they also, like animals, *feed* and
in so doing absorb carbon dioxide and, under the action of sunlight,
split it up into carbon and oxygen, giving the oxygen back to the

air and using the carbon in the formation of their own structure. As this process goes on to a much greater extent than does the "breathing" of plants, they perform the part of maintaining a fairly constant composition of the air.

Moisture in the Atmosphere.   Water is present in the atmosphere as a vapour, its presence may be detected in various ways of which perhaps the simplest is to note its effect on "hygroscopic substances."   These are substances which on exposure to moist air or gases absorb water and show a corresponding increase in weight and, in some cases, an obvious dampness.   Examples of these substances with which we ought to be acquainted are, freshly burnt lime, calcium chloride, strong sulphuric acid, freshly ground Portland cement, impure salt, and wood from which all the free moisture has been driven by heat (see Experiment 84).

How to dry a gas.   A perfectly dry gas is sometimes required for experimental purposes (see Experiment 77), and may be prepared by passing the gas through one or more drying tubes such as is shown in fig. 164.   This form consists of a U-tube packed with either calcium chloride or pumice soaked in strong sulphuric acid.   An alternative method is to make the gas bubble through the acid contained in a jar or flask.

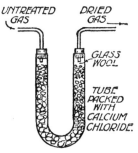

Fig. 164.   A U-tube for drying a gas.

Humidity.   In dealing with the moisture in air we speak of the "humidity of the air"; the "*absolute* humidity" of the air at any moment being "the number of grams (or grains) of water vapour present in a litre (or cubic foot) of the air."

This amount may be *directly* ascertained by passing a measured quantity of air through several drying tubes, which have been previously weighed, the final increase in weight giving the weight of water present in the given volume of air.   (See Problems XII, 9.)

It is not, however, usually necessary that we should know the absolute humidity of the atmosphere but rather that we should be able to compare the variations which take place from day to day, these may be ascertained by *indirect* but less complicated means than those mentioned above.   This, however, will be dealt with more fully in the succeeding volume, but before concluding our reference here, it will be convenient to deal briefly with some of the effects of atmospheric moisture upon building materials and construction.

Some Effects of Variations in Humidity on Building.
Temperature plays a large part in the variations which take place
in the humidity of air from day to day, since warm air can contain
more moisture than cold air.   When air at any particular temperature contains as much water vapour as it is possible for it to
hold, the air is said to be "saturated" and any drop in the temperature will then cause some of the moisture to condense as drops
of water.   If a glass containing cold water (with a few pieces of
ice if possible) be taken into a warm room, the air near the surfaces
of the glass will be cooled to such an extent as to cause the water
vapour to condense on the glass.

The same phenomenon may be noted in *badly ventilated rooms*,
in which the moisture, given off by the occupants of the room and
by the combustion of coal gas, condenses on any cold *non-porous*
surfaces such as windows, cold-water pipes, cement-rendered and
painted wall surfaces.   In public halls this condensation may go
on to such an extent as to disfigure the decorations seriously.   The
obvious cure is better ventilation, but in such fittings as skylights
and conservatories, where it is difficult to prevent it, special
"condensation gutters" should be provided to conduct the moisture away as it collects.

In papered rooms the moisture will not be visible, being
absorbed by the paper, but if excessive in amount, as in bath-
rooms, it may cause the paper to buckle and eventually come
away from the walls.   When the amount of moisture in the air
of the room decreases the moisture in the walls evaporates.   It
is for this reason that very porous papers and wall surfaces are
considered unhygienic by some, since in this way dust and small
organic substances find their way into the pores of the paper
and may eventually prove to be a source of disease.

When much moisture is present in the air, as in the damp days
of early spring and autumn, the "drying powers" of the air are
much reduced since evaporation does not take place so readily.
During such weather plaster, lime, concrete and bricks dry very
slowly and it is unwise to occupy new houses, unless special
precautions are taken (by ventilation and the lighting of fires)
to dry out the surplus moisture.   If possible new, well-seasoned
joinery should not be fixed in houses in such a condition, since
it absorbs the moisture and swells, shrinking after the house
has been occupied for some time and showing unsightly open
joints.

In very dry weather mortar and concrete dry very rapidly and
this reduces their ultimate strength.   To prevent this the bricks
should be sprayed or soaked in water before use, so that they may
not absorb the water from the mortar too rapidly, and all fresh

concrete should be covered with wet bags or otherwise protected from the drying effects of the air and of direct sunshine.

Hygroscopic Moisture. Nearly all building materials contain some free water which is known as "hygroscopic moisture." The amount varies with the state of the weather, being generally least during the summer months. The presence of this moisture need not be detrimental but the *variation* in the amount held in this way affects some materials considerably; chief amongst these is timber. With the increase or decrease of moisture timber expands or contracts, and particular notice should be taken of the methods adopted in actual construction to allow these variations in size to take place without fracturing the wood or weakening the piece of construction.

Similar movements take place in earth which is near the surface and which is unprotected—by paving or draining, say—from the effects of rain, wind and sun. If the foundations of a house are not carried down to a sufficient depth the stability of the house will be affected by these movements, particularly if the house is built upon clay, the variations being considerable from season to season. (See Problems XII, 12.)

A similar effect is noticeable in deep excavations which have to be kept open for some time. After exposure the sides of the excavation shrink and unless the timbering is carefully watched and the struts wedged up from day to day they may drop out completely, resulting possibly in a dangerous collapse.

The following experiment will show that wood as ordinarily used contains 12 to 15 per cent. of moisture, that unseasoned wood contains about 50 per cent., and we may conclude from this that the seasoning of timber consists largely of the drying out of surplus moisture.

Experiment 84. To ascertain the amount of free moisture present in seasoned and unseasoned timber. Prepare some specimens from the woods to be tested, in the shape of square prisms about $\frac{1}{2}'' \times \frac{1}{2}'' \times 3''$. Weigh each one carefully and then place in a "water oven," see fig. 165;

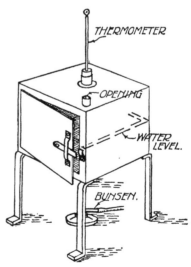

Fig. 165. A water oven.

the temperature of the oven should not be allowed to rise above 90° C.   After about one hour in the oven the pieces should be weighed and then placed in the oven again and the weighings repeated at intervals until no further loss is apparent.   The amount lost is then calculated as a percentage on the weight of the wood *after drying* and will give the measure of the amount of free moisture orig'nally contained in the pores of the wood.   To ascertain the percentage amount of moisture in large test pieces of timber, it is convenient to bore a hole into the timber and *carry out the test on the chips* thus produced, collecting them on a "watch glass" or "clock face" for the purpose.   Repeat the experiment on specimens obtained from wood recently felled and also from wood partly seasoned.

Experiment 85.   To show that hygroscopic substances attract moisture. Cut two small equal-sized pieces of rubber brick and soak one in a saturated solution of salt (see p. 177).   Then dry both specimens in the water oven and obtain their weight when dry.   Place the specimens in the open air, but protected from direct rain, and after a period of a week or a fortnight weigh them again.   Both will show an increase in weight due to hygroscopic moisture, but a greater amount will have been attracted to the brick containing the salt, showing that salt—as contained in sea sand—is from this point of view undesirable in building.   (See Problems XII, 10.)

Experiment 86.   To show the effect of variations of moisture on the shape of timber.   Obtain pieces of timber (sizes according to size of water oven available) with sections as shown at A, B, C, and D, fig. 166.   Cut from each piece three specimens not more than ½ inch "long" (measured along the grain). Of each set place one in water, another in the water oven and the third in air. After the lapse of at least an hour place each set of specimens together and note the results.

JOIST SECTIONS.

SECTIONS OF FLOOR BOARDS.

Fig. 166.   The effect of moisture on the shape of timber.

The relation between the variations in shape of timber and its structure will be dealt with more fully in the succeeding volume, but the student of Building Construction should here consider (*a*) the effect of the variations, as shown at A and B, on both "solid floor strutting" and on "herring bone strutting," and (*b*) the advantage to be obtained by using flooring boards with "standing grain" (annual rings almost vertical) as shown at D, as compared with the section shown at C.

PROBLEMS XII

1.   How would you proceed to show that only one constituent of the air assists combustion while the other does not?

2.   Calculate the volume of hydrogen to be burned in Experiment 80 to produce 1 gm. of water.   Take the density of hydrogen as 0·09 gm. per litre.

3. Describe the difference between an ordinary bat-wing burner and a bunsen burner. Which gives the best light and which the most heat for equal quantities of gas? Why does a Méker or similar burner give a higher temperature than either of the other two?

4. Mention two substances produced when we breathe or when coal or coal gas is burned. How would the presence of these substances be indicated in a badly ventilated room with painted walls?

5. How would you distinguish between oxygen, hydrogen, nitrogen and air?

6. How would you show (a) that carbon dioxide is heavier than air, and (b) that it is soluble in water?

7. How would you show that carbon dioxide and water are present in the air in a room?

8. (a) Compare the density of carbon dioxide with that of air, given that the former weighs 1·974 gms. per litre and the latter 1·293 gms. per litre. (b) Calculate the weight of carbon dioxide which may be added to the air in a room, the cubic capacity of which is 200 cubic metres, if the percentage volume of this gas may change from ·04 per cent. to ·06 per cent.

9. 8 litres of air were drawn through a series of drying tubes, which at the commencement of the experiment weighed 159·542 gms. and at its close weighed 159·581 gms. Calculate the absolute humidity of the air. (See p. 171.)

10. Two test pieces of rubber brick were treated as described in Experiment 85. The untreated piece weighed 220 gms. when dried and 222 gms. after exposure in a damp room for a week. The other piece after soaking in a salt solution and being dried weighed 235 gms., and 251 gms. after exposure in the same room. Calculate the percentage increase in weight in each case and explain the reason for the difference.

11. A piece of timber weighed 10·12 gms. before drying and 9·25 gms. after drying as described in Experiment 84. Calculate the percentage amount of moisture present in the original timber.

12. A crack in the upper part of a house, which is built on clay, is observed to open in summer and close again in winter. What is the probable cause of this movement and how might it have been prevented?

13. Stone containing iron often shows red discoloration on its exposed surfaces, how would you explain this?

14. Describe how you would ascertain the percentage moisture content of a piece of unseasoned timber.

Describe what would happen to timber constructions if timber is used in this condition. To what figure should the percentage moisture content be reduced before it is reasonably safe finally to frame up pieces of timber construction, such as a panelled door?

CHAPTER XIII

SOME PROPERTIES OF NATURAL WATERS

Natural Waters. So far in considering the properties of water we have dealt with the case of chemically pure water; we have seen it to be a colourless, tasteless and odourless liquid which boils at 100° C. and freezes at 0° C. Such water, however, has a remarkable power of dissolving other substances to form solutions and there are few substances which pure water cannot to some extent dissolve; hence it is not surprising that water is never found in a pure state in nature, since in its passage through the air as vapour and rain and through the ground as spring or river water, it is at all times in contact with substances which may pass into a state of solution in the water and render it less pure.

Gases in Water. In falling through the air rain comes into contact with oxygen, nitrogen, carbon dioxide and other gases, all of which may be expected to be dissolved in the water of the rain drops to whatever extent is possible for each gas (since they are present in the air as a *mixture* of gases and not as a gaseous compound, see p. 155). In passing through the ground, where gases are similarly present—particularly carbon dioxide, which in "ground air" may be present in a ratio about 250 times higher than in atmospheric air—these gases are still further dissolved. It is these dissolved gases which give a bright appearance to all natural waters and also to artificially prepared mineral waters, e.g. soda water, though it does not necessarily follow that the presence of all such gases is desirable. Pressure has a considerable effect upon the amount of gases dissolved in this way, the amount increasing with the increase of pressure. Thus when the stopper is removed from a bottle of soda water the pressure is reduced and the dissolved gas (carbon dioxide) rises rapidly to the surface.

Experiment 87. To compare distilled water and spring water for dissolved gases. Fill two small beakers with the waters to be compared and place them under a bell-jar standing on a greased plate (to make an air-tight joint), see fig. 167. Connect the jar to an air-pump and exhaust the air from the jar, thus *reducing the pressure*. Under this reduced pressure the dissolved gases will be seen to form as bubbles in the natural water, while in the distilled water (or recently boiled water) no such effect is noticed.

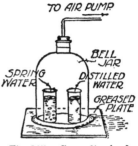

Fig. 167.   Gases dissolved in water.

We have already seen, by the evidence of the acid test (p. 170), that carbon dioxide may be driven off by boiling; the other gases present may also be driven off in this way. If spring water be heated in a flask fitted with a delivery tube the gases may be collected over a beehive shelf as already explained. Analysis of such gases shows that the carbon dioxide may form as much as one-quarter of the whole volume, while the oxygen and nitrogen are not present in the same proportions as in air (see p. 155).

It is to the dissolved gases in water that the corrosion of iron "water pipes" is due, hence it is necessary that they should be coated with some impervious and lasting substance to prevent this corrosion and the consequent discoloration of the water.

Advantage is taken of the presence of oxygen in water in some methods of treating sewage. The sewage to be treated is diluted with large quantities of fresh water, the oxygen of which oxidises the organic matter, converting it into carbon dioxide and water and thus rendering it harmless (there are other actions which we need not consider here). Another and later method is to force compressed air into the sewage so as to hasten the process of oxidation. Contaminated stream water may be rendered harmless by similarly absorbing oxygen from the air as it tumbles over rocks, etc.

Solids in Solution. When any substance, like salt or sugar, is placed in water it dissolves forming a "solution"; if more of the substance be added and the mixture stirred continually a point will be reached when no more of the substance can be dissolved, the surplus settling to the bottom. The clear liquid standing above the particles at the bottom of the vessel is a "saturated solution." The saturated solution may be separated from the undissolved particles by pouring the contents of the vessel carefully into a glass funnel in which has been placed a "filter paper"— a porous paper which allows the solution to pass through but not the solids. The "filtrate" may be caught in a dish below, and, if the liquid be slowly heated over a water bath, see fig. 177, the water is evaporated and "crystals" of the original substance are left behind.

The solubility of a substance is measured by the number of grams which 100 grams of water can dissolve at a stated temperature.

Experiment 88. To compare approximately the solubility of various substances. Place into separate test tubes, containing equal quantities of water, a gram each of salt, sugar, alum, powdered gypsum and chalk. Shake the tubes for some time and compare the residues after settlement.

This is only a very rough test but it will help the reader to realise the variations in solubility for the various substances.

If a soluble and an insoluble substance be mixed together, they may be separated once more by "dissolving out" the soluble substance. This is what occurs when sand, which is known to contain salt, is washed in running water so as to render it suitable for building purposes. (See Problems XIII, 5 and 6.)

The Effect of Impurities on the Solvent Powers of Water. In addition to the solvent powers of *pure water* it should be noted that some impurities add still further to these powers; this is particularly so with dissolved carbon dioxide. Pure water is not capable of dissolving limestone (calcium carbonate); when, however, the water is charged with carbon dioxide it has this power and the impurities dissolved by this means have most important effects upon the water from our point of view.

Experiment 89. To show the effect of dissolved carbon dioxide on the solvent powers of water. Prepare a solution of equal parts of lime water and distilled water, place some of this in a beaker and pass carbon dioxide through it as shown in fig. 168.

Lime water is a saturated solution of calcium hydrate (slaked lime) and in the presence of carbonic acid (formed as we have seen by the passage of carbon dioxide through the water, see p. 170) this calcium hydrate is converted into calcium carbonate ("limestone") *which is insoluble in water.*

After the gas has been passing through the lime water for some little time the presence of the insoluble carbonate is shown by the turbidity or milky appearance of the water. If left at this stage the solid would settle or be "precipitated" as a fine powder.

Fig. 168. Passing carbon dioxide through lime water.

On continuing to pass the gas through the liquid the milkiness will gradually pass away. The *excess of carbon dioxide* has given the water the power of dissolving the calcium carbonate. (Keep the liquid thus obtained for use in Experiment 93.)

The Hardness of Water. Water containing impurities which prevent it lathering freely with soap is known as a "hard water," as compared with a "soft water," which lathers freely. With a hard water much soap is wasted before a lather is formed, the waste soap forming a dirty insoluble curd on the surface of the water.   Hence, apart from other reasons, the use of hard water for domestic purposes is distinctly objectionable.

The hardness of water is due to the presence of salts of lime and magnesia which the water has dissolved, in its passage through the rocky strata in which these substances are present as limestone.   Before discussing methods by which the hardness may be reduced or removed we will explain briefly and in as simple a way as possible one of the methods usually adopted for measuring the **degrees of hardness** of various waters.

The method is briefly to prepare a solution of soap of standard strength (see any book on analytical chemistry) and ascertain how much of this is used up by samples of different waters before a "permanent lather" (lasting 3 minutes) is obtained on shaking the mixture in a bottle.

Experiment 90.   To illustrate the meaning of hardness and to compare various waters.   (Note.   For this preliminary experiment "standard soap solution" need not be used, but for it may be substituted a solution of Castile soap in diluted methylated spirits.)

Fill a burette with the soap solution just prepared and fix it in a stand as shown in fig. 169.   Into three or four clean stoppered bottles place *equal quantities*, say 50 or 60 gms., of the following waters: (a) distilled water, (b) rain water, (c) tap water, (d) a very hard water.   Take the reading of the burette and run the solution slowly into each sample of water, shaking occasionally to find when a permanent lather is obtained.   Set down the amounts used in each case, this will give a rough indication of the comparative hardness of the waters tested.

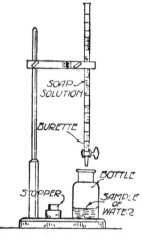

Fig. 169.   Testing the hardness of water.

Experiment 91.   To ascertain the degrees of hardness on "Clarke's scale" for the samples just treated.   (For this experiment standard soap solution must be used.)

Each bottle should be rinsed out with water and then dried before being used.   The procedure is the same, but exactly 70 c.cms. of each sample must be used.   *The degree of hardness on Clarke's scale will be found by subtracting 1 from the number of cu.cms. of soap solution necessary to produce a permanent lather.*

Temporary and Permanent Hardness.   We have seen how carbon dioxide may be driven off from water by boiling.   If a water, containing substances which have been dissolved *in virtue of the presence of the carbon dioxide,* be so treated the loss of the gas will result in the precipitation of these substances.

The removal of these substances from solution causes a reduction in hardness. That portion of the hardness which can be removed by boiling is called the "temporary hardness." The hardness remaining is known as the "permanent hardness" and is due to the presence of salts which can be dissolved by water without the aid of carbon dioxide. The permanent hardness may be partly removed by the use of washing soda (sodium carbonate), but it leaves the water unfit for drinking purposes.

It is the precipitation of insoluble bodies which causes the "fur" to form on the insides of pipes and boilers in hot water systems and in steam boilers, and the great expense involved in cleaning and the possible dangers associated with the gradual closing of the pipes are reasons why soft waters are preferable for domestic purposes.

A certain degree of hardness is, however, essential if lead piping is to be used in the water supply system. Very soft water containing dissolved gases of an acid nature on coming into contact with lead will form *an oxide of lead which is soluble* and which would eventually produce lead poisoning in those who drank the water. The use of moderately hard water results in the deposit of a protecting layer of lead carbonate on which the insoluble solids already mentioned are deposited, thus preventing further action.

About 5 to 8 degrees of hardness is considered a good average for general use.

Experiment 92. To distinguish between temporary and permanent hardness. Obtain the "total hardness" of a fairly hard water. Boil a portion of the water and allow it to cool. Ascertain the hardness of this portion now that the temporary hardness has been removed by boiling. This gives the permanent hardness. The temporary hardness is obtained by subtracting the permanent hardness from the "total hardness." Boil a further portion of the water and whilst it is still hot add a small quantity of a solution of washing soda (sodium carbonate), allow the liquid to cool and once more test for hardness.

Test of a fairly soft tap water.

Total Hardness ... ... = 7·4 degrees (Clarke's scale)
Permanent Hardness ... ... = 6·7 ,, ,, ,,
∴ Temporary ,, ... = 0·7 ,, ,, ,,
Hardness after the addition of washing soda = 1·1 ,, :, ,,

Experiment 93. To show that the addition of lime results in the removal of temporary hardness. This is the method adopted where water has to be softened on a large scale for trade purposes. Take the liquid used in Experiment 89, which is now really an artificially prepared hard water. Divide it into three portions. (*a*) Obtain the total hardness of one portion. (*b*) Boil the second portion and obtain the permanent hardness. (Note the return of the milky appearance due to the loss of the carbon dioxide and the consequent precipitation of the insoluble carbonates.)

(c) Add lime water slowly to the third portion until on shaking there is *a white precipitate*. Obtain the hardness of this treated water (after settlement) and note that the reduction is similar to that obtained in (b) by boiling.   The lime has taken up the excess of carbon dioxide in solution to form calcium carbonate, which is precipitated along with the other carbonates which are now no longer soluble.

Suspended Impurities in Water.   In addition to the soluble matters of which we have already spoken, both river and spring waters usually contain insoluble bodies in a fine state of division such as sand, clay, and vegetable and animal bodies.   These are usually removed by allowing the water to stand in large reservoirs, so that the larger bodies may have time to settle, and also by passing the water through filters, consisting usually of layers of sand, in which the action is partly *mechanical* (hence the term "mechanical filtration")—removing further suspended bodies, partly *chemical* — oxidising vegetable substances present, and partly *biological*, resulting in the removal of micro-organisms which would be harmful if present in drinking water.

PROBLEMS XIII

1. Explain why it is that natural waters are never pure. How may pure water be obtained?

2. Two bottles were filled with spring water into which was put some iron nails. Before corking the bottles up the water in one was boiled for some time. After a time the nails were noticed to rust in the bottle containing the unboiled water but not in the other. Explain this.

3. In what way does the "air" dissolved in water differ from atmospheric air? How does this go to prove that air is a mixture of gases?

4. In order to find the solubility of salt and alum a saturated solution of each was obtained some of which was, in each case, run into an evaporating dish, the water evaporated and the remaining substance weighed.

From the following experimental data obtained calculate (a) the solubility of salt, and (b) the solubility of alum.

	Salt	Alum
Weight of dish	32·54	32·54
„ „ and solution ...	39·83	38·92
„ „ and dry substance	34·80	33·35

5. To obtain the percentage amount of salt in a mixture of sand and salt the salt was dissolved out and the sand then dried and weighed. Calculate the percentage amount of salt present in the mixture from the following values:

Weight of mixture of salt and sand	= 7·10 gms.
„ filter paper	= 0·88 „
„ „ „ and dry sand	= 6·24 „

6.   You are given a mixture of sand, salt and chalk, explain how you would obtain (a) the percentage amount of salt, (b) get rid of the chalk and hence obtain the percentage amount of sand.

7.   Describe a simple experiment to show that the amount of gases dissolved in water is affected by the pressure.

8.   What gases would you expect to find dissolved in water obtained from peaty moors?   Would such a water be likely to be hard?

9.   Explain why such water as is described in the last question will, when passing through limestone districts, burrow below the ground and form the underground caverns often found in such districts.   Would this water be hard after passing through such a district?

10.   Explain what is meant by temporary, permanent and total hardness.

How may temporary hardness be removed (a) when the water is for domestic use, and (b) when it is only to be used for trade purposes?

11.   Describe the effect of hard and soft waters on lead and iron pipes. How may iron pipes be protected?

12.   Explain why "furring" in a hot water system is usually most pronounced at the point where the water enters the boiler and is rapidly raised in temperature.

13.   Water is said to be a powerful solvent. Explain this statement. Give at least three instances of the advantages and disadvantages of this characteristic of water in connection with the supply of water for domestic purposes.

14.   Describe the differences in the properties of water which is "permanently" hard and water which is only "temporarily" hard. State the nature of the impurities usually responsible for each condition and explain how they were probably introduced into the water.

15.   What is lime water? When carbon dioxide is passed through lime water for some time, the lime water first becomes milky in appearance and then clear again. How would you show that this is now a hard water? If this hard water be boiled it becomes milky again. Explain this, and say what effect the boiling has had upon the hardness.

CHAPTER XIV

THE PREPARATION AND USE OF LIME

Limestones. Lime is prepared from some variety of limestone. This is a rock which is found in great abundance all over the globe, its characteristic feature being that it consists in part, or almost entirely, of calcium carbonate. Whilst it is not our intention to discuss at this stage the formation and structural uses of this stone, it will be of interest to note that, generally, the stones may be classified under two heads according to their mode of formation as *chemically* or *organically* formed, that is they may have been formed by the precipitation of calcium carbonate held in solution by water (not the only mode of chemical formation), or they may consist largely of calcareous remains, such as the shells or skeletons of marine or fresh-water organisms.

Limestone, marble, iceland spar, calc spar, chalk, sea-shells, coral, and egg-shells may all be classed together as substances consisting largely of calcium carbonate. A strong acid has the power of uniting with the calcium oxide (lime) and releasing the carbon dioxide. This fact is utilised generally as a simple test for the presence of the *carbonate* and as a particular test for *distinguishing limestones* from other stones.

Experiment 94. To make a simple test for the presence of calcium carbonate in various substances. Obtain samples of the substances mentioned in the last paragraph, add a piece of old lime mortar, a piece of sandstone and a piece of granite. Fill up a burette with dilute hydrochloric acid, place each specimen in turn beneath the burette and allow a few drops of the acid to fall upon it. Brisk effervescence may be taken as an indication of the presence of calcium carbonate. No action will either indicate that none of the carbonate is present or that this particular test must be amplified to prove its presence. (Hot acid is necessary with magnesian limestone.)

That carbon dioxide is given off during this action will be shown in Experiment 96.

The Preparation of Lime. If the calcium carbonate is heated to a high temperature—"calcination"—the carbon dioxide is driven off and calcium oxide (lime) remains. This is the basis of the preparation of lime for use on buildings.

Experiment 95. To illustrate the calcination of limestone. Take about a gram of powdered marble and place it in a porcelain crucible (without the lid). Place the crucible in a crucible furnace, see fig. 170, heated by a Méker burner or one having an air blast attached. Heat thus for at least 30 minutes. Remove the crucible and its contents from the furnace and allow it to cool in a desiccator, see fig. 171. This is a piece of apparatus

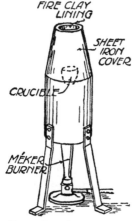

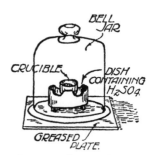

Fig. 170. The calcination of limestone in a crucible furnace.

Fig. 171. Lime cooling in a
desiccator.

designed to prevent the absorption of moisture from the air, the air in the desiccator being kept dry by the action of concentrated sulphuric acid contained in the large porcelain dish.

When cool weigh the dish and its contents and note the decrease in weight. (See Problems XIV, 1 and 2.)

Let a few drops of water fall on the lime, note the vigorous action which takes place, the heat generated and the increase in volume—compare with quicklime.

Test some of the slaked lime with some dilute hydrochloric acid—no effervescence—compare with the original marble.

Dip a piece of red litmus into the slaked lime and note that the paper turns blue, showing that the solution of the slaked lime (lime water) is "alkaline" (see p. 192).

Experiment 96. To show that carbon dioxide is lost during the calcination of marble. Fit up a piece of apparatus similar to that shown in fig. 151, but arranged so that a current of air from an aspirator or bellows may pass through the apparatus, see fig. 172. Place some powdered marble in the tube and strongly heat it, letting the resulting gas and air pass through some lime water. The resulting turbidity will prove the presence of carbon dioxide. (It is easy to show that the air alone from the aspirator would take a considerable time to cause the lime water to become turbid.)

The Slaking of Lime. The addition of water to lime is familiar to the builder as the "slaking of lime" and the product "slaked lime" (calcium hydrate) is used in the preparation of mortar and plaster. It is important that this slaking be thoroughly carried out, otherwise small particles of unslaked lime may remain and later cause the work to "blow," that is small pieces will

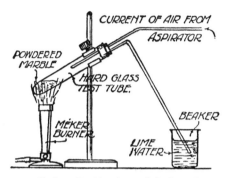

Fig. 172. Carbon dioxide given off during calcination.

burst away from or lift the face of the work owing to the expansion of the lime when it slakes. The same difficulty occurs when small pieces of limestone are embedded in the clay from which bricks are manufactured; during the burning of the bricks this is converted to quicklime, which slakes as soon as moisture reaches it.

Experiment 97. To show the increase in volume which takes place when lime slakes. Fill a small crucible brim-full with fresh lime and cover with water; see fig. 173. As soon as the lime begins to slake note the steady increase in volume. The final increase will be very considerable and will be quite apparent. It is difficult to measure the actual increase accurately, but it is about 150 to 200 per cent. with pure lime.

Fig. 173. The expansion of lime on slaking.

When fresh lime is left exposed to the air it slakes owing to the presence of moisture in the atmosphere and gradually falls into a powder. This is known as "air-slaking." (See Problems XIV, 9.)

We have spoken of the bad effects resulting from unslaked lime in mortar, plaster or bricks; the following simple experiment will illustrate this fact in a striking manner.

Experiment 98. To show the bursting force of slaking lime. Cut from some "rubber" bricks some pieces about $4'' \times 3'' \times 3''$. With an iron drill bore a $\frac{1}{2}''$ hole in one of the faces to a depth of about $2''$. Enlarge this inside with a small cold chisel and tightly pack the space thus formed with fresh lime, see fig. 174. Close the hole with a well-fitting cork and immerse the brick entirely in water as shown. These bricks are very porous and absorb water rapidly; after a short while the water reaches the lime and

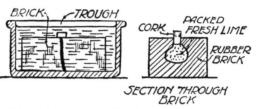

Fig. 174. A brick fractured by the expansion of slaking lime.

slaking commences, the expansion following results in the fracture of the brick. A similar method for blasting coal and stone was formerly used, "lime cartridges" being used in place of the more powerful explosives used at the present time.

The Setting of Lime Mortar. Lime mortar consists of a mixture of slaked lime and sand in the proportions of 1 to 3 parts of sand by bulk to 1 of slaked lime. Such a mixture, as we have seen in Chap. IV, is very porous and, upon its exposure to air, it loses its surplus water rapidly when the mixture is said to "set." A further action also takes place, termed the "hardening" of the mortar, which may go on for years; this is a chemical action which results from the absorption of carbon dioxide from the air—which can penetrate the mass because of its porosity—and the consequent reconversion of the hydrated lime to calcium carbonate and water. The presence of calcium carbonate in old mortar may be detected by the acid test as explained in Experiment 94.

The reader is warned that this is an extremely elementary explanation of the setting and hardening of lime mortar and probably refers only to mortars prepared from limestones which are almost pure calcium carbonate, these produce what are known as "fat limes." Limestones which are not pure, but which contain impurities in the form of silica (oxide of silicon) and alumina (oxide of aluminium), form on calcination a lime consisting of silicates and aluminates of lime in addition to free lime. Such limes have the power of hardening under water and hence are known as "hydraulic limes." This power varies with the amount of the aforementioned impurities present and this fact furnishes a convenient method for classifying these limes.

The setting of hydraulic limes and cements is not capable of simple explanation and is in fact a most complex chemical problem; more will be said concerning it in the succeeding volume; meanwhile it will be well if the reader does not conclude that the explanation given above of the setting of fat limes applies in this case.

The usual classification is as follows:

	Class	% of impurities	Power of setting under water
Non-hydraulic Lime	Fat lime	Less than 5	Not at all
Hydraulic Limes	Feebly hydraulic	5 to 12	Firm in 15 to 20 days
	Ordinarily hydraulic	12 to 20	Firm in 6 to 8 days
	Strongly hydraulic	20 to 30	Firm in 20 hours

Rate of Slaking. The amount of impurities present in a lime has considerable effect upon the rapidity of slaking, and the following experiment will illustrate how this fact may be utilised to classify limes roughly into groups very similar to those given above.

Experiment 99. To classify limes according to their rate of slaking. To give satisfactory results freshly burnt samples should be used, hence it is better to prepare them in the laboratory. This may be done by heating pieces of the original limestones to a red heat for several hours in a muffle furnace. If a large furnace is not available small pieces sufficient for this experiment may be prepared in the crucible furnace shown in fig. 170.

Take pieces of marble, mountain limestone, magnesian limestone, and Lias limestone and convert them to lime as explained above. Place approximately equal-sized pieces in evaporating dishes. Place these dishes on burette stands and by means of the burettes allow water to drop on the limes as fast as it is absorbed.

Note carefully the *time* from the addition of the water until *the first signs of slaking* appear. In the case of the purer limes slaking will commence almost as soon as the water is added. With the impure limes the action is long in starting and the signs of chemical action less easy to detect. In all cases the best guide is the *cracking* of the lime.

PROBLEMS XIV

(Refer also to Problems X, 6 and 8.)

1. If the loss of weight on calcination for a particular limestone be 40 per cent. calculate the amount of lime which can be obtained from 1 ton of this limestone.

2. For pure calcium carbonate the loss on calcination is 44 per cent. With some limestones the loss is less than this. Explain this fact simply.

3. Using the values obtained in Problems X, 6, calculate the amount (by weight) of slaked lime which would be got from 1 cwt. of the lime.

4. If dilute hydrochloric acid is poured on slaked lime there is no effervescence and the hydrate is dissolved. When mortar made from this hydrated lime has been allowed to set and harden for some months there will be effervescence on the addition of the acid. Explain this.

5. If you know that when dilute hydrochloric acid is poured over old lime mortar all the lime present is dissolved, how would you proceed to test an old lime mortar in order to ascertain approximately the amount of sand originally used?

6. In an experiment such as is mentioned in question 5 the following values were obtained:

Weight of mortar = 10·24 gms.

Weight of residue, after dissolving the mortar in dilute acid and drying the residue = 6·9 gms.

Calculate the approximate proportions of lime to sand as used in the mortar.

7. Describe the object of adding sand to mortar and plaster.

8. A plastered wall surface shows numerous small blisters some months after it has been finished.   Explain what is the probable cause.

9. A jar is *completely filled* with fresh lime and a glass plate laid loosely over it.   After a week or so the lime rises in the jar and lifts the plate up. Explain what has taken place.

10. What effect would you expect a fire to have on a concrete floor, the concrete of which has been made with a limestone aggregate?   Is the action chemical or physical?

11. How would you distinguish between a limestone and a sandstone? If these stones were used in a manufacturing town where traces of *acid gases* are known to be in the air, which would you expect to weather best and why? (Refer to Experiment 94.)

12. How would you proceed to convert a small piece of limestone into lime in the building laboratory?

Describe the properties of lime, particularly those which make it of use in building.

13. Describe what takes place when lime is slaked. What happens if small pieces of unslaked lime are enclosed near the surfaces of bricks or of plastering?

Limes are commonly classified according to their purity. Briefly describe this classification and mention any simple experiment which would enable you roughly to grade some samples of lime according to purity.

14. When limestone is burned quicklime is produced. Before being used in mortar the quicklime is slaked. On being mixed with sand to form mortar, the mortar will set on exposure to air.

Describe the characteristics of the materials formed at each of the stages mentioned and also explain the nature of the chemical actions which take place.

CHAPTER XV

ATOMS AND MOLECULES. CHEMICAL NOTATION. CHEMICAL CALCULATIONS

Atoms. The idea that matter is made up of extremely small particles called *atoms* (meaning "indivisible") has been held for a very long time. While modern scientific investigations have shown that it is wrong to think of atoms as hard little balls of matter, yet for all practical purposes it is still reasonably correct, and of course rather helpful, to think of atoms as very minute packets or particles of matter. It is probable that chemical action takes place only between these very small particles.

As developed by Dalton (*c.* 1800), and later by others, modern atomic theory may be said to lay it down that *an atom is the smallest particle of an element which can take part in chemical change,* which of course is another way of saying that the atom is the *unit* of chemical change, this unit never being divided into fractional parts. On this simple but striking conception a great deal of chemical theory is built up.

We know that *the atoms of an element are identical in every respect.* For example each atom in an element has the same weight.

We also know that *the atoms of different elements have different characteristics.* In particular the atoms of different elements have different weights.

Atomic weights. The actual weight of an atom is so extremely small that, even if it is stated numerically, it is almost impossible for anyone to grasp its meaning in any practical sense. The *relative weights* of the atoms of different elements are, however, of very great theoretical and practical importance in the subject of chemistry and these, fortunately, can be stated in a form which is simple and easy to grasp. For this purpose a series of figures have been worked out which give the relative weights of the elements. These are known as the *atomic weights* and their approximate values (given only to the nearest half integer) are given in the accompanying table for a number of the commoner elements.

Common elements and their approximate atomic weights*

Element	Symbol	Atomic weight (approx.)
Aluminium†	Al	27
Antimony†	Sb	120
Calcium†	Ca	40
Carbon	C	12
Chlorine	Cl	35·5
Copper†	Cu	63·5
Gold†	Au	197
Hydrogen	H	1
Iron†	Fe	56
Lead†	Pb	207
Magnesium†	Mg	24
Mercury†	Hg	200
Nitrogen	N	14
Oxygen	O	16
Phosphorus	P	31
Potassium†	K	39
Silicon	Si	28
Silver†	Ag	108
Sodium†	Na	23
Sulphur	S	32
Tin†	Sn	119
Zinc†	Zn	65·5

* The approximate values greatly simplify the necessary calculations, while they are also sufficiently accurate for all practical purposes.

† These elements are usually classed as *Metals* (see Chap. XVI). At normal temperatures they are all solids except mercury.

It will be seen from the table that *the approximate atomic weight of hydrogen is* 1. Since hydrogen is the lightest known element it will be seen how convenient it is to use its atomic weight as unity in considering the relative or atomic weights of the elements. (Compare with this arrangement that of using the density of water as 1 in speaking of the relative densities of substances. See Chap. I.)

We may thus say that *the atomic weight of an element is the number of times an atom of that element is heavier than hydrogen.*

Thus the atomic weight of oxygen being 16, we can say that an atom of oxygen is 16 times the weight of an atom of hydrogen. Similarly an atom of lead, which is nearly the heaviest atom among the metals, is seen to be 207 times as heavy as the hydrogen atom.

Chemical symbols. It is common practice in chemistry to write down a *symbol* instead of the full name of an element. The symbol used is usually the first or the first and one other letter of the common or Latin name of the element. Thus "C" is the symbol for the element carbon, "Fe" the symbol for iron (*ferrum*), "Pb" the symbol for lead (*plumbum*), and so on. The table gives the symbols for the elements included in the list.

It is important to note, however, that these symbols are something more than a mere shorthand for the chemical names of the elements. Thus the symbol of an element is also taken to represent one atom of that element with its associated atomic weight. Then H will stand for one atom of hydrogen, of an atomic weight of 1. Similarly Cl will stand for one atom of chlorine, with an atomic weight of 35·5.

In addition the symbols may also be used to represent so many *parts by weight* of the element named. Thus H may stand for 1 part by weight of hydrogen, while Cl may stand for 35·5 parts by weight of chlorine. In these cases the weights may be in any convenient unit—pound, gramme, etc.—provided the same unit is used throughout a calculation.

Molecules. When two or more atoms of the same or different elements combine chemically to form a small particle of some substance, then we speak of these particles as *molecules*. The molecule of a substance consists really of a group of atoms which is capable of existing in a free state. It is in fact important to remember that atoms do not normally exist in a free state as individuals, but only in these groups which we call molecules. This is true even of the elements. Hydrogen and oxygen for instance are normally made up of pairs of atoms, hence the molecules of these substances are represented by the formulae H_2 and O_2 respectively.

Hence we may define the *molecule as the smallest particle of matter which can exist in a free state.*

Chemical formulae. The use of the term "symbol" is restricted to the atoms of the elements. The combination of symbols necessary to represent the composition of a molecule of a substance is called its *chemical formula*.

Thus, if an atom of hydrogen (H) combines with an atom of chlorine (Cl) to form hydrochloric acid, then a *molecule* of this latter substance is represented by the *chemical formula* HCl. Again water is known to contain 2 atoms of hydrogen (H) to 1 atom of oxygen (O), so that a molecule of water may be represented by the chemical formula H_2O. The small number 2, given after and just below the letter H, indicates that 2 atoms of hydrogen are included in the molecule of water.

If we wish to indicate that several molecules of a substance are to be taken then this is done by placing the required number in front of the formula for the substance. Thus $10H_2O$ represents 10 molecules of water, each containing 2 parts (1×2) by weight of hydrogen to 16 parts (16×1) by weight of oxygen.

The composition of a compound substance by weight. The principles already laid down enable us to calculate the proportions, by weight, of the different elements which may be present in a chemical compound. Thus we may consider the substance sulphuric acid, the formula for which is H_2SO_4. From this formula we see that each molecule of sulphuric acid contains two atoms of hydrogen, one atom of sulphur and four atoms of oxygen. Making use of the table of atomic weights, and multiplying the atomic weight in each case by the number of atoms we obtain the following results:—

Element		Atomic wt.		No of atoms		Totals
Hydrogen	=	1	×	2	=	2
Sulphur	=	32	×	1	=	32
Oxygen	=	16	×	4	=	64
			Total parts by weight		=	98

Thus we see that in 98 parts by weight of sulphuric acid we have 2 parts by weight of hydrogen, 32 parts by weight of sulphur and 64 parts by weight of oxygen.

The figure 98 is known as the *molecular weight* (really the sum of the atomic weights included in the molecule) of sulphuric acid.

As has already been stated these "parts" may be expressed in any unit of weight provided the same unit is used throughout. Thus we may say, that in 98 lb. of sulphuric acid there are 2 lb. of hydrogen, 32 lb. of sulphur and 64 lb. of oxygen. The composition of other substances by weight may be similarly calculated. (See Problems XV.)

Chemical equations. As was stated in Chap. x, in all cases where chemical action takes place, matter is neither created nor destroyed. In addition, in this chapter we have seen that chemical action takes place between whole atoms, so that molecules of the substances used in or resulting from the action can never be shown with fractions of atoms in its composition. Thus it is clear that, in order to conform to the law of the indestructibility of matter and the requirement that action only takes place between whole atoms, the same atoms must be present in the resulting substances as were present in the original substances wherever chemical action takes place. We are thus able to write down, in the form of an equation, a short statement describing the complete action.

This is known as a *chemical equation*. On the left-hand side appear the formulae for the original substances, while on the right-hand side appear the formulae for the resulting substances.

Thus, in Exper. 96, where limestone, or calcium carbonate ($CaCO_3$), was decomposed by the application of heat to produce lime, or calcium oxide (CaO), and carbon dioxide (CO_2), this could be written in the form of a chemical equation as:

$$CaCO_3 \quad = \quad CaO \quad + \quad CO_2$$
(limestone)   (calcium oxide)   (carbon dioxide)

It will be readily seen that the same elements and the same number of atoms of each element are present on each side of the equation, thus satisfying the conditions stated above.

Chemical calculations. We can now go a stage further and, by means of the method described above for calculating the composition of a compound substance by weight, we can calculate the weights of the substances taking part in this action. Using the table of atomic weights the calculations may be set out as follows:

(*a*) *Left-hand side of equation*:

There are 40 parts by weight of Ca.
There are 12 parts by weight of C.
There are (3×16) or 48 parts by weight of O.

∴ There are 100 parts by weight of $CaCO_3$.

(*b*) *Right-hand side of equation*:

(i)   There are 40 parts by weight of Ca.
There are 16 parts by weight of O.

∴ There are 56 parts by weight of CaO.

(ii)   There are 12 parts by weight of C.
There are (16×2) or 32 parts by weight of O.

∴ There are 44 parts by weight of CO_2.

We may therefore say that 100 parts by weight of limestone or calcium carbonate on being heated change to 56 parts by weight of lime and 44 parts by weight of carbon dioxide. As has already been stated any unit of weight may be used. Hence we may say that 100 lb. of limestone will produce 56 lb. of lime.

Or 100 tons of limestone will produce 56 tons of lime.

Or 1 ton of limestone will produce $\frac{56}{100}$, or 0·56 ton, or 1254 lb. of lime.

It will be remembered that in Exper. 96 the *carbon dioxide* was given off in the form of a gas. Although it is not possible to include here even an elementary explanation of the process of reasoning underlying the following statement, it is interesting to note that the volume of this gas could have been calculated by using the statement:

The molecular weight of a gas, when given in grammes, occupies 22·4 litres at normal temperature and pressure.

The phrase "normal temperature and pressure" is usually abbreviated to "N.T.P." and represents a temperature of 0° C. and an atmospheric pressure of 760 mm. of mercury. (See Problems XV.)

The construction of chemical equations and formulae. In setting out the equations and in making these calculations it is necessary to remember:

(1) that the atomic weight of an element is a constant quantity;

(2) that the composition of any chemical substance never varies, the same elements being present in the same proportions every time;

(3) that a chemical equation only has meaning in association with the chemical action which it is intended to represent;

(4) that there must be the same number of atoms of each element on each side of the equation, from which it follows that the same weight of matter must be represented on each side of the equation.

The above conditions should be sufficient to enable the elementary student to construct chemical equations in all cases where he is dealing with familiar substances, of which the chemical formulae are well known. Outside these limits the correct construction of chemical equations and formulae demands knowledge which is outside the scope of this book, and for which the reader should consult books on chemistry which give a more extended treatment.

The treatment given in this chapter, however, should have served to make clearer to the reader the great practical significance of the principal laws of chemical action, which have been referred to from time to time. First, *the law of the indestructibility of matter,* which states that matter cannot be created or destroyed. Second, *the law of constant proportion or of constant composition,* which states that the same compound always consists of the same elements combined in exactly the same proportions. Another law is *the law of multiple proportions* and yet another *the law of reciprocal proportions.* These latter laws need not concern us here and their explanation is in any case beyond the scope of this book. It may be said briefly, however, that they are really dependent upon the fundamental idea that, since chemical combination and decomposition are always in terms of whole atoms, it should be possible to express, in relatively simple numerical terms, the relations between the compositions of the substances taking part in the action.

Temperature changes during chemical action. As was noted in Chap. x temperature changes are always observable during chemical action.   Thus when coal is burnt or lime is slaked heat is given out. On the other hand, to produce lime from limestone or oxygen from red oxide of mercury (see Exper. 74), heat has to be supplied in order to start and maintain the action.

The chief significance of these temperature changes during chemical action is that they indicate that an interchange of energy is going on.   Thus, if the temperature rises during the action this indicates that energy is being dissipated in the form of heat, while if the temperature falls, or, what is the same thing, heat has to be supplied, then energy in the form of heat is being absorbed.

Thus the resulting substances in any chemical action may have a greater or a smaller store of heat energy than had the original substances; e.g. coal ash has little or no heating capacity as compared with the original coal.   From the point of view of energy therefore the chemical equation is not strictly speaking an equation. It can in fact only be accepted as such so long as it is understood that it takes no account of energy changes.

In building, many chemical actions take place over a long period of time, e.g. the setting of lime mortar, and the temperature changes are therefore too small to be noticeable.   In other cases, as for example in quick-setting cements, the temperature changes are easily detected.   In the latter cases, where for example large masses of concrete are being laid, it is most important that the design of the structure and the conditions under which the concrete is laid should be such as will allow of the dissipation of the heat generated so as not to cause permanent harm to the concrete.   A usual method is to avoid laying large masses of concrete at one time.   Another is to keep the concrete moist and cool, while it sets and attains the first stages of hardening, by the use of coverings which exclude the air and sun and which can be kept moist by periodical wettings.

PROBLEMS XV

1. Explain the terms atom, molecule, mixture and compound.

2. Classify the following substances as elements or compounds, giving the chemical symbol and formula in each case: iron (chemically pure), lead, calcium, lime, carbon, water.

3. Calculate the proportions by weight of the elements in the following compounds: lime, calcium sulphate ($CaSO_4$), chloride of lime ($CaOCl_2$), red lead (Pb_3O_4), silica (SiO_2), salt ($NaCl$).

4. Using the values given in this chapter calculate the volume of gas given off in Exper. 95 if the marble has lost 0·5 gram in weight after heating.

5. Assuming that the calcium carbonate used in Exper. 95 has lost the whole of the gas (CO_2), represented by the loss in weight of 0·5 gram given in Problem 4, calculate the original weight of the carbonate.

6. Construct an equation to show the formation of water from hydrogen and oxygen and indicate on each side of the equation the amount of each element and substance by weight.

7. Given that hydrochloric acid (HCl) acts on calcium carbonate ($CaCO_3$) to produce calcium chloride ($CaCl_2$), carbon dioxide (CO_2), and water (H_2O), construct a chemical equation showing the reactions. Calculate the parts by weight of the substances on each side of the equation.

8. Calculate the weight of lime which may be obtained from 10 tons of pure limestone. Give the chemical equation showing the action taking place.

CHAPTER XVI

METALS AND NON-METALS. ACIDS AND ALKALIES. EFFLORESCENCE. PLASTERS. WEATHERING

Metals and Non-Metals. As we have already stated, all known *simple* substances are contained in a list of about 90 elements. From the chemical point of view it is possible to show that these elements may be arranged in definite groups according to their chemical and physical properties. It is not, however, our intention to enter here into the investigation of such groupings, but there is at least one broad classification of the elements with which we ought to be acquainted. In referring to such substances as iron, lead and copper we speak of them as "metals." Certain of the elements may be grouped as metals and, as it happens, the *physical characteristics* of this particular group of elements are more or less such as we popularly associate with the term "metal":—hardness, heaviness, opacity to light, metallic lustre (when in the lump) and ability to conduct heat and electricity.

All elements which are not metals are classed generally as "non-metals," and examples of these with which we are already acquainted are sulphur, carbon, hydrogen, oxygen and nitrogen. Speaking broadly the non-metallic elements are softer, lighter, more transparent and less able to conduct heat or electricity than the metals, and it is interesting to note that three of the non-metallic elements we have mentioned above are gases at ordinary temperatures, while of the common metals all are solids under the same conditions except mercury.

It is necessary to point out, however, that this is a classification which, as regards physical properties alone, must not be interpreted too rigidly, since there are elements which occupy an intermediate position between metals and non-metals, so far as physical properties are concerned, and which in this sense are difficult to classify.

There is, however, a distinction of a chemical character which, with a few exceptions, makes the classification of the elements into metals and non-metals much more definite. This distinction depends upon the properties possessed by the oxides of the elements and with these we shall now proceed to deal.

Properties of the Oxides. With a few exceptions all the elements may be made to combine with oxygen to form oxides. Some of these oxides are difficult to obtain and cannot be produced by *direct* combination. With several of the commoner elements, however, the oxide may be obtained directly by burning the element in an atmosphere of oxygen and this furnishes us with a convenient method for studying the better known oxides.

Experiment 100. To illustrate the combustion of some elements in oxygen. Obtain a number of deflagrating jars similar to that shown in fig. 175 and in the manner already described (see Experiment 75) fill them all with oxygen and cover with a greased plate. Leave a little water in each jar.

(*a*) Into a deflagrating spoon place a piece of sulphur. Heat the spoon until the sulphur begins to burn, then plunge it quickly into one of the jars of oxygen. The burning will continue much more quickly and with greater brilliance than in air. When the burning has ceased run into the water at the bottom of the jar some "neutral litmus," by means of a pipette, replace the cover and shake the jar and its contents. The liquid will *redden.*

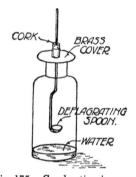

Fig. 175. Combustion in oxygen.

(*b*) Repeat the experiment with a piece of charcoal (carbon) and note that once more the liquid *reddens* but only faintly. Instead of water run into another jar of oxygen some lime water and after burning a piece of charcoal in the gas note that on shaking the jar and its contents the lime water becomes turbid and milky. This latter test shows that carbon dioxide has been produced by combination between the carbon and the oxygen (see p. 167).

(*c*) Repeat the experiment with iron, which may be used in the form of fine wire and ignited by fastening a small piece of sulphur to the end of it, lighting this before lowering the wire into the jar of oxygen. The wire will burn with great brilliance, producing dark brownish-coloured globules which will not affect the litmus solution.

(*d*) Repeat the experiment with **magnesium** ribbon and—if possible—**calcium** (wire or ribbon) and note that in these cases the litmus turns *blue.*

Below we summarise the results of these experiments and we may here state that one of the properties of "acid" liquids is to give a red colour to litmus (a vegetable dye prepared from lichens), while "alkaline" liquids restore the blue colour to reddened litmus.

Combustion of some Elements in Oxygen

Classifi-cation	Element	Compound formed	Effect of solution of oxide on neutral litmus	Classification of solution of oxide
Non-metals	Sulphur	A colourless gas with pungent smell, soluble in water—sulphur di-oxide (SO_2)	Reddened neu-tral litmus	**Acid**
	Carbon	A colourless gas, soluble in water, turns lime water milky—carbon dioxide (CO_2)	Gave a reddish tinge to neu-tral litmus	
Metals	Calcium	A white solid, slightly soluble in water—cal-cium oxide, "lime" (CaO)	Turned neutral litmus blue	**Alkaline**
	Mag-nesium	A white solid, slightly soluble in water—magnesia, magnesium oxide (MgO)	Turned neutral litmus blue	
	Iron	Brownish solid, insol-uble in water—"black scale" or magnetic oxide of iron ($Fe_3O)_4$	No effect on lit-mus since not soluble	Insoluble in water, neu-tral

So far as our experiment has gone we see that *non-metallic oxides* which are soluble in water give *acids*.

On the other hand those *metallic oxides* which are soluble in water give *alkaline solutions*.

Properties of Acids. While it is important to note that not all acids are formed from non-metallic oxides in the manner described above, e.g. hydrochloric acid (HCl) contains no oxygen, all acids possess properties which mark them off from other liquids and particularly from alkaline solutions.

Speaking broadly the properties of acids are:

(*a*) when diluted they have a sour taste and turn blue litmus to red;

(*b*) they dissolve or corrode certain metals, with the liberation of a gas (usually hydrogen) or gases, leaving behind a salt (see below and also p. 159, "killed spirits").

(*c*) they dissolve or act upon such substances as limestone, liberating, in this case, carbon dioxide (see Exper. 82).

Well-known examples of acids are sulphuric acid, or "oil of vitriol" (H_2SO_4), hydrochloric acid, or "spirits of salts" (HCl), and nitric acid, or aqua fortis (HNO_3).

Bases and Alkalies. Bases are the compounds formed when a metal unites with oxygen to form a metallic oxide, such that it will react with an acid to form a salt with water. *Those bases which are soluble are known as "alkalies,"* and their solutions (a) turn red litmus blue, (b) are soft and soapy to the touch and (c) destroy or neutralise acids. The solutions mentioned are formed really by the alkalies uniting with the water (e.g. lime) to form hydrates (or hydroxides) *which are themselves soluble.*

Experiment 101. To show the neutralisation of an acid and the production of a salt. Put into an evaporating dish some sodium hydroxide and add a few drops of blue litmus solution (to act as an "indicator"). Add dilute hydrochloric acid slowly from a burette, see fig. 176, until the colour of the liquid in the dish just turns to a faint pink. If this has been done carefully the acid has now been neutralised by the alkaline solution and if the water present be evaporated a "salt" will be left.

Place the dish and its contents on a water bath, see fig. 177, and evaporate the water slowly. A white solid of fine crystals will be obtained—sodium chloride or common salt.

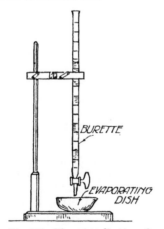

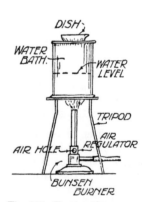

Fig. 176. The neutralisation of an acid.   Fig. 177. Evaporation over a water bath.

Crystallisation. The formation of crystals is an action of considerable importance in the manufacture or in the formation of certain building materials, and in the actions which result from what we call weathering or exposure to atmospheric influences. Thus, for example, the granites and the marbles are stones largely crystalline in their make-up.

As we have seen, it is not difficult to form crystals experimentally. Additional and interesting examples which may be mentioned are the crystals formed from hot saturated solutions of washing soda, or sodium carbonate, and of alum (see "Solids in Solution," Chap. XIII, for outline of experimental method).

The shapes and particularly the angles between the flat surfaces of freely formed crystals are characteristic of the different substances and afford one means of identification. Thus naturally formed rock salt (of which a sample should be available) will show surfaces at right angles to each other.

Water of Crystallisation. Newly formed crystals of washing soda will be clear, like ice. If, however, they be exposed to the air for some time a white powder will form on the angles and surfaces. If they then be heated the crystals will fall into a shapeless mass of white powder.

Similarly the blue cystals of copper sulphate when heated will disintegrate into a mass of white powder (anhydrous copper sulphate). If water be added to this powder it will again turn blue. (See Exper. 30, where anhydrous copper sulphate was used as an indicator of the presence of moisture.)

The above actions arise out of the fact that, in the formation of crystals in the manner described, a certain amount of water may be taken up in the crystal which is not "held" strongly by the crystal. This is known as the "water of crystallisation" and, as we have seen, it is often readily separated from the crystal by exposure to air, by heat, or by a combination of both.

Efflorescence. Those substances which part so readily with some of the water of crystallisation that they do so merely on exposure to air are said to be *efflorescent*.

Deliquescence. Some substances, which in their crystalline form have been deprived of their water of crystallisation, show, on the other hand, such a tendency to re-absorb the moisture that in many cases enough moisture will be attracted from the air to form a solution of the substance. Such substances are said to be *deliquescent*. Thus in describing "how to dry a gas" (see Chap. XII), it was explained that the gas could be passed over calcium chloride $(CaCl_2)$ to absorb the moisture. Common salt usually contains traces of magnesium chloride $(MgCl_2)$ which, if left exposed in a damp atmosphere, will often reduce the salt to a watery mess. It is for this reason mainly that sand from the sea shore is considered unsuitable for use in plaster, mortar or concrete, unless it has been exposed on the shore for long periods, so that the salt has been largely washed out by the rain.

Efflorescence in Buildings. This term is also applied commonly to the formation of a whitish powder on the surface of brick and stone buildings (sometimes also called "whitewash"). The action usually takes place in porous walling materials. In these, water, from rain and moisture from the air, is constantly being absorbed and then given up in evaporation, with changes in the humidity of the air (see Chap. XII). In some cases, due to defective damp-proof courses or faulty construction, an excessive amount of moisture finds its way into the body of the wall. This moisture will tend to escape from all exposed surfaces.

If then soluble substances exist in the pores of the material, these are constantly being dissolved and brought to the exposed surfaces of the material by these moisture movements. There, as already explained, the substances will crystallise and "efflorescence" will appear.

The substances usually causing this effect include the sulphates of calcium, sodium, potassium and magnesium, which are all more or less soluble in water. The formation of these salts may arise from the composition of a stone, from the manufacturing processes of a brick or from reactions taking place in weathering. Thus if traces of sulphuric acid be present (see below), this may act upon any free lime (calcium oxide) which may be present, either in the mortar or in the bricks, or even in the clay during the manufacturing processes of the brick, to form a salt. The salt in this case is calcium sulphate. This is slightly soluble in water and may thus give rise to efflorescence.

Efflorescence is frequently seen on new buildings, and may continue until the salts near the surface are gradually washed out. The process may be hastened by periodic washing with clean water. Efflorescence is also frequently seen during the spring months, when the greater amount of moisture absorbed during the more humid months is being dried out.

Excessive and continued efflorescence in plinths and parapets may usually be taken as an indication of defective damp proofing or other forms of defective construction. Steps should in these cases be taken to get to the root of the trouble.

Efflorescence in buildings is always unsightly. It is usually relatively harmless, but if the crystals tend to form just below the outer surface of the material they may in time force off the outer skin of the material and greatly hasten the normal processes of decay.

Plasters. The basis of nearly all building materials grouped under the term "plaster" is the mineral *gypsum*. This will be familiar to many as the opaque whitish stone used in rock gardens and, in more refined forms, as alabaster. It consists of hydrated calcium sulphate ($CaSO_4.2H_2O$). As this formula indicates each molecule of calcium sulphate ($CaSO_4$) has two molecules of water. These form the water of crystallisation to which reference has been made above.

The gypsum is heated to about 120° C. and this causes some of the water of crystallisation to be driven off in the form of steam, hence the term "boiling," which is frequently applied to this process. (The process may easily be conducted experimentally in the laboratory.) The whitish powder left is mainly a hemihydrate of calcium sulphate ($2CaSO_4.H_2O$). A simple calculation will show that this only has one-third of the water of crystallisation of the hydrate.

Because of the large quantities manufactured from gypsum deposits near Paris, this substance has come to be known as plaster of Paris, though it is also sold under other names. When mixed with water the hemihydrate has the property of setting into a solid mass in from 5 to 10 minutes. In this form it has taken up a certain amount of moisture and has practically reverted to the original hydrate. In setting, the hemihydrate expands slightly.

Thus it is excellent for all casting, since it leaves the mould with sharp clear impressions.

Plaster of Paris is too quick-setting for ordinary plaster work. *Gypsum wall plasters* are, however, manufactured from it by adding some substance which retards the setting. "Retarders" may be added during the manufacture, producing plasters which can be grouped as "retarded hemihydrates." On the other hand an ordinary hemihydrate plaster may be used and a retarder, such as glue or gelatine, may be added to the mixing water. (The effect can be readily demonstrated in the laboratory.)

If the heating of the gypsum is carried further (above 200° C.) then an anhydrous calcium sulphate ($CaSO_4$) is formed. A mineral known as *anhydrite*, with the same formula, is found in a natural state and quarried.

The anhydrous calcium sulphate is known as a "hard-burnt plaster." In this form the plaster is very slow setting but attains greater hardness than the gypsum wall plasters. It forms the basis of all *gypsum cements*. In order to reduce the setting time, "accelerators" such as alum, lime or salt are therefore added, usually during manufacture. These plasters are then known as "accelerated anhydrous plasters." They are sold under various trade names.

The Chemical Aspects of Weathering. The weathering of building materials give rise to scientific problems of great complexity, especially in those cases where the effects are extremely slow and the action is spread out over a great number of years. It is possible, however, to acquire, without much difficulty, a useful understanding of the more common weathering actions which take place. In this a knowledge of the chemical actions and combinations explained in this chapter is of great practical value.

In the first place each of the common metals, copper, iron, lead and zinc, will unite with the oxygen of the air to form an oxide, if fresh surfaces of the metals are exposed. As we have seen, some of these oxides may be protective as in lead and copper, but in other cases the oxidation, or corrosion as it is commonly called, may continue until the metal is destroyed. In the latter cases various protective materials, usually in the form of paints, are applied to protect the surfaces from oxidation. Some of the metallic oxides are themselves valuable in the manufacture of paints, such as lead litharge, red lead and zinc white.

Other oxides and bases are found widely distributed in nature. Some are to be found in all naturally-formed building materials such as stones, slates, clays, limes and sands. Of the acid-forming oxides we may mention silica (SiO_2), alumina (Al_2O_3), carbon dioxide (CO_2) and sulphur trioxide (SO_3). And of the bases lime (CaO), magnesia (MgO), potash (K_2O) and soda (Na_2O). All these are usually found in combination as carbonates, silicates or sulphates.

Considering the great range of conditions to which buildings must be submitted after erection—in their contact with the earths on which they stand, in their exposure to the atmosphere and the weather, and in their liability to contact with all manner of materials in use—it is not surprising to find that all sorts of chemical actions are set up. All these we usually group broadly under the term "weathering." A few of the actions are such as to lend themselves to the simple treatment possible at this stage of our study.

As we saw in Exper. 100, when sulphur is burned in oxygen, sulphur dioxide (SO_2) is formed. This combines readily with water to form sulphurous acid (H_2SO_3). Further exposure to light and air aids the absorption of more oxygen, producing sulphuric acid (H_2SO_4).

Likewise, when carbon is burned in oxygen, carbon dioxide (CO_2) is formed and this combines with water to form a weak acid, carbonic acid (H_2CO_3). (See also Exper. 83.)

Now both sulphur dioxide and carbon dioxide are produced when coal is burned. In towns, therefore, where much coal is burned, these gases are given off in considerable quantities. Combining with the moisture in the air acids are formed as described above. If present in sufficient concentration these acids will attack all exposed metals, as already described, hastening corrosion and other actions. They may also assist in the disintegration of stonework (see Exper. 94). By attacking free lime which may be present in mortar, concrete or bricks. In this way the sulphuric acid may help to form calcium sulphate, giving rise to efflorescence and possibly to rapid deterioration of the surfaces of the building as already explained.

All these actions are seen to be dependent upon the presence of moisture. If therefore, by reason of the accumulation of soot and grime, and by faulty construction, there are places where the water may lodge and the normal action of evaporation be delayed, these actions are likely to take place in a concentrated form and serious damage to result. It is therefore seen to be important that the design and construction of the exposed surfaces of a building should be such as to throw off readily all rain or moisture which may condense upon them. In this way not only will the accumulation of dirt and grime in certain places be avoided, but the natural cleansing effect of the rain will be utilised to its fullest extent. This latter effect may of course be greatly assisted by the periodic washing of the faces of the building with clean water. By such means not only may the fresh appearance of the building be maintained, but the effects of weathering may be reduced and the life of the building extended.

PROBLEMS XVI

1. How would you distinguish between the metals and non-metals? Give a list of three elements in each group.

2. Name four oxides to be found in building materials. Say whether they are acidic or alkaline in their reactions when dissolved in water.

3. How would you distinguish, by chemical or physical tests, between the following substances: water, alcohol, turpentine, sulphuric acid, lime water?

4. Classify the following substances into acids, bases and salts: marble, lime, oil of vitriol, spirits of salts, vinegar, washing soda, calcium sulphate.

5. What do you understand by the term "water of crystallisation"? In this connection give an outline of the manufacture of plaster of Paris.

6. Give the chemical formula for plaster of Paris, and explain the action which takes place when water is added and the plaster sets.

7. Explain the effect known as "efflorescence" on buildings.

8. In the case of a new brick building efflorescence was noticed to be general soon after the building had been completed. In the case of an older brick building the effect was only noticed near the ground level. Explain the probable cause in each case and the steps which may be taken to remove the defects.

9. Explain how acids may come to be formed in the atmosphere and on the faces of buildings in industrial towns. What steps may be taken to reduce the undesirable effects of these acids on the buildings themselves?

CHAPTER XVII

THE BEAM. SHEAR FORCES AND BENDING MOMENTS. THE STRENGTH OF BEAMS

The beam is one of the most important structural units in building. The theory underlying its design and use in modern times, in beams of timber, steel and reinforced concrete, is so extended and so complex that only a very simple introduction can be given in this volume. This introduction, however, is complete so far as it goes. It should bring the reader to a stage where he can calculate the sizes of beams in timber and steel for simple cases. The treatment is based upon that given in Volume II, to which the reader who wishes to have a more extended treatment is referred.

Loaded beams. In Chap. VII we saw that in a simple loaded beam there are three forces acting upon the beam, viz. the load and the two supporting forces or *reactions*. If we represent such a beam by a light bar of wood or metal, and load it with a weight W we know that it will bend as shown in fig. 178. If the same or a similar beam be used as a cantilever we know that it will bend in the reverse direction when loaded, as shown in fig. 179.

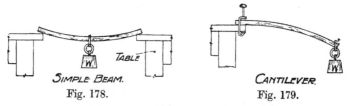

SIMPLE BEAM.　　　　　　　CANTILEVER.
Fig. 178.　　　　　　　　　Fig. 179.

Evidently these changes of form indicate that the material of the beams is being *strained*. We also know that if it is being strained then *stresses* are being set up in the material of the beam to resist these changes of form. From this it is clear that the *external forces* applied to the beam are resisted or balanced by *internal forces*, which are the result of stresses called into play when the material of the beam is strained. It will be convenient to confine our attention in the first place to a simple analysis of the external forces.

External forces acting on a loaded beam. Taking first the simple case of the cantilever shown in fig. 179, one of the effects due to the application of the load W at the end of the cantilever will evidently be that due to the *moment* of the weight W about the point of support (see Chap. VII). Because this and similar moments tend to bend the beam we refer to them as the external *bending moments*.

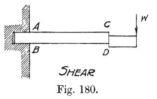

The other effect due to the application of the weight W is that which tends to cause one portion of the beam to slide or shear off from that portion which is nearer to the point of support, as shown for example at section CD in fig. 180. This force is referred to as the external *shear force*.

Fig. 180.

Because a knowledge of the value of the bending moments and shear forces is necessary in the design of beams, and because their values vary from section to section along the beam, it is usual to set them out in diagrams, drawn to scale, which are known respectively as *bending moment diagrams* and *shear force diagrams*. Some examples are given below. The small drawing giving the dimensions and loading of the beam in each case is known as the *space diagram*.

Shear force and bending moment diagrams for a cantilever with a single end load.

The cantilever AB in fig. 181 is shown loaded with a weight W at a span L from the supporting point A. (Note. In these and the following examples we will, for the sake of simplicity, ignore the effects due to the weight of the material of the beam. In relation to the magnitude of the load carried these effects are usually small, though not of course negligible.)

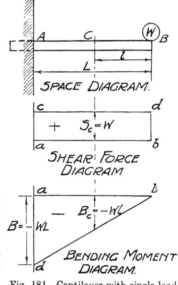

Fig. 181. Cantilever with single load.

At any section C in the length of the beam between B and the supporting point A, the vertical force tending to shear the outer portion of the beam off from the inner portion will be equal to the weight W since no other vertical force is applied to the beam. Thus shear force at $C = S_c = W$. This will be true at any section in the length of the beam, hence the shear force diagram is clearly a rectangle having a base ab representing the length L to some linear scale, and a height ac representing the load W to some force scale.

The turning effect, or bending moment, at the section A due to the load W will evidently be equal to the moment of the load W about A, that is to the load W multiplied by the span L, or to WL. This may be represented on the bending moment diagram by the ordinate ad, set off to a suitable scale.

The value of the bending moment at B immediately beneath the load W will obviously be zero. At any other section such as C, at a distance l from B, the bending moment will be equal to the moment of W about C, or bending moment at $C = B_c = Wl$.

It follows that the bending moment diagram in this case is a triangle in which the value of the bending moments, being zero at B, then increase directly with the distance from B until they reach a maximum value of WL at B.

Scales. In setting out the space diagram and the base lines of the shear and bending moment diagrams a *linear scale*, representing feet or inches, will be used. In setting out the ordinates of the shear force diagram a *force scale*, representing lbs. or tons, will be used. The scale for the ordinates of the bending moment diagram will represent lb. in., lb. feet or ton feet according to the units used (see Chap. VII).

Example. In fig. 181 let L be 12 ft. and W be 3 tons.
Then shear force $= S = W = 3$ tons. This applies at every section in the length of the beam.
The maximum bending moment at A will be

$$W \times L = 3 \text{ ton} \times 12 \text{ ft.}$$
$$= 36 \text{ ton ft.}$$

If l is 5 ft., then

$$B_c = 3 \text{ ton} \times 5 \text{ ft.}$$
$$= 15 \text{ ton ft.}$$

Note regarding signs. It is a great convenience to adopt some method of regarding the signs (positive or negative) to be attached to the different parts of the diagrams. The following simplified definitions are recommended as being suitable and sufficient at this stage.

Shear force. The external shear force will be considered to be positive if it acts downwards to the right of the section being considered.

Thus in fig. 180 the external shear force at CD acts downwards to the right and is therefore positive. Thus the shear forces in the cantilever AB in fig. 181 are all positive and are therefore set up above the base line ab of the shear force diagram.

Bending moment. The external bending moment will be considered to be positive if it tends to bend the beam so that it is concave on its upper surface.

Thus, since in the cantilever AB in fig. 181 the beam is bent so that its upper surface is *convex*, the bending moments at every section are evidently negative. The bending moment diagram abd is therefore set out entirely below the base line ab.

Beam with central load.

A simply supported beam AB carrying a single load W at the centre is shown in fig. 182.

Reactions. As we saw in Chap. vii the supporting loads or reactions in such a case are equal to each other and to half the load, or

$$R_a = R_b = \frac{W}{2}.$$

Shear Force. If we consider the external shear force at any section such as D the only force acting to the right is R_b acting upwards. So that

$$S_d = R_b = -\frac{W}{2}.$$

This is true for any section between the points B and C.

At any section such as E the shear forces acting to the right are R_b acting upwards and W acting downwards. Hence

$$S_e = W - \frac{W}{2} = \frac{W}{2}.$$

This is true for any section between the points A and C.

The shear force diagram therefore consists of two rectangular portions, each with ordinates equal to $\frac{W}{2}$, i.e. to the reactions, that to the left being positive and that to the right being negative.

Bending moment. If we consider the bending moment at any section such as D, situated a distance l from B, we have

Bending moment at $D = B_d$

$$= R_b \times l$$

$$= \frac{W}{2} \times l.$$

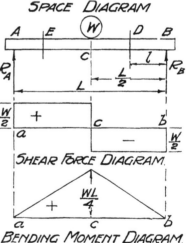

SPACE DIAGRAM

SHEAR FORCE DIAGRAM.

BENDING MOMENT DIAGRAM.

Fig. 182. Beam with central load.

This value clearly increases or decreases as l is made greater or smaller. At B, where $l = 0$, the value of B_b will be 0. At C, where $l = \dfrac{L}{2}$, the value of B_c will be $\dfrac{W}{2} \times \dfrac{L}{2}$.

It may likewise be shown that the magnitudes of the bending moments at the sections between C and A fall off uniformly to a zero value at A. Thus it is seen that the bending moment diagram is a triangle on the base ab, the height at the centre representing the magnitude of the maximum bending moment, which is

$$B_{\max} = \frac{W}{2} \times \frac{L}{2} = \frac{WL}{4}.$$

Since the effect of the load is to cause the beam to bend with its concave surface upwards, the bending moments are everywhere positive, and the diagram is set up wholly above the base line ab.

Example. In fig. 182 let L be 12 ft. and W be 3 tons. Then the reactions are each equal to 3/2 tons, which gives the ordinates of the two portions of the shear force diagram. Also we have

$$B_{\max} = \frac{WL}{4} = \frac{3 \times 12}{4}$$
$$= 9 \text{ ton ft.},$$

which supplies sufficient information to enable us to complete the diagram.

Beam with single load not at the centre.

The load W rests on the beam AB in fig. 183 at a distance y from B and x from A.

Reactions (see Chap. VII). Taking moments about A we have for equilibrium

$$R_b \times L = W \times x.$$
$$\therefore \; R_b = \frac{Wx}{L}.$$

Similarly

$$R_a = \frac{Wy}{L}.$$

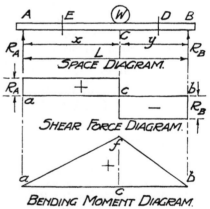

Fig. 183. Concentrated load not at the centre.

Evidently these values give the magnitudes also of the shear forces, which are once again negative to the right of C and positive to the left.

Bending Moment. As in the preceding case it is easy to show that the bending moment diagram is a triangle, the maximum value occurring at C immediately under the load. Also that

$$B_c = B_{max} = R_b \times y$$
$$= \frac{Wx}{L} \times y$$
$$= \frac{Wxy}{L}.$$

Beam with several concentrated loads.

The beam AB in fig. 184 is shown with loads W_1, W_2 and W_3 at distances x, y and z from B.

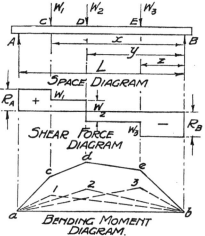

Reactions. The total re-action at either side will be equal to the sum of the re-actions at that side due to the separate loads. Thus

Total reaction at $A = R_a$

$$= \frac{W_1 x}{L} + \frac{W_2 y}{L} + \frac{W_3 z}{L}.$$

The total reaction at

$$B = R_b$$
$$= (W_1 + W_2 + W_3) - R_a;$$

but it is preferable to cal-culate R_b separately so as to act as a check on the cal-culations.

Fig. 184. Beam with several concentrated loads.

Shear force. The reactions R_a and R_b should be set up and down from the base line as shown on the left and right respectively. The diagram can then be completed by stepping down at each load point from the left by an amount equal to the load in each case. The portion to the left of D is positive and that to the right negative.

Bending moment. Each load may be treated separately and the small bending moment diagrams, $a1b$, $a2b$ and $a3b$, set up on the base line as shown. The complete diagram $a c d e b$ can then be set up by adding together the ordinates at each load line.

Another method is to calculate the bending moment at each point due to the action of the several forces. Thus, taking the moments of the forces acting to the right of C we have

Bending moment at C

$$= B_c = R_b x - W_2 (x-y) - W_3 (x-z);$$

from which the value of B_c can be obtained, and similarly at other points. (The case of a cantilever with several concentrated loads can be dealt with similarly.)

Definitions of shear force and bending moment. The last case enables us to give and explain definitions of shear force and bending moment which are of general application.

External shear force. The total external shear force at any section of a beam is equal to the algebraic sum of all the vertical external forces acting to the right (or left) of that section.

Bending moment. The total external bending moment at any section of a beam is equal to the algebraic sum of the moments of all the external forces acting to the right (or left) of that section.

The term "algebraic sum" means that regard must be given to the sign of the quantities. Thus shear forces acting downwards to the right are positive, and bending moments acting anticlockwise to the right of a section are positive. The phrase "to the right (or left) of that section" means that the same result will be obtained on whichever side of the section the forces or moments are summed up, provided of course that due regard is given to the signs.

Beam with a uniformly distributed load. The freely supported beam AB in fig. 185 has a load of w lb. per inch distributed uniformly throughout its length.

If the length L be measured in inches then the total load will be wL lb. Also the reactions, which are obviously equal in magnitude, will be $\frac{wL}{2}$.

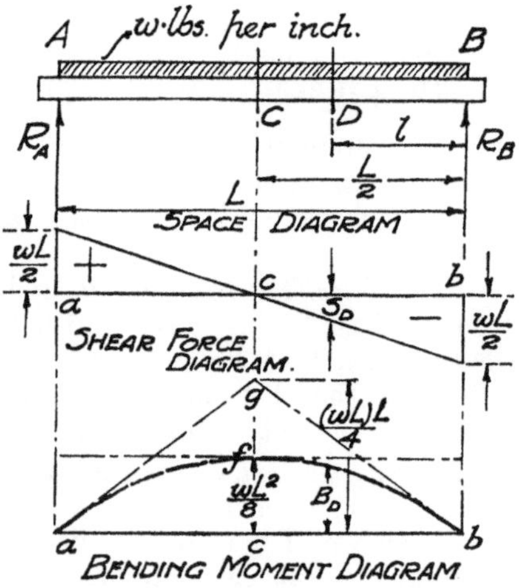

Fig. 185. Beam with uniformly distributed load.

Shear forces. At any point D the shear force will be due to the vertical forces to the right. These are R_b, which is equal to $\frac{wL}{2}$ and is negative, and wl due to the load between B and D, which acts downwards and is therefore positive. Thus

$$S_d = wl - \frac{wL}{2} \text{ lb.}$$

But $\dfrac{wL}{2}$ has a constant value while wl will increase as l is increased. Hence the outline of the shear force diagram must be an inclined straight line. Also at the section C, where the downward acting force wl will have the value $\dfrac{wL}{2}$, we have

$$S_c = \frac{wL}{2} - \frac{wL}{2} = 0.$$

The results are similar to the left of C where, however, the shear forces are positive.

Thus the shear force diagram consists of two triangular figures, the shear force having a zero value at the centre section C.

Bending moments. If the moments of the forces to the right of the section D are considered, we have the reaction R_b acting at a distance l, which is equal to $\dfrac{wL}{2} \times l$ and is positive. Then there is the moment of the weight of the load wl. This may be taken to act at its centre of gravity, i.e. at a distance $l/2$ from D. Its moment about D is therefore $wl \times l/2$, and is negative. Hence

$$B_d = \frac{wlL}{2} - \frac{wl^2}{2} = \frac{wl}{2}(L-l).$$

At B, where $l = 0$, and also at A, where $l = L$, the bending moments become zero.

At C, where l becomes $L/2$, we have

$$B_c = \frac{wL}{4}\left(L - \frac{L}{2}\right) = \frac{WL}{8},$$

where $W = WL = $ total load. This is evidently the maximum bending moment.

It is important to note that, as compared with the effect of a concentrated load of the value of W, for which the maximum bending moment would have been $\dfrac{WL}{4}$, the bending moment is reduced to half this amount if the same load is uniformly distributed along the beam.

Students of algebra will recognise that the expression

$$B_d = \frac{wlL}{2} - \frac{wl^2}{2},$$

will give a graph which is part of a parabolic curve. The above facts are used in setting out the bending moment diagram. The triangle agb is set up in which the ordinate gc is equal to $\dfrac{(wL)\,L}{4}$ or $\dfrac{WL}{4}$.

This is then bisected at f. An accurate parabolic curve may then be drawn by geometrical means through the points a, f and b. Usually it will be sufficiently accurate to draw in the curve afb so that it is tangential to each of the three enclosing lines.

Loads distributed only over a portion of the length. In those cases where the distributed load only extends over a portion of the length of the beam, see fig. 124, a similar plan may be followed to obtain the outline of the bending moment diagram over this portion. Thus, if in fig. 185 AB represents that *portion* only of the beam over which the load is distributed, then the load should be first treated as though it were concentrated at the centre C, and the bending moment diagram completed. If now the height of the small triangle $acbg$, which will be formed over AB, is bisected at f this will give the mid-point through which the parabolic portion of the outline must be drawn. The corresponding portion of the shear force diagram will be a sloping line, drawn between the two points at which the other portions of shear force diagram intersect the verticals through A and B, the ends of the distributed load.

Cantilever with uniformly distributed load. The cantilever AB in fig. 186 has a load of w lb. per inch distributed uniformly throughout its length.

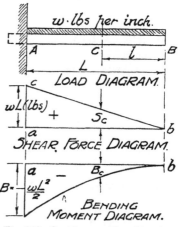

The reaction at A will equal the total load, which will be wL lbs. This is also the value of the shear force at A, which is positive and may therefore be set up above the base line ab of the force diagram.

At any section C distance l from B, the shear force will be $S_c = wl$ lb. From this it is seen that the shear forces increase directly as the distance l from the free end B. The shear force diagram is therefore a triangle abc, the shear forces being zero at B and reaching a maximum value of wL lb. at A.

Fig. 186. Cantilever with uniformly distributed load.

The bending moment at the section C will evidently be due to the load wL acting to the right of C. This may be taken to act at its centre of gravity, at a distance $l/2$ from C. Hence

$$B_c = wl \times \frac{l}{2} = \frac{wl^2}{2} \text{ lb. in.}$$

This expression is the equation to a parabolic curve. The curve may be completed as explained in the last case as soon as the maximum and minimum values of the bending moments have been found.

At B, where $l=0$, we have $B_b=0$. At A, where $l=L$, we have $B_a=\dfrac{wL^2}{2}$, and this is evidently the maximum value.

If we take W to be the total load in the cantilever, its value is evidently wl, and substituting this in the last expression we have

$$B_{\max}=\frac{WL}{2}.$$

From which we see that, as in the case of a simply supported beam, the maximum bending moment is reduced by half if, instead of being concentrated at the end, the load is uniformly distributed throughout the length of the cantilever.

The construction of bending moment diagrams by graphical means.[1] These methods are interesting and in certain cases quicker than those described above. The underlying theory is, however, not easily explained, while additional difficulties arise in the calculation of the scales to be used. The methods described above are therefore to be preferred in the early stages. In addition they give clearer ideas of the nature of the forces being dealt with.

Internal forces in a loaded beam.

Having now analysed the forces acting externally to a loaded beam we will next ascertain what internal forces are set up as a result. These internal forces are clearly the result of strains set up in the material of the beam. The nature of these strains in a bent beam can be demonstrated experimentally.

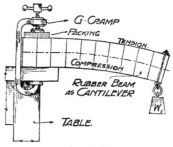

Experiment 102. A beam made of rubber of rectangular section is shown in fig. 187 arranged as a cantilever under a load W. Before loading the cantilever vertical lines equally spaced along its length are marked on the sides of the beam.[2]

Fig. 187.

[1] These methods are fully explained in Volume II.

[2] The effects may also be demonstrated by a small wood beam in which saw cuts at regular intervals are made in the upper and lower thirds of the depth of the beam.

On attaching the load W the cantilever bends. Careful measurement will show that the dividing lines are:

(a) Closer together along the lower edge of the beam,

(b) Further apart along the upper edge, and

(c) At the original distances apart along the line marking the centre of the depth of the beam.

It is evident therefore that the lower fibres of the beam are being shortened because they are in a state of *compression*, while the upper fibres are being extended because they are in a state of *tension*. The fibres lying along the middle layer are evidently not being subjected to either tension or compression since their lengths are unaltered.

If the rubber beam be now supported at each end and loaded in the middle as in a simply supported beam, it will be found that it is the upper fibres which are in compression and the lower fibres in tension.

It is evident, therefore, that in a loaded beam the maximum strains, and therefore the maximum stresses (see Chap. VI), occur in the upper and lower fibres of the beam. Also that these stresses fall off towards the middle layer, where the stresses of this nature are zero. (It is for this reason that the middle layer is referred to as the *neutral layer*.)[1] Thus we see that the external forces acting on the beam are balanced by certain internal forces, which produce certain strains in the material of the beam. We will now ascertain experimentally how these external and internal forces are related.

Experiment 103. To show the balance of external and internal forces in a loaded cantilever.

The following details will explain the construction and use of the apparatus. The block of wood *abcd* is suspended from the frame GH by a spring balance S. This balance is capable of adjustment vertically by means of the wing nut. A small horizontal adjustment is also possible in a slot (not shown).

The lower horizontal member at *fd* is a compression balance C. The upper horizontal member at *ea* consists of two spring balances lying side by side. (Two are necessary to render the apparatus stable.)

Means of adjustment are provided in the length *ae* to take up the movements of the three horizontal balances. When properly adjusted the points *eab* should lie in the same horizontal line.

The apparatus has weight and to allow for this the following procedure is adopted: (a) the apparatus is adjusted as described without the weight W being attached. The

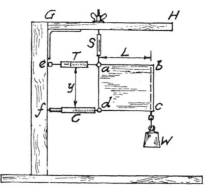

Fig. 188. Equilibrium of a portion of a cantilever

---

[1] It is unfortunately not so easy to demonstrate experimentally that there are also internal shear forces called into play. The next experiment will, however, help to clarify this point.

readings of the balances are noted. (*b*) The weight W is now attached and the apparatus again adjusted so that *eab* is horizontal. The balances are again read. The differences between the two sets of readings will give the values of the forces in S, T and C due solely to the weight W.

In the apparatus just described the block *abcd* is intended to represent the end of a loaded cantilever separated from the remainder of the cantilever at the section *ad*. Clearly then the external vertical shear force will be equal to W acting downwards to the right of *ad*. Also the bending moment will be equal to $(W \times L)$ acting clockwise about the same section.

As the apparatus is arranged the loaded cantilever is supported at the section *ad* by the three forces in S, T and C. Vertically the upward acting force S should balance the downward acting load W. The experimental readings will confirm this, so we may assume that the force S represents the total internal shear forces called into play in the material of the beam. Hence

Total internal shear force = Total external shear force.

The experimental readings will show that the two horizontal forces T and C, measured by the balances, are equal in magnitude. In addition if the distance y between their centre lines be measured, it will be found that

$$T \times y = C \times y = W \times L.$$

If we compare these results with what we noticed in the experiment with the rubber beam, it will be evident that the tensile force T represents the total of all the internal tensile stresses acting above the neutral layer. Also that the compressive force C represents the total of all the internal compressive forces acting below the neutral layer. Hence we see that in the beam

Total compressive forces (C) = Total tensile forces (T).

It should be noted that the experiment demonstrates that the four forces W, S, T and C can produce a state of equilibrium. Moreover this can be checked by applying the Principle of Moments (see Chap. VII). If moments are taken of all the forces about *any point* in their plane (points *a* and *d* give two very convenient points for calculations) the algebraic sum of the moments will be found to be zero.

It is evident then that the external bending moment is balanced or resisted by an internal moment, equal either to $T \times y$ or to $C \times y$.[1] This internal moment is known as the *moment of resistance*, hence for equilibrium we have

External bending moment = Moment of resistance.

Our next step will be to ascertain the magnitude of the moment of resistance in the same terms as those in which we have already found the external bending moments (lb. in. or ton ft. etc.). In the space at our disposal it is not possible to give a complete explanation of this step, but, if certain assumptions are accepted without further proof, it will be possible to carry our treatment to the practical stage enabling us to design simple beams of rectangular section. A full treatment will be found in Volume II.

---

[1] The two forces C and T, which are parallel and equal to each other but act in opposite directions, form what is called a "couple". Couples are fully discussed in Volume II.

The strength of beams of rectangular section. In fig. 189 let the rectangle $AABB$ represent the section of a beam, which is subjected at this section to a bending moment B. Let the line XX across the middle of the section be the line in which the neutral layer cuts across the section—usually called the *neutral axis* of the section. Let the maximum compressive stress in the uppermost fibres of the beam be f_c, and the maximum tensile stress in the lowest fibres of the beam be f_t.

Fig. 189. Internal forces in a loaded beam.

Then, if we assume that the stresses vary uniformly in each case from the maximum stresses to zero at the neutral axis XX, while the maximum stresses f_c and f_t are equal in magnitude, it should be possible to draw a *stress diagram* $Aa \times bB$, as shown in fig. 189, in which aXb is a straight line and crosses AB at X where the stress is zero.

In the upper half of the section, since the maximum compressive stress is f_c the average stress will be $f_c/2$. Similarly in the lower half it will be $f_t/2$. Hence the total compressive force in the upper half will be given by

Total compressive force = area × average stress

$$= \left(b \times \frac{d}{2}\right)\left(\frac{f_c}{2}\right)$$

$$= f_c\left(\frac{bd}{4}\right).$$

Similarly   Total tensile force $= f_t\left(\frac{bd}{4}\right)$.

These two forces are evidently the parallel forces which we designated C and T respectively in Experiment 103. Hence if f stand for the *maximum stresses* (either f_c or f_t) we have

$$C = T = f\left(\frac{bd}{4}\right).$$

In the stress triangle AaX it is not difficult to show that the resultant force C will act at the centre of gravity of the stress triangle, that is at a height of $\frac{2}{3}Ax$ or $\frac{2}{3}\left(\frac{d}{2}\right)$ above the neutral axis XX. Similarly for force T. Hence the total distance between the two parallel forces C and T is $2\left(\frac{2}{3}\times\frac{d}{2}\right)$, which equals $\frac{2d}{3}$.

Evidently we now have both the magnitude and the position of the forces C and T, and we can calculate the magnitude of the moment of the internal forces, that is, the *resistance moment*.

Taking moments about a point in the line of action of C we have

$$\text{Moment of Resistance} = T \times \frac{2d}{3}$$

$$= f_t\left(\frac{bd}{4}\right)\frac{2d}{3}$$

$$= f_t\left(\frac{bd^2}{6}\right),$$

or if we use the common value f we have

$$\textbf{Moment of Resistance} = f\left(\frac{bd^2}{6}\right).$$

The expression $\frac{bd^2}{6}$ is known as the *modulus of the section* (in this case of a rectangular section) and is usually represented by the letter Z. Hence we have

External bending moment = Moment of resistance

= stress × modulus of section,

or $\qquad\qquad\qquad B = fZ.$

Moment of inertia. At a later stage the reader may come to use this term as well as Z. It is usually represented by the letter I. Its significance cannot be explained in simple terms. Its use is not necessary at this stage but it may be a convenience to explain how the two terms are related in a mathematical sense, so that we may find Z when only I is given.

If Z and I are the "section modulus" and the "moment of inertia" respectively of a given section of depth d, then, *if the section is symmetrical about the neutral axis*, it can be shown that:

$$Z = \frac{I}{d/2}.$$

For a rectangular section $I = \frac{bd^3}{12}$.

Hence Z for a rectangular section $= \frac{bd^3}{12} \div \frac{d}{2} = \frac{bd^2}{6}$, as before.

(**Caution.** Always use the inch as the linear unit when using I and Z.)

Strength of rolled steel beams.

Structural steel intended for use as beams is rolled to standard sections, chiefly of an **I** section. By this means the upper and lower "flanges", being concentrated at the uppermost and lowest parts of the section, are subjected in use almost entirely to the maximum bending stresses. This makes both for efficiency and economy.

For these sections the values of both I and Z are obtained from the British Standard Specification No. 4, "Channels and Beams for Structural Purposes". A few typical sections are listed below.

British Standard Beams (I section).

Size (inches)	Wt. per ft.	Moment of Inertia (I)	Modulus of section (Z)
4×3	10	3·66	1·83
6×3	12	20·99	7·00
8×4	18	55·63	13·91
$10 \times 4\frac{1}{2}$	25	122·34	24·47
12×5	32	221·07	36·84

Working stresses. The following values may be used in design.

Structural timber.

Nature of stress	Non-graded timber	Graded timber[1]
Tension	800 lb. sq. in.	1200 lb. sq. in.
Compression	800 ,,	1200 ,,
Shear	90 ,,	100 ,,

Structural Steel.

Tension	8 tons per sq. in.	
Compression	8 ,,	
Shear	5 ,,	

Shear stresses in rectangular beams. The relations between external shear forces and internal shear stresses cannot be simply explained. It must suffice for the present to state that, *in beams of rectangular section, the maximum shear stress occurs at the neutral layer and is equal to 3/2 times the average shear stress over the section*, or

$$\text{Max. shear stress} = \frac{3}{2} \left(\frac{\text{shear force}}{\text{area of section}} \right) = \frac{3}{2} \left(\frac{S}{b \times d} \right).$$

Shear stresses in rolled steel beams. It is assumed that the web takes all the shear stress, which is nearly uniform; hence, approximately,

$$\text{Shear stress} = \frac{S}{\text{area of web}}.$$

---

[1] May be taken to mean carefully selected, high grade timber. Common grades of building timber should be assumed to be non-graded unless otherwise specified.

We are now in a position to make the necessary calculations for beams of rectangular or of standard **I** section. Some examples have been included in the Problems given below, with a few explanatory notes where these appear to be necessary.

Experiment 104. Testing the strength of beams. The accurate testing of the strength of beams cannot be satisfactorily carried out until the theory of loaded beams has been carried to a higher stage than is possible in this volume. It will be found informative, however, to carry out some simple tests on a series of small beams, made up in the principal building materials used for this purpose. The tests may be carried out with very simple apparatus, but the use of a small testing machine is desirable. The tests should be carried to the point of failure. They should give valuable indications of the action of the various materials and their special characteristics at failure. The following notes should be helpful.

Timber beams. The deflections will be considerable before failure takes place. Failure will occur by tension, showing a characteristic splinter fracture.

Beams in cast iron, stone, brick and plain concrete. All these materials are weaker in tension than in compression. Failure will occur in tension and suddenly. Deflection is usually very slight. (Bricks are sometimes tested by being supported as a beam and loaded transversely.)

Beams in structural mild steel. Because of the remarkable elastic qualities of steel the beams may bend and buckle to an extreme stage but show no actual fracture.

Beams in reinforced concrete. The horizontal reinforcement is intended to take the tensile stresses, the compressive strength of the concrete being thus fully developed. Failure will usually occur by compression in the upper half of the beam, unless the beam is relatively deep, when failure by shear (showing sloping cracks) may occur.

PROBLEMS XVII

1. In fig. 183, if $L=12$ ft., $W=3$ tons and $y=4$ ft., find the reactions at A and B and the bending moment at C.

2. In fig. 184 let $L=15$ ft., $x=12$ ft., $y=9$ ft., $z=4$ ft., $W_1=1$ ton, $W_2=2$ tons, $W_3=3$ tons. Find the reactions at A and B and the bending moments at c, d and e.

3. In fig. 185, if $L=12$ ft. and $l=4$ ft., while w is 100 lb. per inch, find the reactions, the maximum bending moment and the bending moment at D. (Note. All lengths should be reduced to one unit of length, either feet or inches. Inches are used in this case so that $L=144$ in.; $l=48$ in.)

4. Find the bending moment at section C in the beam shown in fig. 124.

5. If in fig. 188 the distance y is 8 in. and L is 12 in., what should be the magnitudes of the forces S, C and T when W is 12 lbs.?

6. Find the values of the modulus of section (Z) and the moment of inertia (I) for a rectangular section of a beam 12 in. deep and 6 in. wide.

If this beam spans an opening of 25 ft. and is of graded timber which can safely carry a bending stress of 1200 lb. per sq. in., find the central load to give this stress. What will be the maximum internal shear stress?

7. If the beam in question 6 had been a rolled steel beam 12 in. × 5 in. (see Table for value of Z) what central load would produce a maximum bending stress of 8 tons per sq. in.? What will be the maximum shear stress in the web, if the web is 10·75 in. deep and 0·35 in. thick?

8. A timber floor consists of 8 in. × 3 in. joists spaced at 16 in. centres over a span of 10 ft. If the bending stresses must not exceed 800 lb. per sq. in. what load will the floor carry per sq. ft. of area? [Note. Find the uniformly distributed load to give the required stress, from the formulae $B = \dfrac{WL}{8}$ and $B = fZ$, being careful about units. Then the load W is evidently spread over an area equal to the (span × spacing of joists). Load per square foot can be found from this.]

EXAMINATION PAPERS

Union of Lancashire and Cheshire Institutes*

SENIOR BUILDING COURSE (FIRST YEAR)

BUILDING SCIENCE

1939

1. Explain why, in selecting a sand for mortar, it is preferable to choose one whose particles are well varied in size. What happens, as regards volume, when the sand and cement are mixed dry to form a mortar?

State, approximately, the quantity of dry mixture obtainable from 1 cu. ft. of cement mixed with 3 cu. ft. of sand.

2. Describe the action of a lift-and-force pump, and illustrate your description with a sketch.

3. Determine the nature and magnitude of the force in each member of the framework shown in Fig. 1.

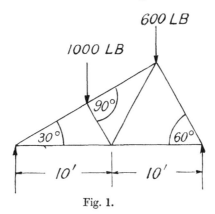

Fig. 1.

4. Describe what is meant by the statement that a machine has a mechanical advantage of 100. Illustrate your description by reference to a screw jack.

If the efficiency of such a machine is 35 %, what distance must the effort be moved in order to raise the load $\frac{1}{2}$ in.?

* These papers are reproduced by kind permission of the Union of Lancashire and Cheshire Institutes.

5. Give examples of heat distribution in buildings by (a) convection, and (b) radiation. Describe how the heat is distributed in each case.

6. Determine the reactions at the supports of the beam shown in Fig. 2 (a).

Four forces act at a point as shown in Fig. 2 (b) and are in equilibrium. The magnitudes of the forces, A and B, are unknown. Determine these magnitudes and show, by means of arrowheads, the directions along the given lines in which these forces act.

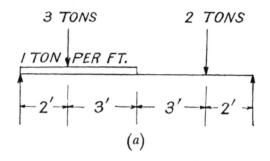

(a)

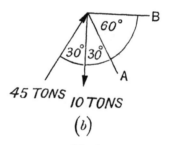

(b)

Fig. 2.

7. Compare the capacity of the following materials to absorb water: hard sandstone, common brick, slate.

Give examples to illustrate how their differences in this respect affect their uses in building.

8. State the principal cause of the corrosion of steel exposed to the atmosphere, and describe the change which takes place. Give *three* examples of methods which are adopted in building or structural work to overcome this difficulty, either by protecting the steel or by using an alternative material.

9. A beam is loaded as shown in Fig. 3. Determine the values of the shear force and bending moment at the point *A*.

Describe, briefly, the manner in which stresses will be set up within the beam to resist this bending moment.

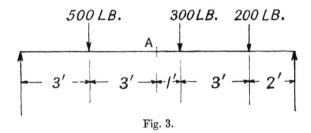

Fig. 3.

10. Give an example, from building work, of a situation in which allowance is made for a material expanding due to a rise in temperature.

A concrete roof slab, 40 ft. long, increases in temperature by 50° F. Determine the increase in length of the slab due to this temperature rise.

[Coefficient of linear expansion of concrete, ·000005 per 1° F.]

Union of Lancashire and Cheshire Institutes

SENIOR BUILDING COURSE (Second Year)

BUILDING SCIENCE

1939

1. Summarise the various methods which may be used to soften water and, for each of the methods you mention, state, briefly, the changes which take place during the softening of the water.

2. Determine the nature and magnitude of the force in each member of the framework shown in Fig. 1.

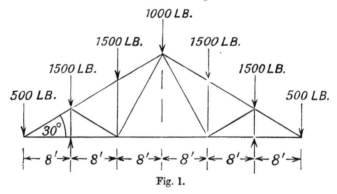

Fig. 1.

3. Describe the behaviour of a bar of mild steel during a test to determine its ultimate tensile strength. Illustrate your description by means of a stress-strain diagram.

Indicate the information, obtainable from the results of the test, which is important to a user of mild steel for structural purposes.

4. A sample of timber is cut to a rectangular block having faces (a) at right angles to the line of the trunk of the tree, (b) tangential to the annual rings, and (c) radial to the annual rings.

Mention the differences in appearance of the faces when seen through a magnifying glass, and describe, briefly, the general structure of the timber responsible for these differences.

Mention the principal change which takes place during seasoning of the timber, and show why this may result in a change of shape of the block.

5. Draw the shear-force and bending-moment diagrams for the beam shown in Fig. 2.

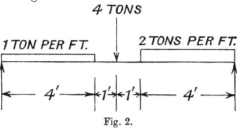

Fig. 2.

6. A timber beam, 3 in. wide, is to be selected to support the loading shown in Fig. 3. The maximum stress in the beam must not exceed 800 lb. per sq. in. Determine a suitable depth for the beam.

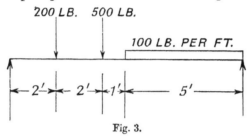

Fig. 3.

7. Mention the principal causes of weathering of building materials.

Describe the manner in which damage is caused, and give some account of methods which may be adopted in practice to protect the materials.

8. A beam is loaded as shown in Fig. 4. It is known that the upper reaction is perpendicular to the beam as shown. Determine the magnitude of the reaction at each support, and the direction of the reaction at the lower support. Neglect the weight of the beam.

9. Describe a crushing test for determining the strength of concrete, brick or stone. Of what value is this information in practice?

10. Explain the development of compressive and tensile stresses in a beam when loads are placed on it and bending takes place. Describe, briefly, any experiment you have seen carried out to show that such stresses are developed, and describe the manner in which these stresses will vary in different parts of the depth of the beam.

11. A properly constructed cavity wall will prevent the penetration of moisture through it. Describe the defects in design and construction of cavity walls which must be guarded against in practice because of their tendency to permit the penetration of dampness.

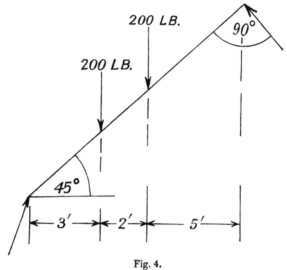

Fig. 4.

Union of Lancashire and Cheshire Institutes

COURSES FOR WOODWORKERS AND
PLUMBERS (Second Year)

SCIENCE AND CALCULATIONS*

1939

1. A simple flushing tank is caused to discharge its contents by a pull on a chain suspended from a lever over the tank. Sketch a vertical section through such a tank, describe the cycle of operations commenced by the pull on the chain, and explain the part played in this cycle by the atmosphere.

2. A roll of sheet lead, weighing 5 cwt., is raised to a scaffold by means of an upper and lower pulley block containing two sheaves each. Show, by means of a diagram, the arrangement of the ropes, and assuming there is no friction, calculate the force which must be exerted on the end of the rope.

3. A hinged platform is loaded as shown in Fig. 1, and is maintained in a horizontal position by a force of P cwt., acting in a chain attached to its free end.

Calculate the value of the force P, and the vertical (downwards) pressure on the hinge.

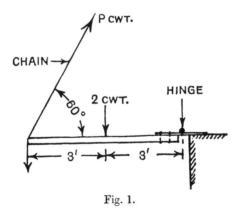

Fig. 1.

* Questions which relate solely to Calculations have been omitted.

4. Explain what is meant by capillary attraction, and show, by the aid of sketches, how its ill effects may be prevented in the case of (a) the sill of a window frame and the bottom rail of the sash, (b) the bottom rail of a timber skylight, and (c) a lead drip.

5. Explain the term "relative density," and the relation between the relative density of timber, its probable durability and tendency to absorb moisture.

A rectangular block of timber, 12 in. long, 6 in. wide, and 3 in. thick, when saturated with moisture weighs 7·25 lb. If its relative density when dry = 0·8, calculate the weight of its water content.

6. Fig. 2 shows a portion of a hot-water system. Copy the figure on to your paper (it may be pricked through the question paper), and indicate by arrows the convection currents which are set up in the system when the water in the boiler is heated. You are given that the pipes indicated at A and B are necessary, but in answering this question they may be ignored.

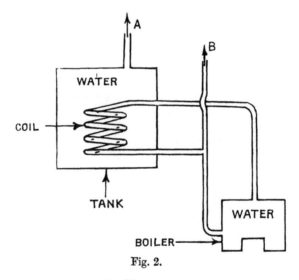

Fig. 2.

7. The formula $B = \dfrac{9wL^2}{fd^2}$ may be used to determine the breadth (B) of a beam of rectangular section to carry a uniformly distributed load.

(a) Evaluate, by means of logarithms, the value of B when w = 217·6, L = 12·2, f = 1200, and d = 9.

(b) Express f (algebraically) in terms of the other quantities.

Union of Lancashire and Cheshire Institutes
COURSE FOR BRICKLAYERS AND MASONS
(Second Year)

SCIENCE AND CALCULATIONS*

1. Fig. 1 shows the outline of a simple roof truss supported by walls at its two ends. Determine, graphically, the tension in the tie and the reactions at the supports.

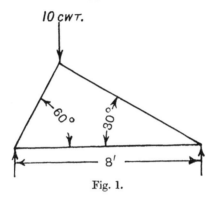

Fig. 1.

2. Fig. 2 shows a vertical section of a sump, into which liquid is flowing at a steady rate, and a pipe which is the only outlet from the sump. Copy the figure on to your paper (it may be pricked

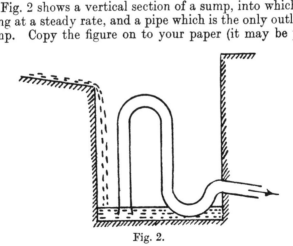

Fig. 2.

* Questions which relate solely to Calculations have been omitted.

through the question paper), and indicate clearly the water levels in the sump and the branches of the pipe when discharge of the contents of the sump is about to occur. Explain the cause of the discharge.

3. Explain the relation between the relative density of a building stone (or brick) and its probable durability.

A building stone has a volume of 1 cu. ft., and when saturated with water weighs 110 lb. If its relative density when dry = 1·6, calculate the weight of its water content.

4. Explain the reason why an interior wall on the ground floor may become damp, and the measures which should be taken to prevent this. Sketch sections of a stone cornice and a stone window sill, showing in each case how they are designed to shed water and prevent it from flowing on to the wall below.

5. A hot-water radiator is used to heat a room. Given that the source of the hot water is in a boiler at a lower level, describe and name the various ways in which the heat is transmitted from the boiler, via the radiator, to the air in the room adjacent to the radiator. Give reasons.

Union of Lancashire and Cheshire Institutes
COURSE FOR PLUMBERS (Second Year)
PLUMBING SCIENCE AND CALCULATIONS*
1939

1. (a) Explain what is meant by the "relative density" of lead, and the "density" of water.

(b) Describe, in detail, how you would determine experimentally the capacity in cubic feet of a movable boiler, provided that you merely had access to a weighing machine and a supply of water.

2. Explain, with the aid of a sketch, the relation between "atmospheric pressure" and the working of a siphon, and describe how you would siphon out the contents of a boiler, with the precautions you would take to ensure extracting the maximum amount of water.

3. A cold-water supply tank has a rectangular base, 3 ft. long and 2 ft. wide, measured internally, and contains water to a depth of 18 in. Calculate the total pressure on the whole of the base, and the intensity of water pressure, in lb. per square inch, in a boiler at a point 24 ft. below the free surface of the water in the tank.

4. Draw a line diagram of a simple hot-water system, showing the boiler, cylinder, and cold-water supply tank, with their connecting-pipes. Indicate, by means of arrows, the direction of flow in each pipe. Explain the reason for a "frost burst" in a cold-water pipe.

5. Explain what is meant by the "specific heat" of a liquid, and why hot water is considered to be a good medium for heating purposes, apart from the question of economy.

A cylinder contains 20 gallons of water, with a temperature of 200 degrees Fahrenheit. If 10 gallons of this are drawn off and replaced by water with a temperature of 50 degrees Fahrenheit, calculate the final temperature of the mixture.

* Questions which relate solely to Calculations have been omitted.

Union of Lancashire and Cheshire Institutes

COURSE FOR PLUMBERS (Third Year)

PLUMBING SCIENCE

1939

1. Outline *three* possible reasons why water, after passing from the mains to a house, may suffer loss of head at the various taps in the house.

Calculate the discharge, in gallons per minute, of water from a 1-in. pipe under a constant head of 30 ft., if there is a loss of 15 per cent. from various causes.

2. A room on the first floor of a house is heated by means of a hot-water radiator, the source of heat being a boiler on the ground floor. Draw a simple diagram to illustrate the system, indicating by means of arrows the convection currents set up in the water of the system and the air of the room. Explain how and where the heat is transmitted by conduction and radiation.

3. Describe, briefly, (a) the advantages claimed for central heating, and (b) the various circumstances which contribute towards loss of heat in a building.

4. Sketch the approximate shape of a "temperature volume" curve for a mass of water, to show the temperature at which it has its minimum volume. Explain what is meant by the "circulating head," and how this affects the working of a hot-water heating system.

5. Sketch a longitudinal section through an "atmospheric relief valve" for a steam main, and explain the mechanical principles involved. What are the merits, from a scientific point of view, of steam-heating systems?

6. Explain the reason for the "hardness" of some waters, and the cause of "permanent hardness." Describe how you would test water for the presence of lead, and give reasons why it may be present.

7. Describe the chief physical and chemical properties of lead and copper, and state the component parts of the alloys known as "plumbers' solder" and "best brass."

8. Obtain, from first principles, a formula for the required thickness (T) of metal in a thin pipe, of diameter D, subjected to an internal fluid pressure of P lb. per sq. in., if the safe tensile strength of the metal is Q lb. per sq. in.

If the safe tensile strength of lead is 475 lb. per sq. in., calculate the value of T for a lead pipe, given that $D = 4$ in., and $P = 45$ lb. per sq. in.

9. (a) What is meant by a "therm" in connection with the supply of gas?

(b) Describe an experiment to produce the flux known as zinc chloride (killed spirits). Name the gas which is evolved during the experiment, and state its physical and chemical properties.

LIST OF EXPERIMENTS IN BUILDING SCIENCE*

Northern Counties Technical Examinations Council

This list of experiments is intended only as a guide to teachers of Building Science. It ought not to prevent teachers using other experiments they feel to be of equal value in the demonstration of fundamental principles. In certain cases (marked × in the list) tests standardised by the British Standards Institution should be adopted; in other cases (marked + in the list) special tests have been devised by the Building Research Station, the Forest Products Research Laboratories, and other similar authorities to whose publications reference should be made. In a few cases suitable apparatus may be constructed in the schools by the exercise of a little ingenuity.

Students should be encouraged to use British and Metric units with equal facility.

It is assumed that adequate supplies of the following measuring apparatus is available:

(1) Length. Rules marked in feet, inches and decimals of inch, and in Metric units. Vernier Scales. Range of Micrometers.

(2) Volume. Measuring Jars graduated in c.c.

(3) Weight. Balances (a) Standard Laboratory type with weights.

        (b) Balance or scales weighing up to 10 lbs.

        (c) Balance or scales weighing up to 50 lbs. rising by ozs. or decimals of 1 lb.

(4) Time. Stop clock or stop watches.

(5) Temperature. Thermometers with Centigrade Scales.
        ,,   ,,   Fahrenheit Scales.

As noted above, standard or special apparatus will be required for the tests so indicated in the list of experiments.

* This list is reproduced by kind permission of the Northern Counties Technical Examinations Council.

A testing machine should be available in S2 and S3 for testing materials in tension and in compression. This machine should have an extensometer suitable for measuring strains in materials. The testing machine should be capable of applying loads of at least 50 tons. Greater power will be needed for testing 6 inch concrete cubes or even 4 inch cubes made of a strong concrete mixture.

The order of the experiments should bear some relation to the order of the lecture work, which may not be the order given in the lists. The lists are not intended to be exhaustive nor is it intended that all experiments need necessarily be performed. As much work as possible, however, should be performed by the students themselves. In some cases it may be convenient to divide the class into groups and to arrange for a portion of the work to be performed by each group. For example, in the determination of densities of materials each group of students may be given a different material and the final results collected by all students. In some cases, however, it may be more effective for the teacher to give a demonstration rather than that each student should perform the experiment independently.

BUILDING SCIENCE (S1)

The items marked * are to be regarded as forming the minimum essential experiments to be carried out by the students individually or in groups.

*1. Determination of volumes of solids, liquids and of powders, applying where applicable methods of direct measurement, measuring vessels, and displacements.

*2. Determination of weights of solids, liquids and of powders.

*3. Determination of density of solids, porous solids, liquids and of powders, using where most convenient the methods:
   (a) Weight/Volume.
   (b) Displacement.
   (c) Principle of Archimedes.

4. Simple demonstration showing porosity and water absorption.

*5. The use of standard sieves for the purpose of grading sands and aggregates.

*6. Determination of voids in a few porous solids and sands.

7. Demonstration of the expansion, contraction and change of shape of timber under varying moisture content.

8. Measurement of the expansion of a few materials under the action of heat.

9. Demonstration of the expansion of water on approaching the freezing point.

10. Demonstration of the increase of weight of iron filings on rusting to show change in composition.

*11. Preparation of CaO from $CaCO_3$ to show loss of weight and change in composition.

12. Slaking of CaO. Show (a) Evolution of heat.
(b) Change in weight.
(c) Change in composition.

*13. Use of reaction balances to demonstrate the values of the reactions at the supports of a simply supported beam.

*14. Use of force boards to demonstrate the triangle and polygon of forces.

15. Show simply the strains produced by loads. By means of graphs show how stress and strain are related.

16. Simple demonstration with wood bricks and balances to illustrate the effect of bonding
(a) in the distribution of pressure at the base,
(b) on the unifying action of a wall or pier.

BUILDING SCIENCE (S2)

In Building Science S2 more attention should be paid to quantitative results than in S1. The items marked * are to be regarded as forming the minimum essential experiments to be carried out by students individually or in groups.

*1. Further determination of porosity of building materials. (General reference B.R.S. Report, 1926.) +

*2. Determination of the permeability of a few building materials. (General reference B.R.S. Report, 1926.) +†

† Standard apparatus is required for these experiments.

3. Demonstration of capillary action in brick and similar porous materials.

4. Determination of rate of evaporation from the surfaces of wet building materials. (B.R.S. Report, 1927, Fig. 10.)   +

5. Effect of repeated freezing on wetted bricks.   ‡

6. Effect of freezing on new concrete.   ‡

7. Sodium sulphate tests on stones and bricks. (General reference B.R.S. Report, 1927 and 1928.)   +

8. Slump test for concrete. (General reference B.R.S. Report, 1926.)   ×†

*9. Preparation and testing of tensile specimens of cement. (B.S.S. for P. Cement.)   ×†

*10. Preparation and testing of concrete cubes of varying density. An attempt should be made to relate the strength to the density by varying the grade of the aggregate.

*11. Preparation and testing of concrete cubes prepared with varying water/cement ratio. Attempt to relate water/cement ratio to strength.

12. Cold Pat and Le Chatelier test for cement. (B.S.S. for P. Cement.)   ×

13. Setting time test for cement. Vicat needle. (B.S.S. for P. Cement.)   ×†

14. Plasticity of plasters and use of Flow Table. (References in B.R.S. Report, 1931, B.R.S. Special Report No. 9. Lime also recommended.)   +†

*15. Determination of moisture content of timber specimens. (Forest Products Research Lab. Leaflet No. 7, 1935.)   +

16. Determination of compressive strength of timbers across and with the grain. (Forest Products Research Lab. Publication, Mech. and Physical Properties of timbers.)

*17. A few determinations of the forces in the members of a pin-jointed plane frame under vertical loads.

† Standard apparatus is required for these experiments.
‡ Access to a refrigerator would be an advantage for these experiments but this is not essential.

18. Demonstration of the conduction, convection and radiation of heat.

19. Simple demonstration of flow of heated water in a closed system.

20. Use of solutions of calcium salts to show efflorescence on bricks and stones.

BUILDING SCIENCE (S3)

In Building Science S3 attention should be directed to the use of constants, determined by experiments. The items marked * are to be regarded as forming the minimum essential experiments to be carried out by the students individually or in groups.

1. Simple chemical experiments to show the composition and action of cements and plasters.

2. Action of dilute acids on stones, bricks and concrete to show action in weathering. +

3. Demonstration of the effect of colour mixes on cements, illustrating the advantage of using a white cement with white and coloured sand.

4. Demonstration of the effect on concrete of the presence of impurities in the materials. For example the effect of such substances as sugar and glue on setting time and strength might be shown.

*5. Portland Cement and rapid hardening cement.
    (a) Fineness test for Cement. ×
    (b) Determination of setting time. ×
    (c) Determination of the increase of compressive strength of concrete cubes with age.

6. Demonstration of the contraction of neat cement mortar over a period, after setting.

7. Demonstration of the expansion and contraction of neat cement mortar with varying moisture content.

8. Demonstration to illustrate the existence of pressure head due to water.

*9. Examination of a typical hardwood and a typical softwood, under the microscope. Prepare sketches of the timber structure and notes relating this structure with strength, seasoning and working properties.

*10. Determination of forces in the members of more complicated pin-jointed frames, under vertical and inclined loads.

*11. Determination of the transverse breaking load on timber specimens of varying section and span. Comparison of results. Relation to the theory of elasticity.

12. Stress-strain curves for various materials in compression and tension.

*13. Complete load extension curve for mild steel.   ×

14. Simple comparison of breaking loads for plain concrete beam and for a similar beam of reinforced concrete, to show effect of reinforcement.

15. Demonstration of the strength of short and long columns of steel or other material, to give a rough comparison for similar cross sections.

*16. Measurement of the deflection of a beam under load, for varying conditions of section, span and load. Comparison of results.

*17. Determination of the centre of gravity of laminae by graphical and experimental methods.

18. Measurement of the natural slope of sand, earth and such materials.

19. Demonstration of the stability of cranes and scaffolds.

*20. Crushing tests should be performed on a number of building materials as time and circumstances permit.

ANSWERS TO PROBLEMS

PROBLEMS I, p. 16.

1. (a) 7 lbs.; (b) 0·119 in.
2. $\frac{1}{16}$ in. or ·0625 in.
3. 0·4 cm.
4. 0·87.
5. 0·931.
6. 62·41.
7. 40·8 lbs. per cu. ft.
8. 0·94.
9. 137 lbs. per cu. ft.
10. 3·1.
11. 0·815 lb.

PROBLEMS II, p. 30.

1. 14·9 lbs.
2. 1824 gms.
3. 0·66 lb. per sq. inch.
4. 5·33 ft.
5. 17·32 lbs. per sq. in.
6. (a) 8·08 ft.; (b) 7·13 ins.
7. 10 tons.
8. 3·865 lbs.
9. (a) 27·7 ft.; (b) 370 ft.
10. 2·6 lb. per sq. in.; 32·68 lb.
11. 62·43 lb.
12. 69 ft.; 5·889 lb.

PROBLEMS III, p. 49.

1. 171 lbs.
2. 0·09 lbs. per sq. in.
3. 0·144 lbs. per sq. in.
4. (a) 6·8″ of mercury; (b) 3·34 lbs. per sq. in.
5. (a) $2\frac{1}{3}$ atmospheres; (b) 34·25 lbs. per sq. in.
6. 21·15 inches of mercury or 10·4 lbs. per sq. in.
7. 924 lbs.
8. 0·266 cu. ft.
9. (a) $\frac{29}{30}$ or 0·966 cu. ft.; (b) 1·24 ozs. per cu. ft.
10. (a) 7·2 tons; (b) 5·2 lbs. per sq. in.
12. 180/100 inch.; 0·065 lb. per sq. in.
13. 14·7 lb. per sq. in.; 5 cu. ft.; 2 cu. ft.
14. (a) $\frac{2}{3}$ cu. ft.; $\frac{5}{6}$ cu. ft.; $\frac{5}{4}$ cu. ft.; (b) 40 cu. ft.
15. 16·9 cu. ft.

PROBLEMS IV, p. 61.

1. 35·5%.
2. (a) 40·3%; (b) 43·8%.
3. (a) 102 cu. ins.; (b) 45·2%.
4. 23% on "20," 47% on "30," 89% on "50," 11% passed all sieves.
5. 15·75%.
6. $364\frac{1}{2}$ lbs. of cement, 12·15 cu. ft. of sand, 24·3 cu. ft. of coarse material.
7. 22·2 cu. ft. of sand; 26·63 cu. ft. of mortar.
8. Theoretical proportions are:—1: 2·43: 4·05, say (approx.) 1 : $2\frac{1}{2}$: 4.
9. Volume of box 17·75 cu. ft.; say 3 ft. 9 ins. by 3 ft. 9 ins. by 15 ins.
10. $8\frac{1}{3}$% of total volume of coarse material.

PROBLEMS V, p. 76

1. A, 2·7%; B, 10·5%; C, 11·8%; D, 5·7%; E, 17%.
2. A, 3·89%; B, 11·5%; C, 13·2%; D, 6·57%; E, 18·3%.
3. (a) 93·8 gallons; (b) 81·4 gallons.
4. A, 8·25%; B, 20·5%.
5. (a) 15·4%; (b) 25%.
6. 0·96 cu. in. per sq. in.
7. 2·35 cu. cms. per sq. cm.
9. 0·00346 cu. ft.

PROBLEMS VI, p. 95.

1. (a) 20 lbs. per sq. in.; (b) 15,250 lbs. per sq. in.
2. (a) 9·78 tons per sq. ft.; (b) 2·44 tons per sq. ft.; (c) 1·375 tons per sq. ft.
3. (a) 5 tons per sq. in. (approx.); (b) 3 tons per sq. in. (approx.).
4. (a) 13·86 lbs.; (b) 16 lbs.   5. 15·2 cwt.
6. In OB compressive force of 11,500 lbs., in OC compressive force of 4200 lbs.
7. (a) Horizontal force of 430 lbs.; (b) Vertical force of 360 lbs.
8. 0·0554; 0·000658.

PROBLEMS VII, p. 116.

1. 9120 lbs., c.g. 2·38 ft. from vertical back and 6·66 ft. from base.
2. T, 8·625 lbs.; P, 1·375 lbs.   3. 6·2 lbs.
4. 6·2 lbs. upwards at 41° to horizontal.
5. (a) 297 lbs.; (b) 390 lbs. upwards at 40° to horizontal.
6. R.H. shore, 1·273 tons; L.H. shore, 2·227 tons.
7. $R_A = 4·131$ tons; $R_B = 3·371$ tons.
8. $R_B = 12·2$ tons; $F = 4·2$ tons.
9. (a) 24·75 cwt.; (b) $R_1 = 8·25$ cwt., $R_B = 16·5$ cwt.
10. AF, compression, 3000 lbs.; BG, compression, 2000 lbs.; FG, compression, 1000 lbs.; FE, tension, 2600 lbs.; GH, tension, 1000 lbs.
11. Reactions 5 lbs. and 15 lbs.; force in tie, 8·7 lbs. tension; force in long rafter, 10 lbs. compression; force in short rafter, 17·3 lbs. compression.
12. 112·5 tons; c.g. is 3·58 ft. from 10 ft. side.

PROBLEMS VIII, p. 130.

1. (a) 2012° F.; (b) 440° F.   2. (a) 318° F.; (b) 14° F.
3. Increase in length, 0·123 in.   4. Increase in length, 0·27 in.
5. 0·0000186.   6. 0·0000161.   7. (a) 0·484 in.; (b) 0·154 in.
8. 0·107 cu. in.   9. 38·67 cu. cms. or 526 gms.   10. 0·191%.
11. Volume at 70° F. = 1·0018.   Increase = 0·18%.
  „ 212° F. = 1·0467.   „ = 4·67%.

PROBLEMS IX, p. 145.

1. 42·27° C.   2. 11 gms.   3. 0·09.   4. 0·56.
5. 815° C.   6. 79° C.
7. (a) 272° C.; (b) 37% lead.   8. 80·55 galls.   9. 9·1d.

PROBLEMS X, p. 155.

5. 1·286 gms. per litre.   6. (a) 43·8%; (b) 24·3%.   7 66·6%.

PROBLEMS XI, p. 164.

2. (a) 0·09 gm. per litre; (b) 1·44; (c) 1·29.   3. 1:8 very nearly.
4. (a) 5 cu. cms.; (b) 25 cu. cms.   5. 0·54 gm.
6. 17,000 cu. cms.   7. (a) 16 cms.; (b) 2840 cu. cms.
8. (a) 4·06 gms.; (b) 4·57 gms.

PROBLEMS XII, p. 174.

2. 1·23 litres.   **8.** (a) 1·525 times as heavy; (b) 78·96 gms.
9. 0·0049 gm. per litre.
10. Untreated specimen, 0·91%; treated specimen, 6·8%.
11. 12%.

PROBLEMS XIII, p. 181.

4. (a) 36; (b) 15.   **5.** 24·5%.

PROBLEMS XIV, p. 187.

1. 12 cwt.   **3.** 139 lbs.   **6.** 1 of lime to 2 of sand (approx.).

PROBLEMS XV, p. 195.

3. 40, 12, 48; 40, 32, 64; 40, 16, 71; 621, 64; 28, 32; 23, 35·5.
4. 0·2545 litre.   **5.** 1·136 gm.
6. $2H_2 + O_2 = 2H_2O$; (weights), $4 + 32 = 36$.
7. $2HCl + CaCO_3 = CaCl + CO_2 + H_2O$; (weights) $73 + 100 = 111 + 44 + 18$.
8. 5·6 tons.

PROBLEMS XVII, p. 221.

1. 1 ton, 2 ton, 8 ton ft.
2. 2·8 ton, 3·2 ton, 8·4 ton ft., 13·8 ton ft., 12·8 ton ft.
3. 7200 lb., 259,200 lb. in., 230,400 lb. in.
4. 26·87 ton ft.
5. 12, 18, 18.
6. 144, 864; 2,304 lb., 24 lb. per sq. in.
7. 8,802 lb., 1·045 ton per sq. in.
8. 129 lb. per sq. ft.

EXAMINATION PAPERS

BUILDING SCIENCE (FIRST YEAR), 1939, p. 223.

1. 3 cu. ft.
3. Reactions: left, 775 lb.; right, 825 lb. Long principal, 1540 lb. and 1030 lb. compression. Short principal, 950 lb. compression. Strut 870 lb. compression. Inclined tie, 870 lb. tension. Horizontal tie: left, 1330 lb. tension; right, 825 lb. tension.
4. 143 in.
6. (a) left, 6·55 tons; right, 3·45 tons; (b) force B, 39·4 tons towards intersection; force A, 32·8 tons towards intersection.
9. Shear force, 33⅓ lb.; bending moment, 1700 lb. ft.   **10.** 0·001 ft.

BUILDING SCIENCE (SECOND YEAR), 1939, p. 226.

2. Reactions, 4000 lb. Principal rafters, from left, 1000; 1500; 1500; all in compression. Horizontals, from left, 870, comp.; 870, comp.; 1150, tension. Verticals, from left, 4000, compression; 1500, compression. Inclined internal members, from left, 2500, tension; 280, tension.
5. Reactions, left 6·8 ton, right 9·2 ton. Total bending moments, centre of left load, 11·6 ton ft. Centre of right load. 14·4 ton ft. Beneath 4 ton load, 32 ton ft.
6. Maximum bending moment occurs under 500 lb. load and is 1940 lb. ft. Required depth $= 7·62$ in.
8. Upper reaction 114 lb. Lower reaction 330 lb., at 14·2° to vertical.

SCIENCE AND CALCULATIONS, p. 229.

2. 1·25 cwt.   **3.** 1·15 cwt.; 1 cwt.   **5.** 1·007 lb.

7. (a) 0·2999; (b) $f = \dfrac{9wL^2}{Bd^2}$.

SCIENCE AND CALCULATIONS, p. 231.

1. Principals; left, 8·7 cwt. compression; right, 5 cwt. compression. Tie, 4·35 cwt, tension. Reactions, left, 7·5 cwt.; right, 2·5 cwt.

3. 10·112 lb.

PLUMBING SCIENCE AND CALCULATIONS, p. 233.

3. 561·9 lb.; 10·41 lb. per sq. in.   **5.** 125° F.

PLUMBING SCIENCE, p. 234.

1. 76 galls. approx.   **8.** $T = \dfrac{DP}{2Q}$; 0·1894 in.

INDEX TO PROBLEMS

INDEX

www.ingramcontent.com/pod-product-compliance
Ingram Content Group UK Ltd.
Pitfield, Milton Keynes, MK11 3LW, UK
UKHW010038140625
459647UK00012BA/1464